W9-BXS-156

ENGLISH
DRAMATIC CRITICISM

SPECIMENS OF ENGLISH
DRAMATIC CRITICISM
XVII—XX CENTURIES

Selected and Introduced by

A. C. WARD

Originally published in 1945 in *The World's Classics* by Humphrey Milford,
Oxford University Press, London, New York, Toronto

Reprinted with the permission of Oxford University Press

Reprinted in 1970 by Greenwood Press
A division of Congressional Information Service
88 Post Road West, Westport, Connecticut 06881

Library of Congress Catalog Card Number 73-138605

ISBN 0-8371-5545-2

Printed in the United States of America

10 9 8 7 6 5 4 3 2

CONTENTS

CONTENTS

viii *CONTENTS*

ACKNOWLEDGEMENTS

of permission to include copyright material

JAMES AGATE: The Author

WILLIAM ARCHER: The Executors of the late William Archer

SIR MAX BEERBOHM: The Author and Messrs. William Heinemann Ltd.

IVOR BROWN: The Author and *New Statesman and Nation*

W. A. DARLINGTON: The Author and *The Daily Telegraph*

ALAN DENT: The Author and Messrs. Macmillan & Co. Ltd.

Articles from THE DAILY TELEGRAPH and MORNING POST: *The Daily Telegraph*

ST. JOHN ERVINE: The Author and *The Observer*

J. T. GREIN: Messrs. John Long Ltd.

Articles from THE IRISH TIMES: Irish Times Ltd.

JOSEPH KNIGHT: Messrs. Sidgwick & Jackson Ltd.

HUBERT GRIFFITH: The Author and *The Observer*

DESMOND MACCARTHY: The Author

H. W. MASSINGHAM: Mr. H. J. Massingham and *New Statesman and Nation*

ALICE MEYNELL: Mr. Wilfrid Meynell

C. E. MONTAGUE: *The Manchester Guardian*

D. L. MURRAY: The Author and *New Statesman and Nation*

Articles from the NEW STATESMAN, THE NATION AND THE ATHENAEUM, and THE WEEK-END REVIEW: *New Statesman and Nation*

BERNARD SHAW: The Author

Articles from THE TIMES: The Times Publishing Company, Limited

SIR HUGH WALPOLE: The Executors to the Walpole Estate

VIRGINIA WOOLF: The Hogarth Press

A few articles from newspapers appear without the authors' names, either to observe a tradition of anonymity, or because the writer has not been identified.

INTRODUCTION

FOR the earliest known dramatic criticism we turn back to the literature of ancient Greece, there to find in Aristotle's Poetics a statement of first principles which, in relation to tragedy, is still valid. But though it is likely that the Poetics will remain for all time the bible of the critics, not all its lessons have so far been learned.

In the present age it has become a fashionable practice in criticism first to conjure a theory from the nebular spaces of the mind and then to adjust the evidence to support the theory. That was not Aristotle's way. He was a deductive critic whose conclusions were based upon a close examination of the output of Greek dramatic poets. In this respect he did work which it has not been necessary to do again, but we need not carry intellectual modesty so far as to suppose that if Aristotle had not arrived at the doctrine of *katharsis* we should have failed to reach it in the meantime. Since the authority of a great man tends to have a deadening effect upon lesser ones who come after, it is well to consider from time to time the shortcomings of the great, though without intent to underestimate their achievements. Nowadays it is less necessary to recall what Aristotle did than what he left undone. In the extant plays of Aeschylus, Sophocles, and Euripides there is available a body of material sufficient for the extraction of a theory of tragedy if the Aristotelian theory did not happen to exist. Where Aristotle fails us as a theatre critic is in saying excessively little about acting and staging. He left us to grope in perpetual semi-darkness in relation to such matters and not all his literary penetration and philosophical depth can compensate the missing information which he might so easily have provided. Those later dramatic critics who have followed Aristotle in neglecting the actor and the visual aspects of theatrical art have no such excuse as can be made for him. To the Greeks drama was far more a spiritual exercise than a holiday spectacle; a rite more than an art. The actor was to them, therefore, somewhat as the celebrant is to us— an official whose activity and personality merge in his office and consequently are of no account apart from it. With the emergence in modern times of a secular art of the theatre, however, values and significances changed. The thing done and its meta-physical implications were challenged in degree of interest and importance by the manner of doing and the personal capacity of the doer. The actor's performance became itself important, and his 'rendering' of a particular part—i.e. the personal force he imposed upon the character—was no less deserving of attention than the author's aim and purpose in creating the character. It was the actor, in fact, who was said to 'create' what he might be supposed merely to interpret.

The literary mind, of course, experiences an immediate impulse to assert that the author's intention is properly the actor's only true concern; that the play is the thing and that to the play the player should always subordinate himself. Yet to this there is an obvious objection. The greater the play the less certain may be the author's exact, or even approximate, intention when he is no longer at hand to direct in that matter. And, also, the greater the play the more is it probable that its full significance will not be entirely comprehended even by the author himself. *Hamlet* no doubt 'means' more than Shakespeare supposed it meant, and an actor is justified in creating the Hamlet of his own vision. The critic's business is then to consider the ability of the performer no less than the credibility of the conception. Even when the author's intention is clear beyond doubt, a merely stereotyped interpretation would become standard unless liberty in interpreting is the understood prerogative of the actor. With a new play before him, instead of an old one, the critic's task is twofold: to assess the merit of the author's material and, as of equal importance, the merit of the player's translation of that material into living terms. This view—that the dramatic critic should treat the actor's work as (potentially at least) on as high a level as the author's—may not command general assent, for writers have long exercised an awful authority, and so long as critics are themselves drawn from the literary fold that authority will not be seriously shaken. But there is a good case for attempting to shake it when the dramatic critic neglects the unique thing he should do for the familiar thing which, at a pinch, he need not do. Each generation can and will undertake its own literary criticism, but when an actor is dead every word of comment by his contemporaries becomes precious. What would we not give for an adequate account by an eye-witness of a performance during the festival of Dionysus at Athens in the fifth century B.C., of a Shakespeare performance during the author's lifetime, or even of certain later occasions in the history of the theatre?

The long-standing impression that English professional dramatic criticism did not begin until the early years of the 19th century should have been removed by the researches of Charles Harold Gray[1] who combed the files of the 17th and 18th century periodical press and found much theatrical news and comment from the 1690s onward. Only a little of this is of general interest, however, and there can be no doubt that Pepys's theatre notes in his Diary, though they are amateur and embryonic, have more of the all-round quality of good dramatic criticism than can be found elsewhere until the 19th century. Pepys's insatiable curiosity made him Argus-eyed and also caused him to develop invisible feelers reaching out in every direction like multiple antennæ. The acuteness of his sensibilities and perceptions gave him a unique sense of occasion, an unexcelled ability to capture the flying moment and bring it down to paper. At one time or another in the course of his frequent playgoing he noted everything to do with the theatre: plays; actors; scenery and costumes; back-stage conditions; the size, composition, manners, and clothes of the audience; the prices of seats (and of oranges); the structure and acoustics of the theatre; the weather—and the draughts blowing round his back and neck. He never became *blasé*, and the intensity of his appreciative powers was such that enjoyment transported and disappointment sickened him. His frequent lack of enthusiasm for Shakespearean plays was no doubt temperamental, though it has to be remembered that a good deal of what went under Shakespeare's name had been subjected to drastic adaptation and decoration, as the reference (19 April 1667) to 'variety of dancing and musique' in *Macbeth* suggests. Among the players Nell Gwynn, his 'pretty

---

[1] *Theatrical Criticism in London to 1795* (Columbia University Press, New York, 1931).

witty Nell', engaged most of his admiration and affection, though he had enough critical disinterestedness to record, even of her, how basely, how like a fool or a changeling, she acted in serious parts.

Pepys's was the first humanistic dramatic criticism and it was long before there was any other. Dryden's *Essay of Dramatic Poesie* (1668) is in the classical style and belongs to the department of literary criticism, though the definition of a play which Dryden puts into the mouth of Lisideius might usefully be memorized by all dramatic critics: '*A just and lively image of human nature, representing its passions and humours, and the changes of fortune to which it is subject, for the delight and instruction of mankind.*' Colley Cibber's *Apology* is perhaps the most disappointing of all autobiographies. Though the author was prominently concerned in all the activities of the contemporary stage, his elephantine style of writing robs the autobiography of most of the vitality we desire. Occasionally, as in the description of Betterton's acting,[1] it becomes vigorous, though still without ceasing to plod. Yet it is an indispensable source-book for students of theatre history. In lighter moods, as in *The Tatler*[2] and *The Spectator*, 18th century dramatic criticism was more urbane than humane. Through its verbal or fictional embroidery, however, we get from time to time a brilliant oblique view of the living stage (e.g. Fielding's allusions to Garrick's Hamlet in the account of Partridge's visit to the theatre[3]). Satirical dramatic criticism in play form, of which Buckingham's *The Rehearsal* was a 17th century example, is at its best in Sheridan's *The Critic* (1779). The farcical

---

[1] See *post*, pp. 46–59.   [2] *Post*, pp. 44–45.
[3] *Post*, pp. 63–68, and (discussed), pp. 142 ff.

humours of this piece contrast agreeably with the heavy moralistic tendency and slow pedestrian tread of late 18th century formal dramatic criticism, such as that of Francis Gentleman. Gentleman, himself an actor and playwright, gave in his *Dramatic Censor* a series of painstaking studies of Shakespearean and other plays. 'No man', he said in his 'Advertisement', 'can be hardy enough to deny, that a well-regulated drama is worthy support in the most polished, learned, or moral state'; while, he added, since the drama of the time was conducive to vice, he intended 'to strip off the serpent's shining coat, and to show the poison which lurks within'. His method involved a long descriptive account of each play, followed by brief comparative notes on various performers in the leading parts, and a final moralizing paragraph. Yet *The Dramatic Censor, or Critical Companion*, dull though it is, has merit as a pioneering work. It treats dramatic criticism as a serious activity—serious in this instance to the point of humorless solemnity. It fails, mainly, because of its apparent total unawareness of æsthetic values, while the retrospective method robs it of the enlivening immediacy which is inseparable from good criticism of a recent and particular performance. Deliberation is not a virtue in a dramatic critic.

To turn from Gentleman to Leigh Hunt is to be at once aware of a quickening of the critical mind and pulse. Enthusiasm had broken in during the thirty years or so which separates the two writers. 'Feel the passion', says Hunt of actors, 'and the action will follow.' Of dramatic critics we might say 'feel the passion and the words will come'. While reading Leigh Hunt we feel something of that anticipatory excitement usual in the theatre before the curtain goes up. His is an excellent complementary performance as well as good criticism, sound and penetrating, apt in phrase and figure, pulsating with the intimacy and warmth of friendly talk. For the first time in English dramatic criticism the life of the stage gave life to a professional critic's prose, and there is an abundant sense of communication across the footlights. To Leigh Hunt the player was no mere puppet to be manipulated by the dramatist puppetmaster. Recognizing that a great performer can give life and credibility even to material only crudely shapen by the playwright, he saw the drama in its proper aspect—as a spectacle in which the illusion of actuality is created by the genius of the players. For the life of the theatre he looked to the actors rather than to the authors, and the 19th century actors justified him by keeping the theatre alive during the generations when playwriting was moribund. William Hazlitt was doubtless a better writer than Hunt, but doubtless also he was less good as a theatre critic. He had in fact the supreme disqualification: he was not in love with the theatre itself. He wrote in 1820,[1] 'Our head is stuffed full of recollections on the subject of the Drama, some of older, some of later date, but all treasured up with more or less fondness; we, in short, love it, and what we love we can talk of for ever. . . . But we love it best at a distance. We like to be a hundred miles off from the acted drama in London.' This is as though a music critic were to declare his dislike of concerts and determine to sit at home and base his criticisms on a reading of the printed score. Hazlitt was a man of letters and his dramatic criticism is a

[1] 'Vulgarity in Criticism' (*The English Stage*).

series of Literary Variations on a Theatrical Theme. He enmeshes the traffic of the stage in a web of words until what has been called in another context the 'living communication with the experience' vanishes. He could weave this web so cunningly that he is sometimes near to deceiving us: 'We never saw Mr. Liston's countenance in better preservation; that is, it seems tumbling all in pieces with indescribable emotions, and a thousand odd twitches and unaccountable absurdities oozing out at every pore. His jaws seem to ache with laughter: his eyes look out of his head with wonder: his face is unctuous all over and bathed with jests; the tip of his nose is tickled with conceit of himself, and his teeth chatter in his head in the eager insinuation of a plot: his forehead speaks, and his wig (not every particular hair, but the whole bewildered bushy mass) "stands on end as life were in it".' Our immediate response to this is to think 'Here, surely, is the actor as he lived and moved and had his being upon the stage', but as we examine further we grow less sure. There is description of facial play, but is there communication with the living experience? Are we not left, after an interval, with a dim impression of a grinning mask from behind which the life had departed? The pictorial-descriptive method in criticism rarely produces a lasting effect even when it is most excellently done, for the image transmitted to the visual memory of the reader is, at best, as impermanent as an unfixed photographic print. This was a method upon which Leigh Hunt did not rely. He gives us no intermediate picture, but, by a subtle tuning of our sensibilities to his own, evokes in us that stirring of the pulse and stimulation of the mind which he had himself experienced. Hazlitt said of Eliza O'Neill's

Lady Teazle that 'it was a piece of laboured heavy *still-life*'. 'Still-life' is not an unsuitable term for his own dramatic criticism. Yet at least he made no false pretence. In saying he loved the drama but not the acted drama, he admitted that the drama appealed to him mainly as literature. But such an attitude is fundamentally mistaken, for the use of the dialogue form presupposes the employment of speakers, therefore of actors, therefore of a stage. It might be urged in Hazlitt's defence that his admission was mere playfulness, and that the essay *On Actors and Acting*[1] tells a different story. As a literary exercise that essay is admirable, but its compliments to the stage come from the moods of his own mind, not from the eager pulsations of enthusiasm.

If Hazlitt was insensitive to the delights of stage representation, what is to be said in this connexion of Charles Lamb? Since we know from *Old China* that he was a one-time playgoer of the right breed, it is the more shocking that when writing *On the Tragedies of Shakespeare* he should have claimed that Shakespeare is better read than acted. This is equivalent to saying that Shakespeare was a fool who wrote for the stage in mistake for the library. We have no evidence that he cared a jot about his plays as reading matter. They were matter for acting. If it were true, as Lamb declared, that by being acted Hamlet must always and inevitably be turned into a Hamlet foreign to Shakespeare's conception, then Shakespeare was a bungler who wasted himself in the composition of unplayable plays. It is true enough of many of us that we stage Shakespeare in our own minds and, in vanity, prefer our representation to any other. That, no doubt, was

[1] See *post*, pp. 101–11.

Lamb's case also, but it is a dubious foundation on which to build a critical argument that the stage-actor's medium is in its nature so coarse that to perform Shakespeare is necessarily to ruin him. Some ten years later Lamb was to make amends for this clever nonsense with the Elia essay *On Some of the Old Actors*, not by withdrawing his general stricture, but by discussing Shakespearean and other acting in terms that leave no room to doubt his affection for the craft. That essay carries us away again from the frigid descriptive zone of Hazlitt back to the genial climate of communication in which we left Leigh Hunt. As Hotspur (says Lamb), Bensley's voice 'had the dissonance, and at times the inspiriting effect of the trumpet. His gait was uncouth and stiff, but no way embarrassed by affectation; and the thorough-bred gentleman was uppermost in every movement. He seized the moment of passion with the greatest truth; like a faithful clock, never striking before the time; never anticipating or leading you to anticipate. He was totally destitute of trick and artifice. He seemed come upon the stage to do the poet's message simply, and he did it with as genuine fidelity as the nuncios in Homer deliver the errands of the gods.' And again, this time of a comedian, 'Care, that troubles all the world, was forgotten in [Dicky Suett's] composition. Had he had but two grains (nay, half a grain) of it, he could never have supported himself upon those two spider's strings, which served him . . . as legs. A doubt or a scruple must have made him totter, a sigh have puffed him down; the weight of a frown had staggered him, a wrinkle made him lose his balance. But on he went, scrambling upon those airy stilts of his, with Robin Good-Fellow, "thorough brake, thorough **briar**", reckless of a scratched face or a torn doublet.' We can never forget those spider-string legs, but the effects Lamb produces in these passages come mainly through non-visual channels. If criticism is communication by translation Lamb's skill in criticism is self-evident. When he falls to discussing the 17th and 18th century comedies[1] he strays happily from plays to players and we are insinuated on intimate terms into the company of Palmer and Smith and John Kemble and the rest.

Many excellent observations on acting occur in the Diary and Journals and correspondence of Henry Crabb Robinson, who was almost as indefatigable a playgoer as Pepys. During his lifetime of more than ninety years he spanned the stage from Mrs. Siddons to Kate Terry, and *The Times* might have done even better to employ him as dramatic critic than as foreign correspondent and (for a few months) editor. Though Crabb Robinson's was a soberer mind than Pepys's and there are very few laughs to be had from him and no engaging human indiscretions to share, he too, was endlessly curious, with a vast mental appetite. A good judge of acting, unlike his friend Charles Lamb he got more from a Shakespearean play in the theatre than in the study, though even on the stage he could see little in *Richard II.* His admiration for Mrs. Siddons was unbounded and as a young man he was once so moved by her acting that he became hysterical in the theatre and had to be restored by a good-natured woman with a smelling bottle! Through his series of references to this great tragic actress we can see her at length ageing and losing her powers. When

[1] See *post,* pp. 112–22.

shortly before her retirement, she played The Lady in *Comus*, Crabb Robinson wrote (5 June 1812): 'For the first time in my life I saw Mrs. Siddons without any pleasure. . . . She was dressed most unbecomingly, and had a low gipsy hat with feathers hanging down the side. She looked old, and I had almost said ugly. Her fine features were lost in the distance. Even her declamation did not please me.' But when he made his final visit to the theatre more than half a century later (12 October 1866) at the age of ninety-one, the pathos of the old man's 'half-deafness' and 'dimness of sight' is mitigated by his remembrance of Mrs. Siddons in the same play long ago. Though now he could see and hear very little of what was happening on the Drury Lane stage 'the recollection of Mrs. Siddons as Constance is an enjoyment in itself'. He ends: 'On the whole, the greatest benefit that I have derived from the evening is that I seem to be reconciled to never going again.'

After the literary brilliance of Leigh Hunt, Hazlitt, and Charles Lamb, the regular dramatic criticism of the generation following—that of John Forster, George Henry Lewes, Henry Morley, Dutton Cook, and Joseph Knight—seems no more than competent. Into the field which had so far been cultivated somewhat casually and patchily by diarists, actors, novelists, moralists, biographers, and literary essayists, there now came a more academic and professionalized class of critics. Forster (Dickens's friend and biographer) was a political writer and historian, G. H. Lewes (George Eliot's house-fellow) a philosopher, Morley a university professor of language and literature. Knight had antiquarian leanings and edited *Notes and Queries* but for both him and Dutton Cook dramatic criticism was for years a major occupation. They were the vanguard of that race of journalists which took up dramatic criticism as a career and made it a distinct branch of newspaper writing. No example of Forster's work is given here, for as a writer on the theatre he was less interesting than the others. Lewes was the most notable and illuminating but none of the four calls for particular introductory comment. The special interest of Knight and Cook is that they were writing while Henry Irving and Ellen Terry were at their best, and it is with those two players that the modern phase of English theatre history begins. Beyond them in the past lie dim stretches of shadowland peopled by figures legendary to us—Macready, Phelps, Kean, the Kembles, Mrs. Siddons, Garrick, Peg Woffington, Cibber, Mrs. Bracegirdle, Mrs. Barry, Betterton, Burbage. . . . Irving, Ellen Terry, Forbes Robertson, Beerbohm Tree and their successors have been so much written about by so many that it is hard to believe they will ever wholly join that earlier ghostly company. Each curious tone of Irving's voice, every mannerism of utterance, every oddity of gait and bearing, have been recorded by his critics, so that he is familiar even to those who never saw him. Of Ellen Terry enough can never be known, but her life and career have been more fully documented than any other actress's; and, most fortunately and happily, her incomparable spirit lives on in her letters to Shaw.[1]

A good many years must pass before impartial witnesses can be produced in the case of Bernard Shaw. He has been a fruitful breeder of partisans,

[1] *Ellen Terry and Bernard Shaw: A Correspondence* (1931).

whose range of disagreement is so wide as to make it almost impossible to believe that so many contrarious assertions could be made of one person. Only the quality of his dramatic criticism need be discussed here. Though he had, even more strongly than Hazlitt, the chief disqualification for the office of dramatic critic—namely, a hearty dislike of theatres—his dramatic criticism is undoubtedly the most satisfying as well as the most brilliant in the English language. Since paradox is the Shavian norm, this particular paradox should arouse no murmur of surprise. Assuming that his expressed disgust and contempt for the London theatres of the 1890s was genuine, how did it come about that his criticisms of the work of those theatres are still among the most absorbing and entertaining of his writings? This is due in the first place to his unshakeable integrity. Being by nature as well as by conviction an honest workman, he produced honest work. He was engaged to write about the theatre: therefore he brought his whole store of information and all his talents to the carrying out of the task. And what a store and what talents! And with what skill and assurance and ease and mastery he deploys his information! To be at once erudite, informative, provocative, and delightful is within the power of only an infinitesimal minority, but Shaw is among that minority; he might himself say he *is* that minority. His criticism of Irving's staging of *King Arthur*[1] is a masterpiece in which each aspect of the production is considered by the light of his knowledge of painting, costume, music, and legend, as well as of acting. This is not a piece of shewing-off by the critic. It is just that the knowledge is there, therefore

[1] *Our Theatres in the Nineties*, Vol. 1.

it is used: it is as simple as that—the simplicity of the craftsman using the tools proper to the job in hand. If there is little in Shaw's work to warm the heart, if he approaches the theatre less as a lover than as an inspired welfare-worker, what is missing is compensated by the presence of honesty, knowledge, skill, audacity, and wit. The edges are sharp, the outline clear and clean. The result is functional criticism of the best kind. But it is useless as a model, for, overriding the qualities that have been listed, there is in Bernard Shaw's make-up the characteristic which is unique to genius: the ability to see himself objectively. The paramount folly of Shaw's critics is that they have been so busy accusing him of self-conceit that they have failed to notice that he is altogether free from *amour-propre*, the chief source of human self-bemusement. The familiar sign of egotism is self-depreciation, a form of invitation to others to praise us as in our hearts we praise our-selves. But Shaw never invited nor desired the praise of others. Why should he? Endowed, as he has told us, with normal sight he had no need to borrow the eyes of others. He could see himself by vision and prevision as an Old Master beside the other Old Masters. He measured his own stature by theirs— and theirs by his. Hence, in the dramatic criticisms, his attitude towards Shakespeare: his refusal to do him reverence as a Great Thinker. If we are sure that Shakespeare *was* a great thinker we should be undisturbed by Shaw's disagreement. If we have accepted as a secondhand article of faith that he was a great thinker we may be incensed by any dis-turbance of that insecure faith. If Shaw's contrary view leads us to inquire for ourselves into the validity or invalidity of Shakespeare's reputation, it has done what criticism should do: it has startled us out of our comfortable mental lassitude. From first to last the explanation of Bernard Shaw is the master paradox of his career—his abnormal normality.

English dramatic criticism in the last two decades of the 19th century had a more familiar appearance in the writings of two others, Clement Scott and William Archer. Though Shaw gave him just and kindly recognition at other times, Scott is now remembered chiefly through the publicity accorded (in Shaw's *Quintessence of Ibsenism*) to his intemperate attack on *Ghosts*.[1] Clement Scott had the kind of inelastic and humorless mind that can easily be made to look foolish, and he was content that the theatre should go round and round in its old groove. He was the average late Victorian, wearing familiar moral and social blinkers.   He kicked violently if any one lifted his blinkers so that he suddenly saw what was outside his usual field of sight, and instinctively he declared (*a*) that what had been shown to him wasn't there at all, or (*b*) that it if was there it was so indecent and/or so horrible that no decent-minded person would consent to be aware of its existence. This is still a common attitude, though it is nowadays encouraged more by cynicism than by the stubborn niceness which led the earlier generation to believe that it was better to preserve an unsullied mind than to set about publicly cleaning the Augean stables scattered over the landscape.

Clement Scott upheld the *status quo*, William Archer was an advocate of the new order. Ibsen was the symbolic bone of contention in this struggle and the Archer brothers happened to be Ibsen's

[1] See *post*, pp. 182–9.

translators. But though William Archer was there-fore more directly concerned in the matter than Shaw, he had too sceptical an intelligence to be a violent partisan. Many of his judgements would now be reversed on appeal, but they are of considerable interest in enabling us to see e.g. how Pinero im-pinged on a generation which was apt to confuse actual social problems with stage-manufactured ones and was inordinately interested in that oddest and dullest of period pieces, the Woman-with-a-Past. The most famous of Archer's judgements was also his wrongest. He put it on record at the outset of his friend's career that Bernard Shaw would never succeed as a playwright. It was, however, through Archer that Shaw became first a dramatic critic and then a playwright, and, as if that were not enough for a lifetime, thirty years later (1921) the black-coated, dour, stiff-collared 65-year-old Archer suddenly blazed into popularity and prosperity with a giddy-plumaged melodrama of outrageous improbability, *The Green Goddess.*

While in the nineties these Ibsenite and anti-Ibsenite eructations were in process *The Times* dramatic critic of that period, A. B. Walkley, was marking out a track in which more than one of his profession has followed since. He was a *littérateur* and a lover of the urbanities in whose regard acting—though perhaps only English acting—partook too much of the nature of life in the raw. He was disposed to watch a play as though it were something transpiring in the privacy of his own mind and stirring remembrances of past writers, chiefly foreign, from Aristotle onward. Rarely did he seem to be fully conscious of the living people moving before him on the stage. Consequently his criticisms had a strong literary bias, with comment on acting as a meagre appendix; and before being reprinted in the books in which they had a second life they were sometimes subjected to an appendicectomy. The *Manchester Guardian* dramatic critic C. E. Montague had at least as strong a literary bias as Walkley, but, as his notice of F. R. Benson's Richard II[1] shows, he was adept in grafting a penetrating and perhaps abstruse literary discussion on to an individual performance by an actor. Of Max Beerbohm who followed Shaw on the *Saturday Review* the departing critic said what no one could better or would wish to change half a century later: 'The younger generation is knocking at the door; and as I open it there steps spritely in the incomparable Max.' Though he was scarcely at his happiest as a dramatic critic, for the theatre somewhat caged the sprite, Max remained incomparable and as youthful in his ripest age as he had been mature in his youth.

The golden period of theatre criticism in England was the twenty-five years that ended in 1914. As well as the writers named here there were the anonymous critics whose work in the daily papers was allotted space on a scale so generous as to excite, now, our envious astonishment. And who that reads e.g. the notice of the Haymarket production of Ibsen's *The Pretenders*[2] will say that the quality was less remarkable than the quantity, or be able wholly to stifle a foolish sigh for the press of yesteryear?

More recently there has been a marked tendency for dramatic criticism to become stubbornly literary and for playwrights' work to be given disproportionate attention in comparison with that of the players.

[1] See *post*, pp. 222–30.   [2] See *post*, pp. 264–72.

But the drama is a composite art born in the theatre. In the playwright's mind it is only germinally existent. A more comprehensive and satisfying kind of criticism might result if all intending critics were required to undergo a portion of their apprenticeship in the practical work of the playhouse; while, since a close acquaintance with audiences on each social level should also be a part of their minimum equipment, critics and their work—and possibly plays and acting too—would benefit if they made a practice of sitting as often in the gallery and pit as in the stalls. An exclusively stall-eyed view of the drama has limitations peculiar to itself.

A. C. W.

Oxford
January 1945

LONDON THEATRES IN THE 1660s[1]

1660

18 *August.*—To the Cockpitt play, the first that I have had time to see since my coming from sea, *The Loyall Subject*, where one Kinaston, a boy, acted the Duke's sister, but made the loveliest lady that ever I saw in my life.

11 *October.*—To the Cockpitt to see *The Moore of Venice*, which was well done. Burt acted the Moore; by the same token, a very pretty lady that sat by me, called out, to see Desdemona smothered.

5 *December.*—To the New Theatre and there I saw *The Merry Wives of Windsor* acted, the humours of the country gentleman and the French doctor done very well, but the rest but very poorly, and Sir J. Falstaffe as bad as any.

31 *December.*—I bought the play of *Henry the Fourth*, and so went to the new Theatre and saw it acted; but my expectation being too great, it did not please me, as otherwise I believe it would; and my having a book, I believe did spoil it a little.

1661

3 *January.*—To the Theatre, where was acted *Beggars' Bush*, it being very well done; and here the first time that ever I saw women come upon the stage.

19 *January*—To the Theatre, where I saw *The Lost Lady*, which do not please me much. Here I was troubled to be seen by four of our office clerks, which sat in the half-crowne box and I in the 1s. 6d.

[1] A short selection from Pepys's many references to the theatres.

28 *January*.—To the Theatre, where I saw again *The Lost Lady*, which do now please me better than before; and here I sitting behind in a dark place, a lady spit backward upon me by a mistake, not seeing me, but after seeing her to be a very pretty lady, I was not troubled at it at all.

12 *February*.—To Salsbury Court play-house, where not liking to sit, we went out again, and by coach to the Theatre, and there saw *The Scornfull Lady*, now done by a woman, which makes the play appear much better than ever it did to me.

23 *February*.—To the Play-house, and there saw *The Changeling*, the first time it hath been acted these twenty years, and it takes exceedingly. Besides, I see the gallants do begin to be tyred with the vanity and pride of the theatre actors, who are indeed grown very proud and rich.

23 *March*.—To the Red Bull (where I had not been since plays come up again) up to the tireing-room, where strange the confusion and disorder that there is among them in fitting themselves, especially here, where the clothes are very poore, and the actors but common fellows. At last into the pitt, where I think there was not above ten more than myself, and not one hundred in the whole house. And the play, which is called *All's lost by Lust*, poorly done; and with so much disorder, among others, that in the musique-room the boy that was to sing a song, not singing it right, his master fell about his eares and beat him so, that it put the whole house in an uprore.

8 *June*.—To the Theatre and there saw *Bartholomew Faire*, the first time it was acted now-a-days. It is a most admirable play and well acted, but too much prophane and abusive.

24 *August*.—To the Opera, and there saw *Hamlet*,

Prince of Denmarke, done with scenes very well, but above all, Betterton did the Prince's part beyond imagination.

30 *August.*—To Drury Lane to the French comedy, which was so ill done, and the scenes and company and every thing else so nasty and out of order and poor, that I was sick all the while in my mind to be there.

31 *August.*—I find myself lately too much given to seeing of plays, and expense, and pleasure, which makes me forget my business, which I must labour to amend.

11 *September.*—Walking through Lincoln's Inn Fields observed at the Opera a new play, *Twelfth Night*, was acted there, and the King there; so I, against my own mind and resolution, could not forbear to go in, which did make the play seem a burthen to me, and I took no pleasure at all in it; and so after it was done went home with my mind troubled for my going thither, after my swearing to my wife that I would never go to a play without her.

21 *October.*—Against my judgment and conscience (which God forgive, for my very heart knows that I offend God in breaking my vows herein) to the Opera, which is now newly begun to act again, after some alteracion of their scene, which do make it very much worse; but the play, *Love and Honour*, being the first time of their acting it, is a very good plot, and well done.

25 *October.*—My wife and I to the Opera, and there saw again *Love and Honour*, a play so good that it has been acted but three times and I have seen them all, and all in this week; which is too much, and more than I will do again a good while.

28 *October.*—To the Theatre, and there saw

Argalus and Parthenia, where a woman acted Parthenia, and came afterwards on the stage in men's clothes, and had the best legs that ever I saw, and I was very well pleased with it.

29 *November.*—Sir W. Pen and I to the Theatre, but it was so full that we could hardly get any room, so he went up to one of the boxes, and I into the 18*d.* places, and there saw *Love at first sight,* a play of Mr. Killigrew's, and the first time that it hath been acted since before the troubles, and great expectation there was, but I found the play to be a poor thing, and so I perceive every body else do.

16 *December.*—To the Opera, where there was a new play (*Cutter of Coleman Street*), made in the year 1658, with reflections much upon the late times; and it being the first time the pay was doubled, and so to save money, my wife and I went up into the gallery, and there sat and saw very well; and a very good play it is. It seems of Cowly's making.

1662

26 *May.*—To the Redd Bull, where we saw *Doctor Faustus,* but so wretchedly and poorly done, that we were sick of it, and the worse because by a former resolution it is to be the last play we are to see till Michaelmas.

29 *September* (*Michaelmas day*).—This day my oaths for drinking of wine and going to plays are out, and so I do resolve to take a liberty to-day, and then to fall to them again.... To the King's Theatre, where we saw *Midsummer Night's Dream,* which I had never seen before, nor shall ever again, for it is the most insipid ridiculous play that ever I saw in my life. I saw, I confess, some good dancing and some handsome women, which was all my pleasure.

2 *October*.—Hearing that there was a play at the
Cockpit (and my Lord Sandwich, who came to town
last night, at it), I do go thither, and by very great
fortune did follow four or five gentlemen who were
carried to a little private door in a wall, and so crept
through a narrow place and came into one of the
boxes next the King's, but so as I could not see the
King and Queene, but many of the fine ladies, who
yet are not really so handsome generally as I used to
take them to be, but that they are finely dressed.
Here we saw *The Cardinall*, a tragedy I had never
seen before, nor is there any great matter in it. The
company that came in with me into the box, were all
Frenchmen that could speak no English, but Lord!
what sport they made to ask a pretty lady that they
got among them that understood both French and
English to make her tell them what the actors said.

20 *October*.—Young Killigrew did so commend
The Villaine, a new play made by Tom Porter, and
acted only on Saturday at the Duke's house, as if
there never had been any such play come upon the
stage. The same yesterday was told me by Captain
Ferrers; and this morning afterwards by Dr. Clerke,
who saw it. . . . I took my wife by coach to the Duke's
house, and there was the house full of company: but
whether it was in over-expecting or what, I know not,
but I was never less pleased with a play in my life.
Though there was good singing and dancing, yet no
fancy in the play, but something that made it less
contenting was my conscience that I ought not to
have gone by my vowe, and, besides, my business
commanded me elsewhere. But, however, as soon as
I came home I did pay my crowne to the poor's box,
according to my vowe, and so no harme as to that is
done, but only business lost and money lost, and my

old habit of pleasure wakened, which I will keep down the more hereafter, for I thank God these pleasures are not sweet to me now in the very enjoying of them.

1 *December.*—To the Cockpitt, with much crowding and waiting, where I saw *The Valiant Cidd* acted, a play I have read with great delight, but is a most dull thing acted, which I never understood before, there being no pleasure in it, though done by Betterton and by Ianthe, and another fine wench that is come in the room of Roxalana; nor did the King or Queen once smile all the whole play, nor any of the company seem to take any pleasure but what was in the greatness and gallantry of the company.

26 *December.*—Dined with many tradesmen that belong to the Wardrobe, but I was weary soon of their company, and broke up dinner as soon as I could, and away, with the greatest reluctancy and dispute (two or three times my reason stopping my sense and I would go back again) within myself, to the Duke's house and saw *The Villaine*, which I ought not to do without my wife, but that my time is now out that I did undertake it for. But, Lord! to consider how my natural desire is to pleasure, which God be praised that he has given me the power by my late oathes to curbe so well as I have done, and will do again after two or three plays more. Here I was better pleased with the play than I was at first, understanding the design better than I did.

27 *December.*—With my wife to the Duke's Theatre, and saw the second part of *Rhodes,* done with the new Roxalana; which do it rather better in all respects for person, voice, and judgment, than the first Roxalana. Not so well pleased with the company at the house to-day, which was full of citizens, there

hardly being a gentleman or woman in the house; a couple of pretty ladies by us that made great sport in it, being jostled and crowded by prentices.

1663

6 *January*.—To the Duke's house, and there saw *Twelfth Night* acted well, though it be but a silly play, and not related at all to the name or day.

23 *February*.—Walked out to see what play was acted to-day, and we find it *The Slighted Mayde*. . . . By and by took coach, and to the Duke's house, where we saw it well acted, though the play hath little good in it, being most pleased to see the little girle dance in boy's apparel, she having very fine legs, only bends in the hams, as I perceive all women do. The play being done, we took coach and to Court, and there got good places, and saw *The Wilde Gallant*, per-formed by the King's house, but it was ill acted, and the play so poor a thing as I never saw in my life almost, and so little answering the name, that from beginning to end, I could not, nor can at this time, tell certainly which was the Wild Gallant. The King did not seem pleased at all, the whole play, nor any body else. . . . It being done, we got a coach and got well home about 12 at night. Now as my mind was but very ill satisfied with these two plays themselves, so was I in the midst of them sad to think of the spending so much money and venturing upon the breach of my vowe, which I found myself sorry for. But I did make payment of my forfeiture presently, though I hope to save it back again by forbearing two plays at Court for this one at the Theatre, or else to forbear that to the Theatre which I am to have at Easter. But it being my birthday and my day of liberty regained to me, and lastly, the last play that

is likely to be acted at Court before Easter, because of the Lent coming in, I was the easier content to fling away so much money.

22 April.—To the King's Playhouse, where we saw but part of *Witt without mony*, which I do not like much, but coming late put me out of tune, and it costing me four half-crownes for myself and company.

8 May.—To the Theatre Royall, being the second day of its being opened. The house is made with extraordinary good contrivance, and yet hath some faults, as the narrowness of the passages in and out of the pitt, and the distance from the stage to the boxes, which I am confident cannot hear; but for all other things it is well, only, above all, the musique being below, and most of it sounding under the very stage, there is no hearing of the bases at all, nor very well of the trebles, which sure must be mended. The play was *The Humerous Lieutenant*, a play that hath little good in it, nor much in the very part which, by the King's command, Lacy still acts instead of Clun. In the dance, the tall devil's actions was very pretty. The play being done, we home by water, having been a little shamed that my wife and woman were in such a pickle, all the ladies being finer and better dressed in the pitt than they used, I think, to be. To my office to set down this day's passage, and, though my oathe against going to plays do not oblige me against this house, because it was not then in being, yet believing that at the time my meaning was against all publique houses, I am resolved to deny myself the liberty of two plays at Court, which are in arrear to me for the months of March and April, which will more than countervail the excess, so that this month of May is the first that I must claim a liberty of going to a Court play according to my oathe.

10 *June.*—To the Royal Theatre by water, and landing, met with Captain Ferrers his friend, the little man that used to be with him, and he with us, and sat by us while we saw *Love in a Maze*. The play is pretty good, but the life of the play is Lacy's part, the clowne, which is most admirable; but for the rest, which are counted such old and excellent actors, in my life I never heard both men and women so ill pronounce their parts, even to my making myself sicke therewith.

12 *June.*—With my wife by water to the Royall Theatre; and there saw *The Committee*, a merry but indifferent play, only Lacey's part, an Irish footman, is beyond imagination. Here I saw my lord Falconbridge, and his Lady, my Lady Mary Cromwell, who looks as well as I have known her, and well clad; but when the House began to fill she put on her vizard, and so kept it on all the play; which of late is become a great fashion among the ladies, which hides their whole face. So to the Exchange, to buy things with my wife; among others a vizard for herself.

1664

1 *January.*—Went to the Duke's house, the first play I have been at these six months, according to my last vowe, and here saw the so much cried-up play of *Henry the Eighth*; which, though I went with resolution to like it, is so simple a thing made up of a great many patches, that, besides the shows and processions in it, there is nothing in the world good or well done.

2 *January.*—After dinner I took my wife out, for I do find that I am not able to conquer myself as to going to plays till I come to some new vowe concerning it, and that I am now come to, that is to say, that

I will not see above one in a month at any of the
publique theatres till the sum of 50s. be spent, and
then none before New Year's Day next, unless that I
do become worth 1,000l. sooner than then, and then
am free to come to some other terms, and so to the
King's house, and saw *The Usurper*, which is no good
play, though better than what I saw yesterday.

8 *March.*—*Heraclius* being acted, which my wife
and I have a mighty mind to see, we do resolve,
though not exactly agreeing with the letter of my
vowe, yet altogether with the sense, to see another this
month, by going hither instead of that at Court,
there having been none conveniently since I made my
vowe; besides we did walk home on purpose to make
this going as cheap as that would have been, to have
seen one at Court, and my conscience knows that it
is only the saving of money and the time also that I
intend by my oaths, and this has cost no more of
either, so that my conscience before God do after
good consultation and resolution of paying my forfeit,
did my conscience accuse me of breaking my vowe, I
do not find myself in the least apprehensive that I
have done any violence to my oaths. The play hath
one very good passage well managed, about two
persons pretending, and yet denying themselves, to
be son to the tyrant Phocas, and yet heir of Mauricius
to the crowne. The garments like Romans very well.
The little girle is come to act very prettily, and spoke
the epilogue most admirably. But at the beginning,
at the drawing up of the curtain, there was the finest
scene of the Emperor and his people about him,
standing in their fixed and different postures in their
Roman habitts, above all that ever I yet saw at any
of the theatres.

2 *August.*—To the King's playhouse, and there

saw *Bartholomew Fayre,* which do still please me; and is, as it is acted, the best comedy in the world, I believe. I chanced to sit by Tom Killigrew, who tells me that he is setting up a nursery; that is, is going to build a house in Moorefields, wherein he will have common plays acted. But four operas it shall have in the year, to act six weeks at a time; where we shall have the best scenes and machines, the best musique, and every thing as magnificent as is in Christendome; and to that end hath sent for voices and painters and other persons from Italy.

4 *August.*—Sir W. Pen . . . did carry me to a play and pay for me at the King's house, *The Rivall Ladys,* a very innocent and most pretty witty play. I was much pleased with it, and it being given me, I look upon it as no breach of my oathe. Here we hear that Clun, one of their best actors, was, the last night, going out of towne (after he had acted the Alchymist, wherein was one of his best parts that he acts) to his country-house, set upon and murdered; one of the rogues taken, an Irish fellow.

8 *August.*—My wife and I abroad to the King's play-house, she giving me her time of the last month's she having not seen any then; so my vowe is not broke at all, it costing me no more money than it would have done upon her, had she gone both her times that were due to her. Here we saw *Flora's Figarys.* I never saw it before, and by the most ingenuous performance of the young jade Flora, it seemed as pretty a pleasant play as ever I saw in my life.

13 *August.*—Mr. Creed dining with me I got him to give my wife and me a play this afternoon, lending him money to do it, which is a fallacy that I have found now once, to avoyde my vowe with, but never

to be more practised I swear. To the new play, at
the Duke's house, of *Henry the Fifth*; a most noble play,
writ by my Lord Orrery; wherein Betterton, Harris,
and Ianthe's parts are most incomparably wrote and
done, and the whole play the most full of height and
raptures of wit and sense, that ever I heard; having
but one incongruity, that King Harry promises to
plead for Tudor to their Mistresse, Princesse Kather-
ine of France, more than when it comes to it he seems
to do; and Tudor refused by her with some kind of
indignity, not with a difficulty and honour that it
ought to have been done in to him.

1665

3 *April.*—To a play at the Duke's, of my Lord
Orrery's, called *Mustapha*, which being not good, made
Betterton's part and Ianthe's but ordinary too, so
that we were not contented with it at all. All the
pleasure of the play was, the King and my Lady
Castlemaine were there; and pretty witty Nell, at the
King's house, and the younger Marshall sat next us;
which pleased me mightily.

1666

8 *December.*—To the King's playhouse, which
troubles me since and hath cost me a forfeit of 10s.,
which I have paid, and there did see a good part of
The English Monsieur, which is a mighty pretty play,
very witty and pleasant. And the women do very
well; but, above all, little Nelly, that I am mightily
pleased with the play, and much with the House, more
than ever I expected, the women doing better than
ever I expected, and very fine women. Here I was in
pain to be seen, and hid myself; but, as God would
have it, Sir John Chichly come, and sat just by me.

28 *December.*—To the Duke's house, and there saw
Macbeth most excellently acted, and a most excellent
play for variety. I had sent for my wife to meet me
there, who did come, and after the play was done,
I out so soon to meet her at the other door that I left
my cloake in the play house, and while I returned to
get it, she was gone out and missed me. I not
sorry for it much did go to White Hall, and got
my Lord Bellassis to get me into the playhouse;
and there, after all staying above an hour for the
players, the King and all waiting, which was absurd,
saw *Henry the Fifth* well done by the Duke's people,
and in most excellent habits, all new vests, being put
on but this night. But I sat so high and far off, that
I missed most of the words, and sat with a wind coming into my back and neck, which did much trouble
me. The play continued till twelve at night; and
then up, and a most horrid cold night it was, and
frosty, and moonshine.

1667

7 *January.*—To the Duke's house, and saw *Macbeth*,
which, though I saw it lately, yet appears a most
excellent play in all respects, but especially in diver-
tisement, though it be a deep tragedy; which is a
strange perfection in a tragedy, it being most proper
here, and suitable. So home, it being the last play
now I am to see till a fortnight hence, I being from
the last night entered into my vowes for the year
coming on.

23 *January.*—To the King's house, and there saw
The Humerous Lieutenant: a silly play I think; only the
Spirit in it that grows very tall, and then sinks again
to nothing, having two heads breeding upon one,
and then Knipp's singing, did please us. . . . Knipp

took us all in, and brought to us Nelly, a most pretty woman, who acted the great part of Cœlia to-day very fine, and did it pretty well: I kissed her, and so did my wife: and a mighty pretty soul she is. We also saw Mrs. Hall, which is my little Roman-nose black girl, that is mighty pretty: she is usually called Betty. Knipp made us stay in a box and see the dancing preparatory to to-morrow for *The Goblins*, a play of Suckling's, not acted these twenty-five years; which was pretty; and so away thence, pleased with this sight also, and specially kissing of Nell.

2 *March.*—To the King's house to see *The Maiden Queene*, a new play of Dryden's, mightily commended for the regularity of it, and the strain and wit; and, the truth is, there is a comical part done by Nell, which is Florimell, that I can never hope ever to see the like done again, by man or woman. The King and Duke of York were at the play. But so great performance of a comical part was never, I believe, in the world before as Nell do this, both as a mad girle, then most and best of all when she comes in like a young gallant; and hath the motions and carriage of a spark the most that ever I saw any man have. It makes me, I confess, admire her.

15 *April.*—To the King's house by chance, where a new play: so full as I never saw it; I forced to stand all the while close to the very door till I took cold, and many people went away for want of room. The King, and Queene, and Duke of York and Duchesse there, and all the Court, and Sir W. Coventry. The play called *The Change of Crownes*; a play of Ned Howard's, the best that ever I saw at that house, being a great play and serious, only Lacy did act the country-gentleman come up to Court,

who do abuse the Court with all the imaginable wit
and plainness about selling of places, and doing every
thing for money. The play took very much.

16 *April*.—Home to dinner, and in haste to carry
my wife to see the new play I saw yesterday, she not
knowing it. But there, contrary to expectation, find
The Silent Woman. However, in; and there Knipp
come into the pit. . . . Knipp tells me the King
was so angry at the liberty taken by Lacy's part[1] to
abuse him to his face, that he commanded they should
act no more, till Moone went and got leave for them to
act again, but not this play. The King mighty angry;
and it was bitter indeed, but very true and witty.
I never was more taken with a play than I am with
this *Silent Woman*, as old as it is, and as often as I have
seen it. There is more wit in it than goes to ten new
plays.

18 *April*.—To the Duke of York's house, and there
saw *The Wits*, a play I formerly loved, and is now
corrected and enlarged: but, though I like the acting,
yet I like not much in the play now.

19 *April*.—To the playhouse, where we saw *Macbeth*, which, though I have seen it often, yet it is one
of the best plays for a stage, and variety of dancing
and musique, that ever I saw.

20 *April*.—To the King's house, but there found the
bill torn down and no play acted, and so being in the
humour to see one, went to the Duke of York's house,
and there saw *The Witts* again, which likes me better
than it did the other day, having much wit in it.
Here met Mr. Rolt, who tells me the reason of no play
to-day at the King's house. That Lacy had been
committed to the porter's lodge for his acting his part
in the late new play, and being thence released to

[1] In *The Change of Crowns* (cf. 15 and 20 April).

come to the King's house, he there met with Ned
Howard, the poet of the play, who congratulated his
release; upon which Lacy cursed him as that it was
the fault of his nonsensical play that was the cause of
his ill usage. Mr. Howard did give him some reply;
to which Lacy answered him, that he was more a fool
than a poet; upon which Howard did give him a blow
on the face with his glove; on which Lacy, having a
cane in his hand, did give him a blow over the pate.
. . . But Howard did not do any thing but complain
to the King of it; so the whole house is silenced, and
the gentry seem to rejoice much at it, the house being
become too insolent.

22 *May.*—To the King's house, where I did give
18*d.*, and saw the two last acts of *The Goblins*, a play I
could not make any thing of by these two acts, but
here Knipp spied me out of the tiring-room, and came
to the pit door, and I out to her, and kissed her, she
only coming to see me, being in a country-dress, she
and others having, it seemed, had a country-dance
in the play, but she no other part: so we parted, and
I into the pit again till it was done. The house full,
but I had no mind to be seen.

17 *August.*—To the King's playhouse, where the
house extraordinary full; and there the King and Duke
of York to see the new play, *Queen Elizabeth's Troubles,
and the History of Eighty Eight.* I confess I have sucked
in so much of the sad story of Queen Elizabeth, from
my cradle, that I was ready to weep for her sometimes; but the play is the most ridiculous that sure
ever came upon the stage; and, indeed, is merely a
show, only shows the true garbe of the Queen in
those days, just as we see Queen Mary and Queen
Elizabeth painted; but the play is merely a puppet
play, acted by living puppets. Neither the design

nor language better; and one stands by and tells us the meaning of things: only I was pleased to see Knipp dance among the milkmaids, and to hear her sing a song to Queen Elizabeth; and to see her come out in her nightgowne with no lockes on, but her bare feet and hair only tied up in a knot behind; which is the comeliest dress that ever I saw her in to her advantage.

22 *August*.—To the King's playhouse, and there saw *The Indian Emperour*; where I find Nell come again which I am glad of; but was most infinitely displeased with her being put to act the Emperour's daughter, which is a great and serious part, which she does most basely. The rest of the play, though pretty good, was not well acted by most of them, methought; so that I took no great content in it.

24 *August*.—Saw *The Cardinall* at the King's house, wherewith I am mightily pleased; but, above all, with Becke Marshall. But it is pretty to see how I look up and down for, and did spy Knipp; but durst not own it to my wife, for fear of angering her, and so I was forced not to take notice of her, and so homeward: and my belly now full with plays, that I do intend to bind myself to see no more till Michaelmas.

5 *October*.—To the Duke of York's, the playhouse, but the house so full, it being a new play, *The Coffee House*, that we could not get in, and so to the King's house: and there, going in, met with Knipp, and she took us up into the tireing-rooms: and to the women's shift, where Nell was dressing herself, and was all unready, and is very pretty, prettier than I thought. And so walked up and down the house above, and then below into the scene-room, and there sat down, and she gave us fruit: and hear I read the questions,

while she answered me, through all her part of *Flora's Figary's,* which was acted to-day. But, Lord! to see how they were both painted would make a man mad, and did make me loath them; and what base company of men comes among them, and how lewdly they talk! and how poor the men are in clothes, and yet what a show they make on the stage by candlelight is very observable. But to see how Nell cursed, for having so few people in the pit, was pretty; the other house carrying away all the people at the new play, and is said, now-a-days, to have generally most company, as being better players. By and by into the pit, and there saw the play, which is pretty good.

19 *October.*—Full of my desire of seeing my Lord Orrery's new play this afternoon at the King's house, *The Black Prince,* the first time it is acted; where, though we came by two o'clock, yet there was no room in the pit, but we were forced to go into one of the upper boxes, at 4*s.* a piece, which is the first time I ever sat in a box in my life. And in the same box came, by and by, behind me, my Lord Barkeley and his lady; but I did not turn my face to them to be known, so that I was excused from giving them my seat; and this pleasure I had, that from this place the scenes do appear very fine indeed, and much better than in the pit. The house infinite full, and the King and Duke of York there. By and by the play begun, and in it nothing particular but a very fine dance for variety of figures, but a little too long. But, as to the contrivance, and all that was witty, which, indeed, was much, and very witty, was almost the same that had been in his two former plays of *Henry the 5th* and *Mustapha,* and the same points and turns of wit in both, and in this very same play often repeated, but in excellent language, and were so excellent that the

whole house was mightily pleased all along till the reading of a letter, which was so long and so unnecessary that they frequently began to laugh, and to hiss twenty times, that, had it not been for the King's being there, they had certainly hissed it off the stage. But I must confess that, as my Lord Barkeley said behind me, the having of that long letter was a thing so absurd, that he could not imagine how a man of his parts could possibly fall into it; or, if he did, if he had but let any friend read it, the friend would have told him of it; and, I must confess, it is one of the most remarkable instances of a wise man's not being wise at all times. After the play done, and nothing pleasing them from the time of the letter to the end of the play, people being put into a bad humour of disliking, which is another thing worth the noting, I home by coach, and could not forbear laughing all the way, and all the evening to my going to bed, at the ridiculousness of the letter, and the more because my wife was angry with me, and the world, for laughing, because the King was there.

23 *October*.—To the King's playhouse, and saw *The Black Prince*: which is now mightily bettered by that long letter being printed, and so delivered to every body at their going in, and some short reference made to it in the play; but, when all is done, I think it the worst play of my Lord Orrery's.

2 *November*.—To the King's playhouse, and there saw *Henry the Fourth*: and contrary to expectation, was pleased in nothing more than in Cartwright's speaking of Falstaffe's speech about 'What is Honour?' The house full of Parliament-men, it being holyday with them: and it was observable how a gentleman of good habit, sitting just before us, eating of some fruit in the midst of the play, did drop down as dead,

being choked; but with much ado Orange Moll did thrust her finger down his throat, and brought him to life again.

28 *December.*—To the King's house, and there saw *The Mad Couple*, which is but an ordinary play; but only Nell's and Hart's mad parts are most excellent done, but especially her's: which makes it a miracle to me to think how ill she do any serious part, as, the other day, just like a fool or changeling; and, in a mad part, do beyond imitation almost. It pleased us mightily to see the natural affection of a poor woman, the mother of one of the children brought on the stage: the child crying, she by force got upon the stage, and took up her child and carried it away off the stage from Hart.

1668

1 *January.*—To the Duke of York's playhouse, and there saw *Sir Martin Mar-all*; which I have seen so often, and yet am mightily pleased with it, and think it mighty witty, and the fullest of proper matter for mirth that ever was writ; and I do clearly see that they do improve in their acting of it. Here a mighty company of citizens, 'prentices, and others; and it makes me observe, that when I began first to be able to bestow a play on myself, I do not remember that I saw so many by half of the ordinary 'prentices and mean people in the pit at 2*s.* 6*d.* a-piece as now; I going for several years no higher than the 12*d.* and then the 18*d.* places, though I strained hard to go in when I did: so much the vanity and prodigality of the age is to be observed in this particular.

6 *February.*—To the Duke of York's playhouse; where a new play of Etheredge's, called *She Would if she Could*; and though I was there by two o'clock,

there was 1000 people put back that could not have
room in the pit: and I at last, because my wife was
there, made shift to get into the 18*d.* box, and there
saw; but, Lord! how full was the house, and how silly
the play, there being nothing in the world good in it,
and few people pleased in it. The King was there:
but I sat mightily behind, and could see but little,
and hear not at all. The play being done, I into the
pit to look for my wife, it being dark and raining, but
could not find her; and so staid going between the
two doors and through the pit an hour and a half, I
think, after the play was done; the people staying
there till the rain was over, and to talk with one another. And, among the rest, here was the Duke of
Buckingham to-day openly sat in the pit; and there
I found him with my Lord Buckhurst, and Sedley,
and Etheredge, the poet; the last of whom I did hear
mightily find fault with the actors, that they were out
of humour, and had not their parts perfect, and that
Harris did do nothing, nor could so much as sing a
ketch in it; and so was mightily concerned: while all
the rest did, through the whole pit, blame the play
as a silly, dull thing, though there was something
very roguish and witty; but the design of the play,
and end, mighty insipid.

27 *February.*—To the King's House, to see *The
Virgin Martyr*, the first time it hath been acted a great
while: and it is mighty pleasant; not that the play is
worth much, but it is finely acted by Beck Marshall.
But that which did please me beyond any thing in
the whole world was the wind-musick when the angel
comes down, which is so sweet that it ravished me,
and indeed, in a word, did wrap up my soul so that
it made me really sick, just as I have formerly been
when in love with my wife; that neither then, nor all

the evening going home, and at home, I was able to think of any thing, but remained all night transported, so as I could not believe that ever any musick hath that real command over the soul of a man as this did upon me: and makes me resolve to practice wind-musick, and to make my wife do the like.

15 *April*.—To the King's playhouse, into a corner of the 18*d*. box, and there saw *The Maid's Tragedy*, a good play. Coach, 1*s*.: play and oranges, 2*s*. 6*d*.

17 *April*.—To the King's house, and saw *The Surprizall*, where base singing, only Knipp, who came, after her song in the clouds, to me in the pit, and there, oranges, 2*s*.

1 *May*.—To the King's playhouse, and there saw *The Surprizall*: and a disorder in the pit by its raining in, from the cupola at top.

2 *May*.—To the Duke of York's playhouse, at a little past twelve, to get a good place in the pit, against the new play, and there setting a poor man to keep my place, I out, and spent an hour at Martin's, my bookseller's, and so back again, where I find the house quite full. But I had my place, and by and by the King comes and the Duke of York; and then the play begins, called *The Sullen Lovers*; *or, The Impertinents*, having many good humours in it, but the play tedious, and no design at all in it. But a little boy, for a farce, do dance Polichinelli, the best that ever anything was done in the world, by all men's report: most pleased with that, beyond anything in the world, and much beyond all the play.

1669

22 *February*.—To White Hall, and there did without much trouble get into the playhouse, them in a good place among the Ladies of Honour, and myself

also sat in the pit; and there by and by come the King and Queen, and they begun *Bartholomew Fayre*. But I like no play here so well as at the common playhouse; besides that, my eyes being very ill since last Sunday and this day se'nnight, with the light of the candles, I was in mighty pain to defend myself now from the light of the candles.

12 *May.*—To the Duke of York's playhouse, and there, in the side balcony, over against the musick. did hear, but not see, a new play, the first day acted, *The Roman Virgin*, an old play, and but ordinary, I thought; but the trouble of my eyes with the light of the candles did almost kill me.

17 *May.*—To the King's playhouse, and saw *The Spanish Curate* revived, which is a pretty good play, but my eyes troubled with seeing it, mightily.[1]

The Diary of SAMUEL PEPYS

[1] This is the last reference to playgoing in the Diary, which was discontinued a fortnight later when Pepys feared he was going blind.

BETTERTON'S BENEFIT

Will's Coffee-House, April 8

ON *Thursday* last was acted, for the benefit of Mr. *Betterton*, the celebrated Comedy call'd *Love for Love*. Those excellent Players Mrs. *Barry*, Mrs. *Bracegirdle*, and Mr. *Dogget*, though not at present concerned in the House, acted on that Occasion. There has not been known so great a Concourse of Persons of Distinction as at that Time; the Stage it self was cover'd with Gentlemen and Ladies, and when the Curtain was drawn, it discovered even there a very splendid Audience. This unusual Encouragement, which was given to a Play for the Advantage of so great an Actor, gives an undeniable Instance, that the true Relish for manly Entertainments and rational Pleasures is not wholly lost. All the Parts were acted to Perfection: The Actors were careful of their Carriage, and no one was Guilty of the Affectation to insert Witticisms of his own, but a due Respect was had to the Audience, for encouraging this accomplished Player. It is not now doubted but Plays will revive, and take their usual Place in the Opinion of Persons of Wit and Merit, notwithstanding their late Apostacy in favour of Dress and Sound. This Place is very much altered since Mr. *Dryden* frequented it; where you used to see *Songs*, *Epigrams* and *Satires*, in the Hands of every Man you met, you have now only a Pack of Cards; and instead of the Cavils about the Turn of the Expression, the Elegance of the Stile, and the like, the Learned now dispute only about the Truth of the Game. But however the Company is alter'd; all have shewn a great Respect for Mr.

Betterton: And the very Gaming Part of the House have been so much touched with a Sense of the Uncertainty of Human Affairs, (which alter with themselves every Moment) that in this Gentleman they pitied *Mark Anthony* of *Rome*, *Hamlet* of *Denmark*, *Mithridates* of *Pontus*, *Theodosius* of *Greece*, and *Henry* the Eighth of *England*. It is well known, he has been in the Condition of each of those illustrious Personages for several Hours together, and behaved himself in those high Stations, in all the Changes of the Scene, with suitable Dignity. For these Reasons we intend to repeat this Favour to him on a proper Occasion, lest he who can instruct us so well in personating feigned Sorrows, should be lost to us by suffering under real ones. The Town is at present in very great Expectation of seeing a Comedy now in Rehearsal, which is the 25th Production of my honoured Friend Mr. *Thomas D'Urfey*; who, besides his great Abilities in the Dramatick, has a peculiar Talent in the Lyrick Way of Writing, and that with a Manner wholly new and unknown to the ancient *Greeks* and *Romans*, wherein he is but faintly imitated in the Translations of the modern *Italian* Opera's.

SIR RICHARD STEELE: *The Tatler*, 1709

THOMAS BETTERTON

BETTERTON was an Actor, as *Shakespear* was an Author, both without Competitors! form'd for the mutual Assistance, and Illustration of each other's Genius! How *Shakespear* wrote, all Men who have a Taste for Nature may read, and know—but with what higher Rapture would he still be *read*, could they conceive how *Betterton play'd* him! Then might they know, the one was born alone to speak what the other only knew, to write! Pity it is, that the momentary Beauties flowing from an harmonious Elocution, cannot like those of Poetry, be their own Record! That the animated Graces of the Player can live no longer than the instant Breath and Motion that presents them; or at best can but faintly glimmer through the Memory, or imperfect Attestation of a few surviving Spectators. Could *how Betterton* spoke be as easily known as *what* he spoke; then might you see the Muse of *Shakespear* in her Triumph, with all her Beauties in their best Array, rising into real Life, and charming her Beholders. But alas! since all this is so far out of the reach of Description, how shall I shew you *Betterton*? Should I therefore tell you, that all the *Othellos*, *Hamlets*, *Hotspurs*, *Mackbeths*, and *Brutus*'s, whom you may have seen since his Time, have fallen far short of him; this still would give you no Idea of his particular Excellence. Let us see then what a particular Comparison may do! whether that may yet draw him nearer to you?

You have seen a *Hamlet* perhaps, who, on the first Appearance of his Father's Spirit, has thrown himself into all the straining Vociferation requisite to

express Rage and Fury, and the House has thunder'd
with Applause; tho' the mis-guided Actor was all
the while (as *Shakespear* terms it) tearing a Passion
into Rags.—I am the more bold to offer you this
particular Instance, because the late Mr. *Addison*,
. while I sate by him, to see this Scene acted, made the
same Observation, asking me with some Surprize, if
I thought *Hamlet* should be in so violent a Passion
with the Ghost, which tho' it might have astonish'd,
it had not provok'd him? for you may observe that
in this beautiful Speech, the Passion never rises
beyond an almost breathless Astonishment, or an
Impatience, limited by filial Reverence, to enquire
into the suspected Wrongs that may have rais'd him
from his peaceful Tomb! and a Desire to know what
a Spirit so seemingly distrest, might wish or enjoin
a sorrowful Son to execute towards his future Quiet
in the Grave? This was the Light into which *Betterton* threw this Scene; which he open'd with a Pause
of mute Amazement! then rising slowly, to a solemn,
trembling Voice, he made the Ghost equally terrible
to the Spectator, as to himself! and in the descriptive
Part of the natural Emotions which the ghastly Vision
gave him, the Boldness of this Expostulation was still
govern'd by Decency, manly, but not braving; his
Voice never rising into that seeming Outrage, or wild
Defiance of what he naturally rever'd. But alas! to
preserve this medium, between mouthing, and meaning too little, to keep the Attention more pleasingly
awake, by a temper'd Spirit, than by mere Vehemence of Voice, is of all the Master-strokes of an Actor
the most difficult to reach. In this none yet have
equall'd *Betterton*. But I am unwilling to shew his
Superiority only by recounting the Errors of those,
who now cannot answer to them, let their farther

Failings therefore be forgotten! or rather, shall I in some measure excuse them? For I am not yet sure, that they might not be as much owing to the false Judgment of the Spectator, as the Actor. While the Million are so apt to be transported, when the Drum of their Ear is so roundly rattled; while they take the Life of Elocution to lie in the Strength of the Lungs, it is no wonder the Actor, whose End is Applause, should be also tempted, at this easy rate, to excite it. Shall I go a little farther? and allow that this Extreme is more pardonable than its opposite Error? I mean that dangerous Affectation of the Monotone, or solemn Sameness of Pronounciation, which to my Ear is insupportable; for of all Faults that so frequently pass upon the Vulgar, that of Flatness will have the fewest Admirers. That this is an Error of ancient standing seems evident by what *Hamlet* says, in his Instructions to the Players, *viz.*

> *Be not too tame, neither,* &c.

The Actor, doubtless, is as strongly ty'd down to the Rules of *Horace* as the Writer.

> *Si vis me flere, dolendum est*
> *Primum ipsi tibi——*

He that feels not himself the Passion he would raise, will talk to a sleeping Audience: But this never was the Fault of *Betterton*; and it has often amaz'd me to see those who soon came after him, throw out in some Parts of a Character, a just and graceful Spirit, which *Betterton* himself could not but have applauded. And yet in the equally shining Passages of the same Character, have heavily dragg'd the Sentiment along like a dead Weight; with a long-ton'd Voice, and absent Eye, as if they had fairly forgot what they were about: If you have never made this Observation,

I am contented you should not know where to apply it.

A farther Excellence in *Betterton*, was, that he could vary his Spirit to the different Characters he acted. Those wild impatient Starts, that fierce and flashing Fire, which he threw into *Hotspur*, never came from the unruffled Temper of his *Brutus* (for I have, more than once, seen a *Brutus* as warm as *Hotspur*) when the *Betterton Brutus* was provok'd, in his Dispute with *Cassius*, his Spirit flew only to his Eye; his steady Look alone supply'd that Terror, which he disdain'd an Intemperance in his Voice should rise to. Thus, with a settled Dignity of Contempt, like an unheeding Rock, he repelled upon himself the Foam of *Cassius*. Perhaps the very Words of *Shakespear* will better let you into my Meaning:

> *Must I give way, and room, to your rash Choler?*
> *Shall I be frighted when a Madman stares?*

And a little after,

> *There is no Terror*, Cassius, *in your Looks!* &c.

Not but in some Part of this Scene, where he reproaches *Cassius*, his Temper is not under this Suppression, but opens into that Warmth which becomes a Man of Virtue; yet this is that *Hasty Spark* of Anger, which *Brutus* himself endeavours to excuse.

But with whatever strength of Nature we see the Poet shew, at once, the Philosopher and the Heroe, yet the Image of the Actor's Excellence will be still imperfect to you, unless Language could put Colours in our Words to paint the Voice with.

Et, si vis similem pingere, pinge sonum, is enjoying an Impossibility. The most that a *Vandyke* can arrive at, is to make his Portraits of great Persons seem to *think*; a Shakespear goes farther yet, and tells you *what* his Pictures thought; a *Betterton* steps beyond 'em both, and calls them from the Grave, to breathe, and be themselves again, in Feature, Speech, and Motion. When the skilful Actor shews you all these Powers at once united, and gratifies at once your Eye, your Ear, your Understanding. To conceive the Pleasure rising from such Harmony, you must have been present at it! 'tis not to be told you!

There cannot be a stronger Proof of the Charms of harmonious Elocution, than the many, even un-natural Scenes and Flights of the false Sublime it has lifted into Applause. In what Raptures have I seen an Audience, at the furious Fustian and turgid Rants in *Nat. Lee's Alexander the Great*! For though I can allow this Play a few great Beauties, yet it is not without its extravagant Blemishes. Every Play of the same Author has more or less of them. Let me give you a Sample from this. *Alexander*, in a full crowd of Courtiers, without being occasionally call'd or provok'd to it, falls into this Rhapsody of Vain-glory.

> *Can none remember? Yes, I know all must!*

And therefore they shall know it agen.

> *When Glory, like the dazzling Eagle, stood*
> *Perch'd on my Beaver, in the Granic Flood,*
> *When Fortune's Self, my Standard trembling bore,*
> *And the pale Fates stood frighted on the Shore,*
> *When the Immortals on the Billows rode,*
> *And I myself appear'd the leading God.*

When these flowing Numbers came from the Mouth of a *Betterton*, the Multitude no more desired Sense to them, than our musical *Connoisseurs* think it essential in the celebrated Airs of an *Italian* Opera. Does not this prove, that there is very near as much Enchantment in the well-governed Voice of an Actor, as in the sweet Pipe of an Eunuch? If I tell

you, there was no one Tragedy, for many Years,
more in favour with the Town than *Alexander,* to
what must we impute this its command of publick
Admiration? Not to its intrinsick Merit, surely, if it
swarms with Passages like this I have shewn you! If
this Passage has Merit, let us see what Figure it
would make upon Canvas, what sort of Picture
would rise from it. If *Le Brun,* who was famous for
painting the Battles of this Heroe, had seen this lofty
Description, what one Image could he have possibly
taken from it? In what Colours would he have shewn
us *Glory perch'd upon a Beaver?* How would he have
drawn *Fortune trembling?* Or, indeed, what use could
he have made of *pale Fates,* or *Immortals* riding upon
Billows, with this blustering *God* of his own making
at the *head* of them? Where, then, must have lain
the Charm, that once made the Publick so partial
to this Tragedy? Why plainly, in the Grace and
Harmony of the Actor's Utterance. For the Actor
himself is not accountable for the false Poetry of his
Author; That, the Hearer is to judge of; if it passes
upon him, the Actor can have no Quarrel to it; who,
if the Periods given him are round, smooth, spirited,
and high-sounding, even in a false Passion, must
throw out the same Fire and Grace, as may be
required in one justly rising from Nature; where
those his Excellencies will then be only more pleasing
in proportion to the Taste of his Hearer. And I am
of opinion, that to the extraordinary Success of this
very Play, we may impute the Corruption of so many
Actors, and Tragick Writers, as were immediately
misled by it. The unskilful Actor, who imagin'd
all the Merit of delivering those blazing Rants, lay
only in the Strength, and strain'd Exertion of the
Voice, began to tear his Lungs, upon every false,

or slight Occasion, to arrive at the same Applause. And it is from hence I date our having seen the same Reason prevalent for above fifty Years. Thus equally misguided too, many a barren-brain'd Author has stream'd into a frothy flowing Style, pompously rolling into sounding Periods, signifying —roundly nothing; of which Number, in some of my former Labours, I am something more than suspicious, that I may myself have made one, but to keep a little closer to *Betterton*.

When this favourite Play I am speaking of, from its being too frequently acted, was worn out, and came to be deserted by the Town, upon the sudden Death of *Monfort*, who had play'd *Alexander* with Success, for several Years, the Part was given to *Betterton*, which, under this great Disadvantage of the Satiety it had given, he immediately reviv'd with so new a Lustre, that for three Days together it fill'd the House; and had his then declining Strength been equal to the Fatigue the Action gave him, it probably might have doubled its Success; an uncommon Instance of the Power and intrinsick Merit of an Actor. This I mention not only to prove what irresistible Pleasure may arise from a judicious Elocution, with scarce Sense to assist it; but to shew you too, that tho' *Betterton* never wanted Fire, and Force, when his Character demanded it; yet, where it was not demanded, he never prostituted his Power to the low Ambition of a false Applause. And further, that when, from a too advanced Age, he resigned that toilsome Part of *Alexander*, the Play, for many Years after never was able to impose upon the Publick; and I look upon his so particularly supporting the false Fire and Extravagancies of that Character, to be a more surprizing Proof of his Skill, than his being eminent in those of *Shakespear*; because there, Truth and Nature coming to his Assistance he had not the same Difficulties to combat, and consequently, we must be less amaz'd at his Success, where we are more able to account for it.

Notwithstanding the extraordinary Power he shew'd in blowing *Alexander* once more into a blaze of Admiration, *Betterton* had so just a sense of what was true, or false Applause, that I have heard him say, he never thought any kind of it equal to an attentive Silence; that there were many ways of deceiving an Audience into a loud one; but to keep them husht and quiet, was an Applause which only Truth and Merit could arrive at: Of which Art, there never was an equal Master to himself. From these various Excellencies, he had so full a Possession of the Esteem and Regard of his Auditors, that upon his Entrance into every Scene, he seem'd to seize upon the Eyes and Ears of the Giddy and Inadvertent! To have talk'd or look'd another way, would then have been thought Insensibility or Ignorance. In all his Soliloquies of moment, the strong Intelligence of his Attitude and Aspect, drew you into such an impatient Gaze, and eager Expectation, that you almost imbib'd the Sentiment with your Eye, before the Ear could reach it.

As *Betterton* is the Centre to which all my Observations upon Action tend, you will give me leave, under his Character, to enlarge upon that Head. In the just Delivery of Poetical Numbers, particularly where the Sentiments are pathetick, it is scarce credible, upon how minute an Article of Sound depends their greatest Beauty or Inaffection. The Voice of a Singer is not more strictly ty'd to Time and Tune, than that of an Actor in Theatrical

Elocution: The least Syllable too long, or too slightly dwelt upon in a Period, depreciates it to nothing; which very Syllable, if rightly touch'd, shall, like the heightening Stroke of Light from a Master's Pencil, give Life and Spirit to the whole. I never heard a Line in Tragedy come from Betterton, wherein my Judgment, my Ear, and my Imagination, were not fully satisfy'd; which, since his Time, I cannot equally say of any one Actor whatsoever: Not but it is possible to be much his Inferior, with great Excellencies; which I shall observe in another Place. Had it been practicable to have ty'd down the clattering Hands of all the ill judges who were commonly the Majority of an Audience, to what amazing Perfection might the *English* Theatre have arrived, with so just an Actor as *Betterton* at the Head of it! If what was Truth only, could have been applauded, how many noisy Actors had shook their Plumes with shame, who, from the injudicious Approbation of the Multitude, have bawl'd and strutted in the place of Merit? If therefore the bare speaking Voice has such Allurements in it, how much less ought we to wonder, however we may lament, that the sweeter Notes of Vocal Musick should so have captivated even the politer World, into an Apostacy from Sense, to an Idolatry of Sound. Let us enquire from whence this Enchantment rises. I am afraid it may be too naturally accounted for: For when we complain, that the finest Musick, purchas'd at such vast Expence, is so often thrown away upon the most miserable Poetry, we seem not to consider, that when the Movement of the Air, and Tone of the Voice, are exquisitely harmonious, tho' we regard not one *Word* of what we hear, yet the Power of the Melody is so busy in the Heart, that we naturally annex Ideas to it of our

own Creation, and, in some sort, become ourselves
the Poet to the Composer; and what Poet is so dull
as not to be charm'd with the Child of his own
Fancy? So that there is even a kind of Language in
agreeable Sounds, which, like the Aspect of Beauty,
without Words, speaks and plays with the Imagination. While this Taste therefore is so naturally
prevalent, I doubt, to propose Remedies for it, were
but giving Laws to the Winds, or Advice to Inamo-
rato's: And however gravely we may assert, that
Profit ought always to be inseparable from the Delight
of the Theatre; nay, admitting that the Pleasure
would be heighten'd by the uniting them; yet, while
Instruction is so little the Concern of the Auditor,
how can we hope that so choice a Commodity will
come to a Market where there is so seldom a Demand
for it?

It is not to the Actor therefore, but to the vitiated
and low Taste of the Spectator, that the Corruptions
of the Stage (of what kind soever) have been owing.
If the Publick, by whom they must live, had Spirit
enough to discountenance, and declare against all
the Trash and Fopperies they have been so frequently fond of, both the Actors, and the Authors,
to the best of their Power, must naturally have serv'd
their daily Table, with sound and wholesome Diet.—
But I have not yet done with my Article of Elocution.

As we have sometimes great Composers of Musick,
who cannot sing, we have as frequently great Writers
that cannot read; and though, without the nicest
Ear, no Man can be Master of Poetical Numbers,
yet the best Ear in the World will not always enable
him to pronounce them. Of this truth, *Dryden*, our
first great Master of Verse and Harmony, was
a strong Instance: When he brought his Play of

Amphytrion to the Stage, I heard him give it his first Reading to the Actors, in which, though it is true, he deliver'd the plain Sense of every Period, yet the whole was in so cold, so flat, and unaffecting a manner, that I am afraid of not being believ'd, when I affirm it.

On the contrary, *Lee*, far his Inferior in Poetry, was so pathetick a Reader of his own Scenes, that I have been inform'd by an Actor, who was present, that while *Lee* was reading to Major *Mohun* at a Rehearsal, *Mohun*, in the Warmth of his Admiration, threw down his Part, and said, Unless I were able to *play* it, as well as you *read* it, to what purpose should I undertake it? And yet this very Author, whose Elocution raised such Admiration in so capital an Actor, when he attempted to be an Actor himself, soon quitted the Stage, in an honest Despair of ever making any profitable Figure there. From all this I would infer, That let our Conception of what we are to speak be ever so just, and the Ear ever so true, yet, when we are to deliver it to an Audience (I will leave Fear out of the question) there must go along with the whole, a natural Freedom, and becoming Grace, which is easier to conceive than describe: For without this inexpressible Somewhat, the Performance will come out oddly disguis'd, or somewhere defectively, unsurprizing to the Hearer. Of this Defect too, I will give you yet a stranger Instance, which you will allow Fear could not be the Occasion of: If you remember *Eastcourt*, you must have known that he was long enough upon the Stage, not to be under the least Restraint from Fear, in his Performance: This Man was so amazing and extraordinary a Mimick, that no Man or Woman, from the Coquette to the Privy-Counsellor, ever mov'd or spoke before him, but he could carry their

Voice, Look, Mien, and Motion, instantly into another Company: I have heard him make long Harangues, and form various Arguments, even in the manner of thinking, of an eminent Pleader at the Bar, with every the least Article and Singularity of his Utterance so perfectly imitated, that he was the very *alter ipse*, scarce to be distinguish'd from his Original. Yet more; I have seen, upon the Margin of the written Part of *Falstaff*, which he acted, his own Notes and Observations upon almost every Speech of it, describing the true Spirit of the Humour, and with what Tone of Voice, Look, and Gesture, each of them ought to be delivered. Yet in his Execution upon the Stage, he seem'd to have lost all those just Ideas he had form'd of it, and almost thro' the Character, labour'd under a heavy Load of Flatness: In a word, with all his Skill in Mimickry, and Knowledge of what ought to be done, he never, upon the Stage, could bring it truly into Practice, but was upon the whole, a languid, unaffecting Actor. After I have shewn you so many necessary Qualifications, not one of which can be spar'd in true Theatrical Elocution, and have at the same time prov'd, that with the Assistance of them all united, the whole may still come forth defective; what Talents shall we say will infallibly form an Actor? This, I confess, is one of Nature's Secrets, too deep for me to dive into; let us content ourselves therefore with affirming, That *Genius*, which Nature only gives, only can complete him. This *Genius* then was so strong in *Betterton*, that it shone out in every Speech and Motion of him. Yet Voice, and Person, are such necessary Supports to it, that, by the Multitude, they have been preferr'd to *Genius* itself, or at least often mistaken for it. *Betterton* had a Voice of that kind, which gave more Spirit to Terror, than to the softer Passions; of more Strength than Melody. The Rage and Jealousy of *Othello*, became him better than the Sighs and Tenderness of *Castalio*: For though in *Castalio* he only excell'd others, in *Othello* he excell'd himself; which you will easily believe, when you consider, that in spite of his Complexion, *Othello* has more natural Beauties than the best Actor can find in all the Magazine of Poetry, to animate his Power, and delight his Judgment with.

The Person of this excellent Actor was suitable to his Voice, more manly than sweet, not exceeding the middle Stature, inclining to the corpulent; of a serious and penetrating Aspect; his Limbs nearer the athletick than the delicate Proportion; yet however form'd, there arose from the Harmony of the whole a commanding Mien of Majesty, which the fairer-fac'd, or (as *Shakespear* calls 'em) the *curled* Darlings of his Time, ever wanted something to be equal Masters of. There was some Years ago, to be had, almost in every Print-shop, a *Metzotinto*, from *Kneller*, extremely like him.

In all I have said of *Betterton*, I confine myself to the Time of his Strength, and highest Power in Action, that you may make Allowances from what he was able to execute at Fifty, to what you might have seen of him at past Seventy; for tho' to the last he was without his Equal, he might not then be equal to his former Self; yet so far was he from being ever overtaken, that for many Years after his Decease, I seldom saw any of his Parts, in *Shakespear*, supply'd by others, but it drew from me the Lamentation of *Ophelia* upon *Hamlet*'s being unlike, what she had seen him.

>   ——————*Ah! woe is me!*
> *T' have seen, what I have seen, see what I see!*

The last Part this great Master of his Profession acted, was *Melantius* in the *Maid's Tragedy*, for his own Benefit; when being suddenly seiz'd by the Gout, he submitted, by extraordinary Applications, to have his Foot so far reliev'd, that he might be able to walk on the Stage, in a Slipper, rather than wholly disappoint his Auditors. He was observ'd that Day to have exerted a more than ordinary Spirit, and met with suitable Applause; but the unhappy Consequence of tampering with his Distemper was, that it flew into his Head, and kill'd him in three Days, (I think) in the seventy-fourth Year of his Age.

An Apology for the Life of COLLEY CIBBER, Written by Himself, 1739.

Mr. Garrick took all the necessary steps and precautions, previous to his appearance on a London stage, to ensure his success when he should come forth a candidate for fame. He had performed a noviciate at Ipswich; and even before his going to that place, he had studied, with great assiduity, a variety of parts on the different walks of acting. The Clown, the Fop, the Fine Gentleman, the Man of Humour, the Sot, the Valet, the Lover, the Hero, nay, the Harlequin, had all been critically examined, and often rehearsed and practised by him in private. After long reflection and much serious weighing of consequences, he fixed upon Richard the Third for his first part in London. He had often declared he would never chuse a character which was not suitable to his person; for, said he, if I should come forth in a hero, or any part which is generally acted by a tall fellow, I shall not be offered a larger salary than forty shillings per week. In this he glanced at the folly of those managers who used to measure an actor's merit by his size.

He could not possibly give a stronger proof of sound judgment, than in fixing his choice on Richard. The play has always been popular, on account of its comprehending such variety of historical and domestic facts, with such affecting scenes of exalted misery and royal distress. Richard was well adapted to his figure; the situations in which he is placed are diversified by a succession of passion, and dignified by variety and splendor of action. A skilful actor cannot wish for a fairer field on which to display his abilities.

On the 19th of October, 1741, David Garrick acted Richard the Third, for the first time, at the playhouse in Goodman's-Fields. So many idle persons, under the title of gentlemen acting for their diversion, had exposed their incapacity at that theatre, and had so often disappointed the audiences, that no very large company was brought together to see the new performer. However, several of his own acquaintance, many of them persons of good judgment, were assembled at the usual hour; though we may well believe that the greatest part of the audience was stimulated rather by curiosity to see the event, than invited by any hopes of rational entertainment.

An actor, who, in the first display of his talents, undertakes a principal character, has generally, amongst other difficulties, the prejudices of the audience to struggle with, in favour of an established performer. Here, indeed, they were not insurmountable. Cibber, who had been much admired in Richard, had left the stage. Quin was the popular player; but his manner of heaving up his words, and his laboured action, prevented his being a favourite Richard.

Mr. Garrick's easy and familiar, yet forcible style in speaking and acting, at first threw the critics into some hesitation concerning the novelty as well as propriety of his manner. They had been long accustomed to an elevation of the voice, with a sudden mechanical depression of its tones, calculated to excite admiration, and to intrap applause. To the just modulation of the words, and concurring expression of the features from the genuine workings of nature, they had been strangers, at least for some time. But after he had gone through a variety of scenes, in which he gave evident proofs of consummate art, and perfect knowledge of character, their

doubts were turned into surprize and astonishment,
from which they relieved themselves by loud and
reiterated applause. They were more especially
charmed, when the actor, after having thrown aside
the hypocrite and politician, assumed the warrior
and the hero. When information was brought to
Richard, that the duke of Buckingham was taken,
Garrick's look and action, when he pronounced the
words,

> ————Off with his head!
> So much for Buckingham!

were so significant and important, from his visible
enjoyment of the incident, that several loud shouts of
approbation proclaimed the triumph of the actor
and satisfaction of the audience. The death of
Richard was accompanied with the loudest gratula-
tions of applause.

The same play was acted six or seven times successively. The receipts of the treasury, which I have
before me, amounted, in seven nights, to no more
than 216*l*. 7*s*. 6*d*.

THOMAS DAVIES: *Memoirs of the Life of David Garrick*,
1781.

MR. PARTRIDGE SEES GARRICK

Mr. *Jones* having spent three Hours in reading and kissing the aforesaid Letter, and being, at last, in a State of good Spirits, from the last-mentioned Considerations, he agreed to carry an Appointment which he had before made into Execution. This was to attend Mrs. *Miller* and her younger Daughter, into the Gallery at the Playhouse, and to admit Mr. *Partridge* as one of the Company. For as *Jones* had really that Taste for Humour which many affect, he expected to enjoy much Entertainment in the Criticisms of *Partridge*; from whom he expected the simple Dictates of Nature, unimproved indeed, but likewise unadulterated by Art.

In the first Row then of the first Gallery did Mr. *Jones*, Mrs. *Miller*, her youngest Daughter, and *Partridge*, take their Places. *Partridge* immediately declared, it was the finest Place he had ever been in. When the first Musick was played, he said, 'It was a Wonder how so many Fidlers could play at one Time, without putting one another out.' While the Fellow was lighting the upper Candles, he cry'd out to Mrs. *Miller*, 'Look, look, Madam, the very Picture of the Man in the End of the Common-Prayer Book, before the Gunpowder-Treason Service': Nor could he help observing, with a Sigh, when all the Candles were lighted, 'That here were Candles enough burnt in one Night, to keep an honest poor Family for a whole Twelvemonth.'

As soon as the Play, which was *Hamlet*, Prince of *Denmark*, began, *Partridge* was all Attention, nor did

he break Silence till the Entrance of the Ghost; upon
which he asked *Jones*, 'what Man that was in the
strange Dress; something', said he, 'like what I have
seen in a Picture. Sure it is not Armour, is it?' *Jones*
answered, 'That is the Ghost.' To which *Partridge*
replied with a Smile, 'Perswade me to that, Sir, if you
can. Though I can't say I ever actually saw a
Ghost in my Life, yet I am certain I should know one,
if I saw him, better than that comes to. No, no, Sir,
Ghosts don't appear in such Dresses as that, neither.'
In this Mistake, which caused much Laughter in
the Neighbourhood of *Partridge*, he was suffered to
continue 'till the Scene between the *Ghost* and *Hamlet*,
when *Partridge* gave that Credit to Mr. *Garrick* which
he had denied to *Jones*, and fell into so violent a
Trembling, that his Knees knocked against each
other. *Jones* asked him what was the Matter, and
whether he was afraid of the Warrior upon the Stage?
'O la! Sir,' said he, 'I perceive now it is what you
told me. I am not afraid of any Thing, for I know it is
but a Play: And if it was really a Ghost, it could do
one no Harm at such a Distance, and in so much
Company; and yet if I was frightened, I am not the
only Person.' 'Why, who', cries *Jones*, 'dost thou
take to be such a Coward here besides thyself?' 'Nay,
you may call me Coward if you will; but if that little
Man there upon the Stage is not frightned, I never
saw any Man frightned in my Life. Ay, ay; *go along
with you!* Ay, to be sure! Who's Fool then? Will you?
Lud have Mercy upon such Fool-Hardiness!—Whatever happens it is good enough for you.—*Follow you?*
I'd follow the Devil as soon. Nay, perhaps, it is the
Devil—for they say he can put on what Likeness he
pleases.—Oh! here he is again.—*No farther!* No,
you have gone far enough already; farther than I'd

have gone for all the King's Dominions.' *Jones* offered to speak, but *Partridge* cried, 'Hush, hush, dear Sir, don't you hear him!' And during the whole Speech of the Ghost, he sat with his Eyes fixed partly on the Ghost, and partly on *Hamlet*, and with his Mouth open; the same Passions which succeeded each other in *Hamlet*, succeeding likewise in him.

When the Scene was over, *Jones* said, 'Why, *Partridge*, you exceed my Expectations. You enjoy the Play more than I conceived possible.' 'Nay, Sir,' answered *Partridge*, 'if you are not afraid of the Devil, I can't help it; but to be sure it is natural to be surprized at such Things, though I know there is nothing in them: Not that it was the Ghost that surprized me neither; for I should have known that to have been only a Man in a strange Dress: But when I saw the little Man so frighted himself, it was that which took Hold of me.' 'And dost thou imagine then, *Partridge*,' cries *Jones*, 'that he was really frightned?' 'Nay, Sir,' said *Partridge*, 'did not you yourself observe afterwards, when he found out it was his own Father's Spirit, and how he was murdered in the Garden, how his Fear forsook him by Degrees, and he was struck dumb with Sorrow, as it were, just as I should have been, had it been my own Case.—But hush! O la! What Noise is that? There he is again.—Well, to be certain, though I know there is nothing at all in it, I am glad I am not down yonder, where those Men are.' Then turning his Eyes again upon *Hamlet*, 'Ay, you may draw your Sword; what signifies a Sword against the Power of the Devil?'

During the second Act, *Partridge* made very few Remarks. He greatly admired the Fineness of the

Dresses; nor could he help observing upon the King's Countenance. 'Well,' said he, 'how People may be deceived by Faces? *Nulla fides fronti* is, I find, a true Saying. Who would think, by looking in the King's Face, that he had ever committed a Murder?' He then enquired after the Ghost; but *Jones*, who intended he should be surprized, gave him no other Satisfaction, than 'that he might possibly see him again soon, and in a Flash of Fire.'

Partridge sat in fearful Expectation of this; and now, when the Ghost made his next Appearance, *Partridge* cried out, 'There, Sir, now; what say you now? Is he frightned now or no? As much frightned as you think me; and, to be sure, no Body can help some Fears. I would not be in so bad a Condition as what's his Name, Squire *Hamlet*, is there, for all the World. Bless me! What's become of the Spirit? As I am a living Soul, I thought I saw him sink into the Earth.' 'Indeed, you saw right,' answered *Jones*. 'Well, well,' cries *Partridge*, 'I know it is only a Play; and besides, if there was any Thing in all this, Madam *Miller* would not laugh so: For as to you, Sir, you would not be afraid, I believe, if the Devil was here in Person.—There, there—ay, no Wonder you are in such a Passion; shake the vile wicked Wretch to Pieces. If she was my own Mother I should serve her so. To be sure, all Duty to a Mother is forfeited by such wicked Doings.—Ay, go about your Business; I hate the Sight of you.'

Our Critic was now pretty silent till the Play, which *Hamlet* introduces before the King. This he did not at first understand, 'till *Jones* explained it to him; but he no sooner entered into the Spirit of it,

than he began to bless himself that he had never
committed Murder. Then turning to Mrs. *Miller*,
he asked her, 'If she did not imagine the King looked
as if he was touched; though he is', said he, 'a good
Actor, and doth all he can to hide it. Well, I would
not have so much to answer for, as that wicked Man
there hath, to sit upon a much higher Chair than
he sits upon.—No wonder he run away; for your
Sake I'll never trust an innocent Face again.'

The Grave-digging Scene next engaged the Attention of *Partridge*, who expressed much surprize at
the Number of Skulls thrown upon the Stage. To
which *Jones* answered, 'That it was one of the most
famous Burial-Places about Town.' 'No wonder
then', cries *Partridge*, 'that the Place is haunted. But
I never saw in my Life a worse Grave-digger. I had
a Sexton, when I was Clerk, that should have dug
three Graves while he is digging one. The Fellow
handles a Spade as if it was the first Time he had ever
had o: ε in his Hand. Ay, ay, you may sing. You
had rather sing than work, I believe.'—Upon *Hamlet*'s
taking up the Skull, he cry'd out, 'Well, it is strange
to see how fearless some Men are: I never could
bring myself to touch any Thing belonging to a
dead Man on any Account.—He seemed frightned
enough too at the Ghost I thought. *Nemo omnibus
horis sapit.*'

Little more worth remembering occurred during
the Play; at the End of which *Jones* asked him,
'which of the Players he had liked best?' To this he
answered, with some Appearance of Indignation at
the Question, 'The King without Doubt.' 'Indeed,
Mr. *Partridge*,' says Mrs. *Miller*, 'you are not of the

same Opinion as the Town; for they are all agreed, that *Hamlet* is acted by the best Player who ever was on the Stage.' 'He the best Player!' cries *Partridge*, with a contemptuous Sneer, 'why, I could act as well as he myself. I am sure if I had seen a Ghost, I should have looked in the very same Manner, and done just as he did. And then, to be sure, in that Scene, as you called it, between him and his Mother, where you told me he acted so fine, why, Lord help me, any Man, that is, any good Man, that had had such a Mother, would have done exactly the same. I know you are only joking with me; but, indeed, Madam, though I was never at a Play in *London*, yet I have seen acting before in the Country; and the King for my Money; he speaks all his Words distinctly, half as loud again as the other.—Any Body may see he is an Actor.

HENRY FIELDING: *Tom Jones*, 1749

'THE BEGGAR'S OPERA': 18TH CENTURY[1]

NOTWITHSTANDING we confess a partiality for music when it is composed of sweet, significant and persuasive sounds, yet the Opera, serious or comic, but especially the former, is a species of the drama not at all defensible; it carries absurdity in its front, and absolutely puts nature out of countenance; to prove this would be superfluous, as we cannot pay any reader so bad a compliment as to suppose that a single hint does not bear satisfactory conviction.

Shocked as every man of real taste, feeling and genius must be, at the predominance of those dear-bought, unessential exotics, Italian operas, Gay resolved to exercise his unbounded talent of satire against them; and that good sense, a little embittered, might go down with more fashionable *gout*, as apothecaries gild pills, he called in music to his aid, and such music too as was relishable by, not caviare to the million; thus, as we have read of an army, who defeated their enemies by shooting back upon them their own arrows, so he struck deep wounds into the emaciated *signori* of that time, by shewing such sterling wit and humour as they were unacquainted with, decorated with the reigning taste of the day—the thought was happy, the execution equal to the design, and the success suitable to both.

In the very name of this piece the author seems to have issued a keen shaft of ridicule, and making the author a beggar is a noble sarcasm on fortune and public taste, which have suffered most excellent talents

[1] See also *post*, pp. 93–5 and pp. 273–5.

to pine under a thousand disadvantages, of un-
merited penury and even contempt: no one knew
better than Gay the neglect which too commonly
attends literary merit; he experienced, felt, and with
great poignancy of expression declared it.

This piece opens with Jonathan Wild, the reigning
thief-maker and thief-taker of that time, under the
title of Peachum, perusing his tyburn-register; his
song, in eight lines, contains more of the spirit of
truth and satire than would animate some poems of
eight score; the succeeding scene with Filch exhibits
many excellent remarks, and his account of the gang,
when looking out for proper sacrifices, is not only an
admirable, but a very useful picture to the profligate;
Mrs. Peachum's expressions of pleasure, that there
has been no murder committed for some time
recommend her to favour; and Peachum's replies
shewing what money will do in criminal prosecutions,
is, we are afraid, too just; mention of Macheath
naturally falls in, and the spectators are prepared
to receive him, at least, as an agreeable highwayman:
his attachment to Polly comes aptly into the conversation, and the plot very properly begins to dawn.
—Speaking of Polly's being in love, Peachum discovers a very suitable selfishness, and where he
remarks of what service she may be to him, by acting
on political principles, the expression, as well as some
preceding ones, glows with satiric meaning—'My
daughter should be to me, like a court-lady to a
minister of state, a key to the whole gang.'

Mrs. Peachum's scene with Filch has nothing but
some strokes of low humour to recommmend it, yet
in that light is very satisfactory, and always works a
very laughable effect.

Polly is introduced by her father under such

circumstances as engage favour; her mother's violent entrance is much in character; the fainting too, and the remedy for it, are powerful burlesques on similar incidents to be met with in graver pieces; the daughter's silence on her marriage being discovered, is a very probable effect of confusion and apprehension, nor does a word of the consequent dialogue fail of due influence; the impatience of the parents, one through pride, the other through interest, give a fine opening for Polly's delicate, interesting apology, of a sincere passion, for the man she has married; and Peachum's design of taking off his new son-in-law, seems the growth of a mind fortified against any feelings of humanity.

It is a matter of wonder how several of our gay ladies and fine gentlemen can hear the following speech without blushing conscious guilt; 'If she had had only an intrigue with the fellow, why the very best families have excused and huddled up an affair of that sort; 'tis marriage, husband, that makes it a blemish.' What Peachum replies has a luxuriancy of merit, 'But money, wife, is the true fuller's earth for reputations; there is not a spot or stain but what it can take out'; what brilliant, what general, what compacted satire! mounted on the unshakable basis of truth, does this short sentence contain? How essentially superior to an assimilation of the same ingredients and Mr. Foote's pleasantry, in the prelude to Mr. Colman's Man and Wife, which difference is only mentioned here to shew how much the happy thought of one man of genius may be enervated by passing through the imagination of another.

The parents endeavouring to persuade their daughter that an impeachment of the man she loves, an is her husband also, must recommend her to their favour, has something in it shocking, yet affords a very engaging, pathetic transition in Polly's character; and her soliloquy upon hearing, unseen, the plan for Macheath's destruction, deserves much better delivery, much more expressive features than it is in general favoured with—the breaks are fine, the sentiments tender, the description lively, all dressed in a naiveté of language, which finds a passage to the heart, by nature's aid alone.

The hero is brought forward with great advantage, the bold spirited symphony which introduces him, has a similar effect to those flourishes of martial music in some tragedies, and he comes very opportunely to give the first act additional life towards its conclusion; Polly's distress for his present danger, very naturally disappears at the sight and affectionate address of her husband, but with equal propriety soon returns again, with a variation which pleasingly touches the audience; his reluctance to fly, and her tender resolution to part for a time, rather than hazard his safety, raise delicate feelings.

As only the first song has been particularized, it may be necessary to observe, that to avoid repetition as much as possible, all the musical part will be taken notice of in our general view of the piece, on closing the remarks.

In the first scene of the second act we are presented with a set of characters not at all respectable by profession, yet amusing, and somewhat instructive from their conversation, which however we deem too full of sound sense, and genteel, keen satire for such personages—besides there are some sophistical justifications of highwaymen, rather dangerous for dissolute minds; in the drama this should be rarely

meddled with, as natural vice gains more confirma-
tion from delusive shew and false arguments, than
natural virtue does from moral instruction—however,
placing even thieves above courtiers in friendly
attachments, as the author has judiciously done in
what follows, must considerably palliate the objection
we have raised: one says, 'Who is there here who
would not die for his friend?' another replies, 'Who
is there here who would betray him for interest?'
To which a third returns, 'Shew me a gang of
courtiers who can say as much.' 'Tis very plain
from this, and many other inimitable passages, that
our author knew courtiers in general exceeding well,
what ever his knowledge of thieves might be.

Macheath's short interview with his gang means
nothing more than acquainting them with the reason
of his disappearance for some time, by Mat o' the
Mint's mentioning Moorfields as the place of their
rendezvous, we may learn that part of the town was
then as reputable as some other spots of it are at
present.—What succeeds this scene, previous to the
introduction of the ladies, and their conversation,
however natural, are by no means proper for public
representation; the dialogue has great spirit, and is
enlivened by several smart repartees, but the subject
of action, and the characters are so much founded
upon licentiousness, as not to be defensible; improper
prejudicial ideas must arise, and we heartily condemn the whole from this principle, that vice is
never more dangerous than when she smiles, cover-
ing her deformities with a veil of pleasantry.

Indeed, apprehending Macheath in the midst of
his jollity, by the treachery of two prostitutes, may
convey good warning to some who associate with
such wretches; yet we are apt to think this scene is

more apt to inflame the passions than to correct the conduct of youth; and delicate taste must be offended at many sentiments too gross for its tender relish.

Lockit's reception of Macheath, and his remarks upon the fetters at different prices, shew the gaoler in true, humourous, yet shocking colours; it being a miserable perversion of justice to treat culprits not according to the enormity of their crimes, but strength of their pockets—the perplexity of Macheath arising from his apprehension of Lucy's reproaches, falls well in, and her timely appearance confirms his fear; however, we must again pass censure upon our author for making Lucy speak of her *load* of infamy, from a promise of marriage, and her jealousy of Polly Peachum, the plot might have been sufficiently wrought up without allusions so very sensual, we mean with respect to the audience; Macheath's endeavouring to soothe her into a good humour that they may serve his particular purpose, though ungenerous, is polite and in character; the words which Lucy speaks at going off, 'I long to be made an honest woman', are a strong and pleasant stroke of ridicule against those who vainly imagine that virtue is comprized in any external ceremony, and that a mere compliance with established custom can sanctify vice.

The satires which occur between Peachum and Lockit concerning their accounts, are masterly; and the song, which we cannot avoid quoting, inimitable:

> When you censure the age,
> Be cautious and sage,
>   Lest the courtiers offended should be:
> If you mention vice or bribe,
> 'Tis so pat to all the tribe,
>   That each cries that was levell'd at me.

We have heard a short anecdote of Sir Robert
Walpole, against whom Gay chiefly brandished his
pen, in respect of this song, which shewed an agreeable and politic presence of mind; being in the stage-
box, at the first representation of the opera, a most
universal encore attended Lockit's song, and all eyes
at the same time were fixed on Sir Robert, who,
noting the matter, joined heartily in the plaudit,
and encored it a second time with his single voice;
which not only blunted the poetical shaft, but gained
a general huzza from the audience.

The thief-taker and gaoler quarrelling upon a
principle of honour, is also admirably sarcastical
upon those known scoundrels who pretend a jealousy
for reputation, and who insolently quarrel upon
principles they are totally unacquainted with—
nothing is commoner than for prostitutes to com-
mence vehement burlesque altercations about virtue,
and gamblers about honesty.

Lucy's interposition with her father in favour of
her gallant, and his obdurate refusal manifest a
strict knowledge of nature, as does her determination
to effect the captain's freedom at any rate; no
incident ever fell in more opportunely than Polly's
entrance at this critical point of time; it reduces
Macheath to a peculiar dilemma, and contrasts the
ladies very agreeably; their different feelings are
expressed with a degree of very nice distinction,
tenderness is well opposed, by vehemence of affection,
and the whole scene furnishes extreme agreeable
action.—Polly's patience so long under such circumstances, and at last breaking out into womanish
resentment, is a good delineation of a female mind,
under some restraint of delicacy, yet susceptible of
provocation upon tender points; the quarrel is well

conceived, judiciously conducted, and wrought into a humourous climax; the timely intervention of Peachum prevents actual hostilities, and causes a pleasing touch of the pathetic; while Lucy's resolution of stealing her father's keys to give Macheath his liberty, puts expectation into a fresh degree of suspense, and concludes the second act at a critical period.

A supposition of his daughter's connivance at the captain's escape, gives rise to Lockit's treating her somewhat roughly at the beginning of the third act; but, in the true spirit of corruption, which we may style *ex officio*, indeed the effect of his nature as well as place, he enquires for the perquisite, and is not a little chagrined at finding the girl possessed of generosity.—In the short subsequent scene, where Filch is introduced, we can by no means approve his gross answer to Lockit's observation, that he looks like a shotten herring, it is certainly only fit for the meridian of St. Giles's.

The character of a highwayman is well preserved in Macheath's making a gaming-house his first asylum after enlargement, and fitting him up with occasional finery of external appearance, shews the author not only a judge of nature, but the stage; for such sort of collectors generally aim at making a gallant figure, to appear what they are not, and change of dress often gives an actor some novelty with the audience; this scene, however, imports little more than to shew the dissipated turn of our hero.

Peachum, Lockit, and the tally-woman, Mrs. Dye Trapes, furnish us with a dish of conversation censurable throughout, though it always pleases by the force of action; the subject is too mean for the public ear, the characters mentioned too despicable for notice, except from the police, and the old lady's secrets, of her abominable trade, infamous; we would therefore recommend some other means of discovering Macheath, and heartily wish a total omission of such stuff as no person can learn anything from, which it would not be better to be ignorant of.

The design of poisoning Polly, in a glass of strong waters, renders Lucy a right Newgate bird, and makes her, though the act is not perpetrated, an object of detestation; and we apprehend unnecessarily, unless we carry the idea of burlesque constantly in view, and consider the author as ridiculing the poisoned bowls of tragedy, so often needlessly administered, and so often miraculously escaped; another Billingsgate sentiment we find furnished to Lucy in this scene, it comes immediately after these words, 'I vow, Polly, I shall take it monstrously ill, if you refuse me.'

Macheath's appearing in custody, surprises and alarms attention; his interview with the real and would-be wife is very expressive of the circumstance, and good performance may call forth some drops of pity for a very unworthy object.—The different applications of the females, to their several fathers, call up tender sensations, but, we apprehend, they are rather misplaced; for as Polly is certainly the leading character, and offers the most pathetic address, hers should have come last by way of climax.

The sensible resolution, and commendable, tho' divided, tenderness of Macheath, in his song as he goes off to the Old-Bailey, recommend him considerably to favour, and are therefore artfully thrown in.

As Italian operas depend a good deal on dancing merit, we find Gay has a stroke even at that, by introducing a hop among the Newgate-gentry, to which, by way of making a strange, yet satirical medley, the condemned hole immediately succeeds; and, like other great men in some serious pieces, the captain sings through all weathers—high spirits, low spirits, love and despair; he has no less than ten airs to go through successively, yet so judiciously varied that he must be a bitter bad vocal performer, indeed, who palls his audience with them; the following short scenes between him and his friends, and that with the ladies, claim no great share of praise, nor do they merit any censure.

That very unexpected turn the catastrophe takes is thus apologized for by the beggar, 'In this kind of drama, 'tis no matter how absurdly things are brought about—so you rabble there, run and cry a reprieve'.—Thus, by a kind of poetical, or rather operatical legerdemain, hey! pass! misery is gone, and leaves joy and cheerfulness in its place.

To examine the plot of this piece by strict rules of criticism, as the author does not by any means pretend to regularity, would be too severe; yet the unities are not too grossly intruded upon, except in one place—there are but three short speeches and a dance between Macheath's being taken to trial and his appearing in the condemned hole, which could scarce happen till a day after at least, as prisoners, though found guilty, are not put there till after sentence.

The dialogue of this opera has great ease, spirit and correctness; the sentiments are always just, though sometimes blameable; the satire inimitable, and the songs without one exception, bating that of

Mrs. Trapes, an unparalleled treasure of brilliant allusions, instructive ideas, shrewd tendency, familiar expression, and unaffected versification: they have the plain outward semblance of common ballads, yet teem with a luxuriance of imagination, truth and policy, most amazingly compacted into an incredible narrow compass, which, in our estimation, entitles them to be stiled the quintessence of merit.

Yet after offering this impartial tribute at the shrine of Gay's genius, it gives us concern to be under a necessity of remarking, that a moral was the last point in his view, if it entered there at all; and, in this respect, a gloomy cloud casts its dark shade over the shine of praise he must otherwise have commanded; if young minds, which indeed the music helps, leave a theatre untainted with any prejudicial impression after seeing the Beggar's Opera; if no foolish young person of either sex admires Macheath as any other than a diverting stage-character; if his shew and false courage do not delude the one sex, nor his gallantry attract the other, then the piece may stand as inoffensive; but we fear it does not often work an effect of such mediocrity, therefore are bold to call it a composition made up of ingredients much more noxious than salutary, so pleasingly relished, so flatteringly gilded, that scarce any eye or taste can resist the powerful, dangerous temptation; it stands, like light and heat, alluring passions, which play like moths around it, till they fall a prey to the delusive object of their delight.

In respect of characters, the men are all arrant scoundrels, and the females, except Polly, vicious jades; necessarily there can be but a very faint degree of light and shade, which undoubtedly constitute not only a great part of dramatic beauty but propriety;

for all angels, or all devils, is but a very partial, uninstructive picture of human nature; but indeed our author's choice of characters would not admit of much variety, wherefore we heartily lament his prostituting such exquisite talents to so unedifying, or rather immoral a subject.

Macheath has something specious, but not one valuable symptom in his composition; his profession is not only to rob men of their property, but females of their characters and peace; there is an appearance of courage, without a spark of reality; for at the trying moment, we find he applies to the true resource of a coward, liquor; in short, he is a contemptible knave, yet an agreeable gallant, and therefore, as we have already observed, the more dangerous and censurable for public exhibition.

In the performance of this part, spirited boldness of figure, flashy gentility of deportment, and an expressive, not a refined taste of singing, are necessary, under this idea of requisites, we cannot say that any singer within our knowledge has represented him in a capital manner; Mr. BEARD's appearance and manner of singing were all that could be wished, but his speaking was intolerable, and he appeared too much of the gentleman; Mr. LOWE's voice was more happy, but his expression less characteristic, and his speaking, if possible, worse; Mr. VERNON's musical knowledge is extensive, his merit in acting great, but his figure rather inadequate, and his voice totally so; Mr. MATTOCKS is far too faint in appearance and every degree of expression.

If the managers of Drury-lane would do themselves and the public justice, Mr. BANNISTER, who looks, walks and sings the part, take all together,— better than any who have been mentioned, should undoubtedly be put in possession of it; and indeed of many others, which are miserably mutilated by the present possessors.—Mr. DIGGES, whom we mentioned in our remarks upon Richard the Third, was not without great merits in the captain.

Peachum and Lockit are admirably drawn for their stations, and with a very natural distinction; the former being more in the world, has more extended ideas, more shrewdness, and is a knave of greater latitude; Mr. MACKLIN and Mr. YATES were indisputably superior to any competitors in these parts; but for general dryness and a just cynical turn of humour, Mr. MACKLIN stood, in our opinion foremost; at present it does not deserve notice at either house.

Lockit is obvious and easy to hit, yet all we have seen never exceeded mediocrity; some sink him into an absolute black-guard, which there is no reason for; and others soften the natural gloom of his station too much; the late Mr. BERRY was, we apprehend, the most tolerable of any person for several years.— Filch is well described by the author, and never was, nor never need be, better expressed than by Mr. PARSONS of Drury-lane, who, if it would not seem an aukward compliment, looks, deports, and sings the pickpocket to perfection.

Polly is an agreeable young woman, imprudent, yet delicate, and constant in affection; she commits a breach of filial duty, 'tis true, in point of her secret marriage, but such parents as hers appear to deserve little confidence; no character in the drama has furnished so many young adventurers as this, several of whom have made ample provision for themselves through her introduction into life; and, upon the whole, there never was a part in which so many unequal performers made a tolerable stand; out of a large number in our recollection, the following ladies deserved considerable praise, Miss NORRIS, Miss FALKNER, and Mrs. CHAMBERS.

Mrs. PINTO sung it better, and brought more money, by far, than any person since the first season of exhibition; Mrs. ARNE also had great musical merit, but neither of them possessed a shadow of acting—Mrs. CIBBER, was to the eye, heart and ear, worth all we have mentioned, and the only sensible female singer that we remember—were the understanding to be pleased with sensibility of countenance, emphasis, and sound, we could wish to see Miss MACKLIN do the part at present.

Lucy is a character, who, through weakness of vice, has forfeited her virtue, she is composed of violent passions, and, as we have shewn, of a bad heart; yet, even with moderate merit, must please in acting; Mrs. CLIVE, though she squalled the songs, did the part more justice than any body else. We presume Mrs. MATTOCKS would shew more character and spirit in it than any one now on the stage.

Mrs. Peachum was extremely well represented by Mrs. MACKLIN, and does not suffer injury from Mrs. VINCENT; but, we apprehend, would be much better in possession of Mrs. GREEN; as to Mrs. Dye, and the other ladies, we shall take no notice of them, as we cordially wish they were never to be seen again.

From observations already made, we have shewn that there is scarce any moral deducible from the BEGGAR'S OPERA; that it is, upon the whole, a loathsome, infectious carcase, clothed in an angelic garb; that it is founded upon solid sense and satiric truth, yet rises into a superstructure of licentiousness; that it is highly entertaining, not at all instructive;

that it is an exquisite burlesque upon Italian operas, and not a little so upon virtue; that it is inflammatory with humour, and vulgar with eloquence; in short, it is one of those bewitching evils, which offended reason must wish had never been brought to light, while delighted taste must lament the very idea of its annihilation.

FRANCIS GENTLEMAN: *The Dramatic Censor; or, Critical Companion,* 1770

MRS. SIDDONS

To write a criticism on Mrs. Siddons is to write a panegyric, and a panegyric of a very peculiar sort, for the praise will be true. Like her elder brother, she has a marked and noble countenance, and a figure more dignified than graceful, and she is like him in all his good qualities, but not any of his bad ones. If Mr. Kemble studiously meditates a step or an attitude in the midst of passion, Mrs. Siddons never thinks about either, and therefore is always natural, because on occasions of great feeling it is the passions should influence the actions. Attitudes are not to be studied, as old Havard used to study them, between six looking-glasses: feel the passion, and the action will follow. I know it has been denied that actors sympathise with the feelings they represent, and among other critics Dr. Johnson is supposed to have denied it. The Doctor was accustomed to talk very loudly at the play upon divers subjects, even when his friend, Garrick, was electrifying the house with his most wonderful scenes, and the worst of it was that he usually sat in one of the stage boxes: the actor remonstrated with him one night after the representation, and complained that the talking 'disturbed his feelings': 'Pshaw! David', replied the critic, '*Punch has no feelings.*' But the Doctor was fond of saying his good things as well as lesser geniuses, and to say a good thing in not always to say a true one or one that is intended to be true. To call his friend a puppet, to give so contemptuous an appellation to a man whose powers he was at other times happy to respect, and whose death he lamented as having 'eclipsed the gaiety of nations', must be considered as a familiar pleasantry rather than a betrayed opinion. The best way to solve the difficulty is to apply to an actor himself, but as I am not in the way of such an application, I think the complaint made by Garrick will do as well, since he talks of his feelings as the means necessary to his performance. It appears to me that the countenance cannot express a single passion perfectly, unless the passion is first felt. It is easy to grin representations of joy, and to pull down the muscles of the countenance as an imitation of sorrow, but a keen observer of human nature and its effects will easily detect the cheat. There are nerves and muscles requisite to expression, that will not answer the will on common occasions; but to represent a passion with truth, every nerve and muscle should be in its proper action, or the representation becomes weak and confused, melancholy is mistaken for grief, and pleasure for delight. It is from this feebleness of emotion so many dull actors endeavour to supply passion with vehemence of action and voice, as jugglers are talkative and bustling to beguile scrutiny. I have somewhere heard that Mrs. Siddons has talked of the real agitation which the performance of some of her characters has made her feel.

To see the bewildered melancholy of Lady Macbeth walking in her sleep, or the widow's mute stare of perfected misery by the corpse of the gamester Beverley, two of the sublimest pieces of acting on the English stage, would argue this point better than a thousand critics. Mrs. Siddons has the air of never being the actress; she seems unconscious that there is a motley crowd called a pit waiting to applaud her, or that there are a dozen fiddlers waiting for her exit.

This is always one of the marks of a great actor. The player who amuses himself by looking at the audience for admiration may be assured he never gets any. It is in acting as in conferring obligations: one should have the air of doing nothing for a return.

If Mrs. Siddons has not every single requisite to a perfect tragedian, it is the amatory pathetic. In the despair of Belvidera, for instance, she rises to sublimity, but in the tenderness of Belvidera she preserves too stately and self-subdued an air. She can overpower, astonish, afflict, but she cannot win: her majestic presence and commanding features seem to disregard love, as a trifle to which they cannot descend. But it does not follow that a tragedian unable to sink into the softness of the tender passion is the more to be respected for his undeviating dignity and spirit; it does not follow that he has a loftier genius. Love, though humble, never moves our contempt; on the contrary, it adds new interest to character at other times dignified. In real life the greatest heroes and sages have acquired an extraordinary charm from their union of wisdom and tenderness, of conquest and gallant submission: and as we doubly admire the wise Plato for his amatory effusions and the chivalrous spirit of Henry the Great for the tenderness of his love, so on the stage the tragedian who unites the hero and the lover, that is, who can display either character as it is required, is the more admirable genius. Besides, the figure of Mrs. Siddons is now too large and too matronly to represent youth; we hope that by the next season she will have given up the performance of characters suited neither to her age nor her abilities.

After this one defect, I have in vain considered and reconsidered all the tragedies in which I have seen her, to find the shadow of another. She unites with her noble conceptions of nature every advantage of art, every knowledge of stage propriety and effect. This knowledge, however, she displays not with the pompous minuteness of Mr. Kemble, but with that natural carelessness which shows it to be the result of genius rather than grave study. If there is a gesture in the midst, or an attitude in the interval of action, it is the result of the impassioned moment; one can hardly imagine there has been any such thing as a rehearsal for powers so natural and so spirited. Of the force of such mere action I recollect a sublime instance displayed by Mrs. Siddons in the insipid tragedy of *The Grecian Daughter*. This heroine has obtained for her aged and imprisoned father some unexpected assistance from the guard Philotas: transported with gratitude, but having nothing from the poet to give expression to her feelings, she starts with extended arms and casts herself in mute prostration at his feet. I shall never forget the glow which rushed to my cheeks at this sublime action.

These are the effects Mr. Kemble should study, and not the clap-provoking frivolities of ending every speech with an energetic dash of the fist, or of running off the stage after a vehement declamation, as if the actor was in haste to get his pint of wine. If the brother and sister are compared, the palm both of genius and of judgment must undoubtedly be given to Mrs. Siddons. I question whether she understands her authors so intimately, but she gives double effect to their important passages, and their un-important ones are allowed to sink into their proper mediocrity: where everything is raised into signifi-cance, the significance is destroyed. If an artist would study the expression of the passions, let him lay by the pictures of Le Brun, and copy the looks of Mrs. Siddons.

LEIGH HUNT: *Critical Essays on the Performers of the London Theatres,* 1807

OTHERS—AND MRS. SIDDONS

❧

IN 1812 Kemble revived and adapted, with a splendour, in those days, unparalleled, the play of *Julius Caesar*. No piece was ever more effectively cast: Brutus had for its representative John Kemble; Cassius, Young; Antony, Charles Kemble; Casca, Fawcett; First Citizen, Simmons; and Portia, Mrs. Powell. I have never spoken with any one fortunate enough to have seen that play rendered, as it then was, who has not admitted it to have been the greatest intellectual recreation he ever enjoyed.

It was, really, difficult to believe that one had not been transported, while in a state of unconsciousness, from the purlieus of Bow Street, and the vicinity of Covent Garden Market, to the glories of the Capitol, and the very heart of the Julian Forum; so complete, in all its parts, was the illusion of the scene. When but six years old, I saw the play, on the first night of its representation; and I was allowed to see it again in 1817, with the same cast, minus Mrs. Powell. And although I was then but eleven, the impression left upon my mind has never been effaced. If it appear a thing incredible, that any play, however well put on the stage, however gorgeous its accessories, and however spirited the acting, should have left definite and durable traces on the brain of a child of such tender years, it must be mentioned that he had not only inherited a turn for the stage, but had read and re-read the play in question over and over again, had committed its chief speeches to memory, had rehearsed them by heart, and often represented the characters before small but select audiences composed of all the squabs, bolsters and pillows available in the house. The consequence was that, when I saw *Julius Caesar* for the second time I attended to the stage-business, and more particularly to the by-play, with an intentness and enquiring interest, which it amuses me even now to recall. Owing to my reproductions in the privacy of my little bedroom of the effects I had seen and heard on the boards of the great theatre, I was tolerably qualified, in my own opinion at least, to distinguish between the comparative merits of each actor. And there was, perhaps, nothing which elicited more of my boyish admiration than the fidelity with which the players of prominent parts indirectly indicated the peculiar idiosyncrasies of each (and this, too, before they had opened their lips) by their very mien and movement. Ordinary actors, on first making their entrance in the second scene of the first act, march in procession towards the course, with all the precision of the Grenadier Guards, stepping in time to the martial music which accompanies them. And even on the part of leading actors, I have noted a tameness of deportment (as mechanical as if they were automata), until speech has stirred them into action.

In the play I am writing of, as then enacted, one would have imagined that the invariable white toga, common to all the male performers, beautiful as it is when properly worn and tastefully adjusted, would have rendered it difficult, at first, for any but frequenters of the theatre to distinguish, in the large number of the dramatis personae on the stage, John Kemble from Daniel Terry, or Charles Young from Charles Kemble. Whereas I feel persuaded that any intelligent observer, though he had never entered the walls of a theatre before, if he had but studied the play in his closet, would have had no difficulty in recognizing in the calm, cold, self-contained, stoical dignity of John Kemble's *walk*, the very ideal of Marcus Brutus; or in the pale, wan, austere, 'lean and hungry look' of Young, and in his quick and nervous *pace*, the irritability and nervous impetuosity of Caius Cassius; or in the handsome, joyous face and graceful *tread* of Charles Kemble—his pliant body bending forward in courtly adulation of 'Great Caesar'— Mark Antony himself; while Fawcett's sour, sarcastic countenance would not more aptly pourtray 'quick-mettled' Casca, than his abrupt and hasty *stamp* upon the ground when Brutus asked him 'What had chanced that Caesar was so sad?' In support of my theory of the mute eloquence of gait and movement, Charles Young used to speak in terms of almost wanton admiration of a boldly conceived point he saw Mrs. Siddons once make while playing the comparatively inferior part of Volumnia for her brother's benefit.

In the second scene of the second act of *Coriolanus*, after the victory of the battle of Corioli, an ovation in honour of the victor was introduced with great and imposing effect by John Kemble. On reference to the stage directions of my father's interleaved copy, I find that no fewer than 240 persons marched in stately procession across the stage. In addition to the recognized dramatis personae (thirty-five in number), there were vestals, and lictors with their fasces, and soldiers with the spolia opima, and sword-bearers, and standard-bearers, and cup-bearers, and senators, and silver eagle-bearers with the S.P.Q.R. upon them, and trumpeters, and drummers, and priests, and dancing girls, &c., &c.

Now in this procession, and as one of the central

figures in it, Mrs. Siddons had to walk. Had she been content to follow in the beaten track of her predecessors in the part, she would have marched across the stage, from right to left, with the solemn, stately, almost funeral, step conventional. But at the time, as she often did, she forgot her own identity. She was no longer Sarah Siddons, tied down to the directions of the prompter's book—or trammelled by old traditions—she was Volumnia, the proud mother of a proud son and conquering hero. So that, when it was time for her to come on, instead of dropping each foot at equi-distance in its place, with mechanical exactitude and in cadence subservient to the orchestra; deaf to the guidance of her woman's ear, but sensitive to the throbbings of her haughty mother's heart, with flashing eye, and proudest smile, and head erect, and hands pressed firmly on her bosom as if to repress by manual force its triumphant swellings, she towered above all around, and rolled and almost reeled across the stage; her very soul as it were dilating and rioting in its exultation; until her action lost all grace and yet became so true to nature, so picturesque and so descriptive, that pit and gallery sprang to their feet, electrified by the transcendent execution of an original conception.

JULIAN CHARLES YOUNG: *A Memoir of Charles Mayne Young, Tragedian. Second edition*, 1871.[1]

---

[1] The author's system of punctuation introduced many more commas than, for reasons of intelligibility and comfort in reading, have been included here.—ED.

✦

THE BEGGAR'S OPERA was acted at Covent Garden
last night, for the purpose of introducing Miss Stephens
in the character of Polly. The play itself is among
the most popular of our dramas, and one which the
public are always glad to have some new excuse for
seeing acted again. Its merits are peculiarly its own.
It not only delights, but instructs us, without our
knowing how, and though it is at first view equally
offensive to good taste and common decency. The
materials, indeed, of which it is composed, the
scenes, characters, and incidents, are in general of
the lowest and most disgusting kind; but the author,
by the sentiments and reflections which he has put
into the mouths of highwaymen, turnkeys, their wives
and daughters, has converted the motley group into
a set of fine gentlemen and ladies, satirists, and
philosophers. What is still more extraordinary,
he has effected this transformation without once
violating probability, or 'o'erstepping the modesty
of nature'. In fact, Gay has in this instance turned
the tables on the critics; and by the assumed license
of the mock-heroic style, has enabled himself to
do justice to nature, that is, to give all the force, truth,
and locality of real feeling to the thoughts and
expressions, without being called to the bar of false
taste and affected delicacy. We might particularly

---

[1] Talfourd said that this criticism 'restored *The Beggar's
Opera*, which had long been treated as a burlesque
appendage to the Newgate Calendar, to its proper station'.
—ED.

See also *ante*, pp. 69–83 and *post*, pp. 273–5.

refer to Polly's description of the death of her lover, and to the song, 'Woman is like the fair flower in its lustre', the extreme beauty and feeling of which are only equalled by their characteristic propriety and *naiveté*. Every line of this sterling Comedy sparkles with wit, and is fraught with the keenest and bitterest invective.

It has been said by a great moralist, 'There is some soul of goodness in things evil'; and *The Beggar's Opera* is a good-natured, but severe comment on this text. The poet has thrown all the gaiety and sunshine of the imagination, the intoxication of pleasure, and the vanity of despair, round the short-lived existence of his heroes, while Peachum and Lockit are seen in the background, parcelling out their months and weeks between them. The general view of human life is of the most refined and ab-stracted kind. With the happiest art, the author has brought out the good qualities and interesting emotions almost inseparable from humanity in the lowest situations, and with the same penetrating glance, has detected the disguises which rank and circumstance lend to exalted vice. It may be said that the moral of the piece (which some respectable critics have been at a loss to discover), *is to show the vulgarity of vice*; or that the sophisms with which the great and powerful palliate their violations of integrity and decorum, are, in fact, common to them with the vilest, most abandoned and contemptible of the species. What can be more galling than the argu-ments used by these would-be politicians, to prove that in hypocrisy, selfishness, and treachery, they are far behind some of their betters? The exclamation of Mrs. Peachum, when her daughter marries Mac-heath, 'Hussey, hussey, you will be as ill used and as much neglected as if you had married a Lord', is worth all Miss Hannah More's laboured invectives on the laxity of the manners of high life!

The innocent and amiable Polly found a most interesting representative in Miss Stephens, Her acting throughout was simple, unaffected, graceful, and full of tenderness. Her tones in speaking, though low, and suited to the gentleness of the character, were distinct, and varied with great flexibility. She will lose by her performance of this part none of the reputation she has gained in Mandane. The manner in which she gave the song in the first act, 'But he so teased me', &c., was sweetness itself: the tones undulated through the house, amidst murmurs of rapturous applause. She gave equal animation and feeling to the favourite air, 'Cease your funning'. To this, however, as well as to some other of the songs, a more dramatic effect might perhaps be given. There is a severity of feeling, and a plaintive sadness, both in the words and music of the songs in this Opera, on which too much stress cannot be laid.

WILLIAM HAZLITT: *Morning Chronicle*,
23 October 1813

KEAN AS RICHARD THE THIRD

THERE is a feeling for which but little credit is allowed to critics, and which it may be thought great affectation for us to profess: we shall however venture to express it in spite of the incredulity of prejudice. We know then no greater pleasure than to hail the triumph of genius, and to watch over the progress of a growing fame. A mind of common generosity feels itself humiliated, when it is forced to crush unopposing weakness; to do execution even on resolute and stout offenders, though just, is after all but dirty work; but to be able to bestow rewards on exalted merit, seems for the time not only to place us on a level with the subject of our praise, but even to elevate us above our ordinary nature. We must not however attempt to explain the feeling too nicely, lest it should appear rather selfish than benevolent; but be it selfishness or be it kindness, it was never excited so strongly in our breast as by the display of the talents of Mr. Kean.

In our criticism on his *Shylock*, we promised to retract our praise, if we saw any reason:—something we do wish to alter in that paper, but not the praise. We said that his voice was disagreeable and his figure insignificant. We did not then know that he was labouring under a severe cold, and the tasteless gaberdine of the old Jew concealed that person which was expanded by the heroism of *Richard*: here his soul seemed to enlarge and o'er-inform its tenement, which, under its inspiring influence, became at once impressive and picturesque. Then his fine and somewhat Italian countenance, all intellect and sensibility, excited equally those almost incompatible sensations of high admiration and perfect sympathy. We cannot recollect any performance,—the very finest exhibitions of Mrs. Siddons not excepted,—which was so calculated to delight an audience, and to impress it with veneration for the talents of the actor, as the *Richard* of Mr. Kean.

The great characteristics of *Richard* are a daring and comprehensive intelligence, which seizes its object with the grasp of a giant,—a profound acquaintance with the human soul, which makes him appreciate motives at a glance,—a spirit immoveably fearless, because, how can a mighty being tremble among animals who are but as atoms to his towering superiority?—Besides this, he is a villain; that is, he moves onward to his purpose careless of ordinary duties and ordinary feelings; and yet, when we observe his horrid march, we neither shudder with disgust nor overwhelm him with execrations. Why is this? because he seems to belong to a class above mankind: he is the destroying demon whom we regard with awe and astonishment, and not the mere murderer whose meanness and vulgarity almost rob crime of its horrors. Such are the leading features of the character which Mr. Kean has represented: the full force of Shakespeare's mind seems to have been exercised in the portraiture, and we should think that none but a man of kindred intellect could give an adequate image of such a model. This, however, Mr. Kean has done. He had not been on the stage two minutes, nor repeated half a dozen lines, before there was an universal feeling that no common being had now come forward to challenge our attention. When he finished the soliloquy, he left the audience in admiration of the power of his understanding: he was soon to appear in another light —the lover of a woman whose husband and father he has murdered. What acting can render tolerable this nauseous scene, in which female weakness has been exaggerated merely as a foil to the overbearing influence of *Richard's* mind? Kemble whines it in a way which no ear can endure; Cooke was harsh, ungentlemanly, and coarse. Mr. Kean made it all probable and perfectly natural. An enchanting smile played on his lips, while a courteous humility bowed his head. His voice, though hoarse with cold, was yet modulated to a tone, which no common female mind ever did or ever could resist. Gentle yet self-respected, insinuating yet determined, humble yet over-awing, he presented an object by which the mere human senses must from their very constitution be subjected and entranced. To go through all his excellencies would be to write a pamphlet; we were however particularly struck with that sure test of a superior mind, his daring to adopt the simplicities and familiarities of the commonest every-day life. There was no mock-heroic in his acting. One of the finest touches which we remember was his method of repeating the passage, 'Chop off his head', where he is speaking of Lord Hastings. This is usually given with much pomp and ferocity of utterance. Mr. Kean, who understood that *Richard* could only feel contempt for such a wavering, silly character as Hastings, delivered the order in a way which shewed that he equally despised his victim, and any consequences which might ensue from his murder. He laughed, spoke in a jeering accent, and accompanied his speech with a familiar tap on the arm of his poor subservient creature, who is ready to execute all he demands. In the tent-scene, he gave another striking example of this peculiar beauty: he stands for some moments fixed in reverie, drawing figures on the sand: this was a boldness which nothing but the consciousness of great talent could venture upon; for no common man dare keep the audience waiting without a speech or a startling attitude. In the heroic parts, he animated every spectator with his own feelings;—when he exclaimed that 'a thousand hearts were swelling in his bosom', the house shouted to express their accordance to a truth so nobly exemplified by the energy of his voice, by the grandeur of his mien. His death-scene was the grandest conception, and executed in the most impressive manner; it was a piece of noble poetry, expressed by action instead of language. He fights desperately: he is disarmed, and exhausted of all bodily strength: he disdains to fall, and his strong volition keeps him standing: he fixes that head, full of intellectual and heroic power, directly on his enemy: he bears up his chest with an expansion, which seems swelling with more than human spirit: he holds his uplifted arm in calm but dreadful defiance of his conqueror. But he is but man, and he falls after his sublime effort senseless to the ground. We have felt our eyes gush on reading a passage of exquisite poetry, we have been ready to leap at sight of a noble picture, but we never felt stronger emotion, more overpowering sensations, than were kindled by the novel sublimity of this catastrophe. In matters of mere taste, there will be a difference of opinion, but here there was no room to doubt,—no reason could be impudent enough to hesitate. Every heart beat an echo responsive to this call of elevated nature, and yearned with fondness towards the man who, while he excited admiration for himself, made also his admirers glow with a warmth of conscious superiority, because they were able to appreciate such an exalted degree of excellence.

THOMAS BARNES: *The Examiner*, 27 February 1814

ON ACTORS AND ACTING

PLAYERS are 'the abstract and brief chronicles of the time'; the motley representatives of human nature. They are the only honest hypocrites. Their life is a voluntary dream; a studied madness. The height of their ambition is to be *beside themselves*. To-day kings, to-morrow beggars, it is only when they are themselves that they are nothing. Made up of mimic laughter and tears, passing from the extremes of joy or woe at the prompter's call, they wear the livery of other men's fortunes; their very thoughts are not their own. They are, as it were, train-bearers in the pageant of life, and hold a glass up to humanity, frailer than itself. We see ourselves at second-hand in them: they show us all that we are, all that we wish to be, and all that we dread to be. The stage is an epitome, a bettered likeness of the world, with the dull part left out: and, indeed, with this omission, it is nearly big enough to hold all the rest. What brings the resemblance nearer is that, as *they* imitate us, we, in our turn, imitate them. How many fine gentlemen do we owe to the stage! How many romantic lovers are mere Romeos in masquerade! How many soft bosoms have heaved with Juliet's sighs! They teach us when to laugh and when to weep, when to love and when to hate, upon principle and with a good grace! Wherever there is a playhouse, the world will go on not amiss. The stage not only refines the manners, but it is the best teacher of morals, for it is the truest and most intelligible picture of life. It stamps the image of virtue on the mind by first softening the rude materials of which it is composed, by a sense of pleasure. It regulates the passions, by giving a loose to the imagination. It points out the selfish and depraved to our detestation; the amiable and generous to our admiration; and if it clothes the more seductive vices with the borrowed graces of wit and fancy, even those graces operate as a diversion to the coarser poison of experience and bad example, and often prevent or carry off the infection by inoculating the mind with a certain taste and elegance. To show how little we agree with the common declamations against the immoral tendency of the stage on this score, we will hazard a conjecture that the acting of the *Beggar's Opera* a certain number of nights every year since it was first brought out has done more towards putting down the practice of highway robbery, than all the gibbets that ever were erected. A person, after seeing this piece, is too deeply imbued with a sense of humanity, is in too good humour with himself and the rest of the world, to set about cutting throats or rifling pockets. Whatever makes a jest of vice leaves it too much a matter of indifference for any one in his senses to rush desperately on his ruin for its sake. We suspect that just the contrary effect must be produced by the representation of *George Barnwell*, which is too much in the style of the Ordinary's sermon to meet with any better success. The mind in such cases, instead of being deterred by the alarming consequences held out to it, revolts against the denunciation of them as an insult offered to its free-will, and, in a spirit of defiance, returns a practical answer to them, by daring the worst that can happen. The most striking lesson ever read to levity and licentiousness is in the last act of *The Inconstant*, where young Mirabel is preserved by the fidelity of his mistress, Orinda, in the disguise of a page, from the hands of assassins, into whose power he had been allured by the temptations of vice and beauty. There never was a rake who did not become in imagination a reformed man, during the representation of the last trying scenes of this admirable comedy.

If the stage is useful as a school of instruction, it is no less so as a source of amusement. It is a source of the greatest enjoyment at the time, and a never-failing fund of agreeable reflection afterwards. The merits of a new play, or of a new actor, are always among the first topics of polite conversation. One way in which public exhibitions contribute to refine and humanise mankind, is by supplying them with ideas and subjects of conversation and interest in common. The progress of civilisation is in proportion to the number of common-places current in society. For instance, if we meet with a stranger at an inn or in a stage-coach, who knows nothing but his own affairs—his shop, his customers, his farm, his pigs, his poultry—we can carry on no conversation with him on these local and personal matters: the only way is to let him have all the talk to himself. But if he has fortunately ever seen Mr. Liston act, this is an immediate topic of mutual conversation, and we agree together the rest of the evening in discussing the merits of that inimitable actor, with the same satisfaction as in talking over the affairs of the most intimate friend.

If the stage thus introduces us familiarly to our contemporaries, it also brings us acquainted with former times. It is an interesting revival of past ages, manners, opinions, dresses, persons and actions— whether it carries us back to the wars of York and Lancaster, or half-way back to the heroic times of

Greece and Rome, in some translation from the French, or quite back to the age of Charles II in the scenes of Congreve and of Etherege (the gay Sir George!)—happy age, when kings and nobles led purely ornamental lives; when the utmost stretch of a morning's study went no farther than the choice of a sword-knot, or the adjustment of a side curl; when the soul spoke out in all the pleasing elegance of dress; and beaux and belles, enamoured of themselves in one another's follies, fluttered like gilded butterflies in giddy mazes through the walks of St. James's Park!

A good company of comedians, a Theatre-Royal judiciously managed, is your true Herald's College; the only Antiquarian Society that is worth a rush. It is for this reason that there is such an air of romance about players, and that it is pleasanter to see them, even in their own persons, than any of the three learned professions. We feel more respect for John Kemble in a plain coat than for the Lord Chancellor on the woolsack. He is surrounded, to our eyes, with a greater number of imposing recollections: he is a more reverend piece of formality; a more complicated tissue of costume. We do not know whether to look upon this accomplished actor as Pierre, or King John, or Coriolanus, or Cato, or Leontes, or the Stranger. But we see in him a stately hieroglyphic of humanity; a living monument of departed greatness; a sombre comment on the rise and fall of kings. We look after him till he is out of sight, as we listen to a story of one of Ossian's heroes, to 'a tale of other times'!

The most pleasant feature in the profession of a player, and which, indeed, is peculiar to it, is that we not only admire the talents of those who adorn it, but we contract a personal intimacy with them. There is no class of society whom so many persons regard with affection as actors. We greet them on the stage; we like to meet them in the streets; they almost always recall to us pleasant associations; and we feel our gratitude excited, without the uneasiness of a sense of obligation. The very gaiety and popularity, however, which surround the life of a favourite performer, make the retiring from it a very serious business. It glances a mortifying reflection on the shortness of human life, and the vanity of human pleasures. Something reminds us that 'all the world's a stage, and all the men and women merely players'.

It has been considered as the misfortune of first-rate talents for the stage, that they leave no record behind them except that of vague rumour, and that the genius of a great actor perishes with him, 'leaving the world no copy'. This is a misfortune, or at least a mortifying reflection, to actors; but it is, perhaps, an advantage to the stage. It leaves an opening to originality. The *semper varium et mutabile* of the poet may be transferred to the stage, 'the inconstant stage', without losing the original felicity of the application:—it has its necessary ebbs and flows, from its subjection to the influence of popular feeling, and the frailty of the materials of which it is composed, its own fleeting and shadowy essence, and cannot be expected to remain for any great length of time stationary at the same point, either of perfection or debasement. Acting, in particular, which is the chief organ by which it addresses itself to the mind— the eye, tongue, hand by which it dazzles, charms, and seizes on the public attention—is an art that seems to contain in itself the seeds of perpetual renovation and decay, following in this respect the order of nature rather than the analogy of the productions of human intellect;—for whereas in the other arts of painting and poetry, the standard works of genius, being permanent and accumulating, for awhile provoke emulation, but, in the end, overlay future efforts, and transmit only their defects to those that come after; the exertions of the greatest actor die with him, leaving to his successors only the admiration of his name, and the aspiration after imaginary excellence; so that, in effect, no one generation of actors binds another; the art is always setting out afresh on the stock of genius and nature, and the success depends (generally speaking) on accident, opportunity, and encouragement. The harvest of excellence (whatever it may be) is removed from the ground, every twenty or thirty years, by Death's sickle; and there is room left for another to sprout up and tower to any equal height, and spread into equal luxuriance—to 'dally with the wind, and court the sun'—according to the health and vigour of the stem, and the favourableness of the season. But books, pictures, remain like fixtures in the public mind, beyond a certain point encumber the soil of living truth and nature, distort or stunt the growth of original genius. When an author dies, it is no matter, for his works remain. When a great actor dies, there is a void produced in society, a gap which requires to be filled up. The literary amateur may find employment for his time in reading old authors only, and exhaust his entire spleen in scouting new ones: but the lover of the stage cannot amuse himself, in his solitary fastidiousness, by sitting to witness a play got up by the departed ghosts of first-rate actors; or be contented with the perusal of a collection of old play-bills:—he may extol Garrick, but he must go to see Kean; and, in his own defence, must admire, or at least tolerate, what he sees, or stay away against his will. If, indeed, by any spell or power of necromancy, all the celebrated actors, for the last hundred years, could be made to appear again on the boards of Covent Garden and Drury Lane, for the last time, in their most brilliant parts, what a rich treat to the town, what a feat for the critics, to go and see Betterton, and Booth, and Wilks, and Sandford, and Nokes, and Leigh, and Penkethman, and Bullock, and Estcourt, and Dogget, and Mrs. Barry, and Mrs. Montfort, and Mrs. Oldfield, and Mrs. Bracegirdle, and Mrs. Cibber and Cibber himself, the prince of coxcombs, and Macklin, and Quin, and Rich, and Mrs. Clive, and Mrs. Pritchard, and Mrs. Abington, and Weston, and Shuter, and Garrick, and all the rest of those who 'gladdened life', and whose death 'eclipsed the gaiety of nations'! We should certainly be there. We should buy a ticket for the season. We should enjoy *our hundred days* again. We should not miss a single night. We would not, for a great deal, be absent from Betterton's Hamlet or his Brutus, or from Booth's Cato, as it was first acted to the contending applause of Whigs and Tories. We should be in the first row when Mrs. Barry (who was kept by Lord Rochester, and with whom Otway was in love) played Monimia or Belvidera; and we suppose we should go to see Mrs. Bracegirdle (with whom all the world was in love) in all her parts. We should then know exactly whether Penkethman's manner of picking a chicken, and Bullock's mode of devouring asparagus, answered to the ingenious account of them in the *Tatler*; and whether Dogget was equal to Dowton—whether Mrs. Montfort or Mrs.

Abington was the finest lady—whether Wilks or Cibber was the best Sir Harry Wildair,—whether Macklin was really 'the Jew that Shakespeare drew', and whether Garrick was, upon the whole, so great an actor as the world have would have made him out! Many people have a strong desire to pry into the secrets of futurity; for our own parts, we should be satisfied if we had the power to recall the dead, and live the past over again, as often as we pleased!— Players, after all, have little reason to complain of their hard-earned, short-lived popularity. One thunder of applause from pit, boxes, and gallery, is equal to a whole immortality of posthumous fame; and when we hear an actor (Liston), whose modesty is equal to his merit, declare that he would like to see a dog wag his tail in approbation, what must he feel when he sets the whole house in a roar! Besides, Fame, as if their reputation had been entrusted to her alone, has been particularly careful of the renown of her theatrical favourites: she forgets, one by one, and year by year, those who have been great lawyers, great statesmen, and great warriors in their day; but the name of Garrick still survives with the works of Reynolds and of Johnson.

Actors have been accused, as a profession, of being extravagant and dissipated. While they are said to be so, as a piece of common cant, they are likely to continue so. But there is a sentence in Shakespeare which should be stuck as a label in the mouths of our beadles and whippers-in of morality: 'The web of our life is of a mingled yarn, good and ill together: our virtues would be proud if our faults whipped them not: and our crimes would despair if they were not cherished by our virtues.' With respect to the extravagance of actors, as a traditional character, it is not to be wondered at. They live from hand to mouth, they plunge from want into luxury; they have no means of making money *breed,* and all professions that do not live by turning money into money, or have not a certainty of accumulating it in the end by parsimony, spend it. Uncertain of the future they make sure of the present moment. This is not unwise. Chilled with poverty, steeped in contempt, they sometimes pass into the sunshine of fortune, and are lifted to the very pinnacle of public favour; yet even there they cannot calculate on the continu ance of success, but are, 'like the giddy sailor on the mast, ready with every blast to topple down into the fatal bowels of the deep!' Besides, if the young enthusiast, who is smitten with the stage, and with the public as a mistress, were naturally a close *hunks,* he would become or remain a city clerk, instead of turning player. Again, with respect to the habit of convivial indulgence, an actor, to be a good one, must have a great spirit of enjoyment in himself —strong impulses, strong passions, and a strong sense of pleasure: for it is his business to imitate the passions, and to communicate pleasure to others.

A man of genius is not a machine. The neglected actor may be excused if he drinks oblivion of his disappointments; the successful one if he quaffs the applause of the world, and enjoys the friendship of those who are the friends of the favourites of fortune, in draughts of nectar. There is no path so steep as that of fame: no labour so hard as the pursuit of excellence. The intellectual excitement, inseparable from those professions which call forth all our sensi- bility to pleasure and pain, requires some correspond- ing physical excitement to support our failure, and not a little to allay the ferment of the spirits attendant on success. If there is any tendency to dissipation beyond this in the profession of a player, it is owing to the prejudices entertained against them—to that spirit of bigotry which in a neighbouring country would deny actors Christian burial after their death, and to that cant of criticism which, in our own, slurs over their characters, while living, with a half-witted jest. Players are only not so respectable as a profession as they might be, because their profession is not respected as it ought to be.

A London engagement is generally considered by actors as the *ne plus ultra* of their ambition, as 'a consummation devoutly to be wished', as the great prize in the lottery of their professional life. But this appears to us, who are not in the secret, to be rather the prose termination of their adventurous career: it is the provincial commencement that is the poetical and truly enviable part of it. After that, they have comparatively little hope or fear. 'The wine of life is drunk, and but the lees remain.' In London they become gentlemen, and the King's servants; but it is the romantic mixture of the hero and the vagabond that constitutes the essence of the player's life. It is the transition from their real to their assumed characters, from the contempt of the world to the applause of the multitude, that gives its zest to the latter, and raises them as much above common humanity at night as in the daytime they are depressed below it. 'Hurried from fierce extremes, by contrast made more fierce,'—it is rags and a flock bed which give their splendour to a plume of feathers and a throne. We should suppose that if the most admired actor on the London stage were brought to confession on this point, he would acknowledge that all the applause he had received from 'brilliant and overflowing audiences' was nothing to the light-headed intoxication of unlooked-for success in a barn. In towns, actors are criticised: in country places, they are wondered at, or hooted at: it is of little consequence which, so that the interval is not too long between. For ourselves, we own that the description of the strolling player in *Gil Blas*, soaking his dry crusts in the well by the roadside, presents to us a perfect picture of human felicity.

WILLIAM HAZLITT: *The Examiner*, 15 January 1817

ON THE ARTIFICIAL COMEDY OF THE
LAST CENTURY

THE artificial Comedy, or Comedy of manners, is quite extinct on our stage. Congreve and Farquhar show their heads once in seven years only, to be exploded and put down instantly. The times cannot bear them. Is it for a few wild speeches, an occasional license of dialogue? I think not altogether. The business of their dramatic characters will not stand the moral test. We screw every thing up to that. Idle gallantry in a fiction, a dream, the passing pageant of an evening, startles us in the same way as the alarming indications of profligacy in a son or ward in real life should startle a parent or guardian. We have no such middle emotions as dramatic interests left. We see a stage libertine playing his loose pranks of two hours' duration, and of no after consequence, with the severe eyes which inspect real vices with their bearings upon two worlds. We are spectators to a plot or intrigue (not reducible in life to the point of strict mortality) and take it all for truth. We substitute a real for a dramatic person, and judge him accordingly. We try him in our courts, from which there is no appeal to the *dramatis personæ*, his peers. We have been spoiled with—not sentimental comedy—but a tyrant far more pernicious to our pleasures which has succeeded to it, the exclusive and all devouring drama of common life; where the moral point is every thing; where, instead of the fictitious half-believed personages of the stage (the phantoms of old comedy) we recognise ourselves, our brothers, aunts, kinsfolk, allies, patrons, enemies,—the same as in life,—with an interest in what is going on so hearty and substantial, that we cannot afford our moral judgment, in its deepest and most vital results, to compromise or slumber for a moment. What is *there* transacting, by no modification is made to affect us in any other manner than the same events or characters would do in our relationships of life. We carry our fire-side concerns to the theatre with us. We do not go thither, like our ancestors, to escape from the pressure of reality, so much as to confirm our experience of it; to make assurance double, and take a bond of fate. We must live our toilsome lives twice over, as it was the mournful privilege of Ulysses to descend twice to the shades. All that neutral ground of character, which stood between vice and virtue; or which in fact was indifferent to neither, where neither properly was called in question; that happy breathing-place from the burthen of a perpetual moral questioning—the sanctuary and quiet Alsatia of hunted casuistry—is broken up and disfranchised, as injurious to the interests of society. The privileges of the place are taken away by law. We dare not dally with images, or names, of wrong. We bark like foolish dogs at shadows. We dread infection from the scenic representation of disorder; and fear a painted pustule. In our anxiety that our morality should not take cold, we wrap it up in a great blanket surtout of precaution against the breeze of sunshine.

I confess for myself that (with no great delinquencies to answer for) I am glad for a season to take an airing beyond the diocese of the strict conscience,—not to live always in the precincts of the law-courts,—but now and then, for a dream-while or so, to imagine a world with no meddling restrictions—to get into recesses, whither the hunter cannot follow me—

> —————————Secret shades
> Of woody Ida's inmost grove,
> While yet there was no fear of Jove——

I come back to my cage and my restraint the fresher and more healthy for it. I wear my shackles more contentedly for having respired the breath of an imaginary freedom. I do not know how it is with others, but I feel the better always for the perusal of one of Congreve's—nay, why should I not add even of Wycherley's—comedies. I am the gayer at least for it; and I could never connect those sports of a witty fancy in any shape with any result to be drawn from them to imitation in real life. They are a world of themselves almost as much as fairy-land. Take one of their characters, male or female (with few exceptions they are alike), and place it in a modern play, and my virtuous indignation shall rise against the profligate wretch as warmly as the Catos of the pit could desire; because in a modern play I am to judge of the right and the wrong. The standard of *police* is the measure of *political justice*. The atmosphere will blight it, it cannot live here. It has got into a moral world, where it has no business, from which it must needs fall headlong; as dizzy, and incapable of making a stand, as a Swedenborgian bad spirit that has wandered unawares into the sphere of one of his Good Men, or Angels. But in its own world do we feel the creature is so very bad?— The Fainalls and the Mirabels, the Dorimants and the Lady Touchwoods, in their own sphere, do not offend my moral sense; in fact they do not appeal to it at all. They seem engaged in their proper element.

They break through no laws, or conscientious restraints. They know of none. They have got out of Christendom into the land—what shall I call it?—of cuckoldry—the Utopia of gallantry, where pleasure is duty, and the manners perfect freedom. It is altogether a speculative scene of things, which has no reference whatever to the world that is. No good person can be justly offended as a spectator, because no good person suffers on the stage. Judged morally, every character in these plays—the few exceptions only are *mistakes*—is alike essentially vain and worthless. The great art of Congreve is especially shown in this, that he has entirely excluded from his scenes, —some little generosities in the part of Angelica perhaps excepted,—not only any thing like a faultless character, but any pretensions to goodness or good feelings whatsoever. Whether he did this designedly, or instinctively, the effect is as happy, as the design (if design) was bold. I used to wonder at the strange power which his Way of the World in particular possesses of interesting you all along in the pursuits of characters, for whom you absolutely care nothing —for you neither hate nor love his personages—and I think it is owing to this very indifference for any, that you endure the whole. He has spread a privation of moral light, I will call it, rather than by the ugly name of palpable darkness, over his creations; and his shadows flit before you without distinction or preference. Had he introduced a good character, a single gush of moral feeling, a revulsion of the judgment to actual life and actual duties, the impertinent Goshen would have only lighted to the discovery of deformities, which now are none, because we think them none.

Translated into real life, the characters of his, and

his friend Wycherley's dramas, are profligates and strumpets,—the business of their brief existence, the undivided pursuit of lawless gallantry. No other spring of action, or possible motive of conduct, is recognised; principles which, universally acted upon, must reduce this frame of things to a chaos. But we do them wrong in so translating them. No such effects are produced in *their* world. When we are among them, we are amongst a chaotic people. We are not to judge them by our usages. No reverend institutions are insulted by their proceedings,—for they have none among them. No peace of families is violated,—for no family ties exist among them. No purity of the marriage bed is stained,—for none is supposed to have a being. No deep affections are disquieted,—no holy wedlock bands are snapped asunder,—for affection's depth and wedded faith are not of the growth of that soil. There is neither right nor wrong,—gratitude or its opposite,—claim or duty,—paternity or sonship. Of what consequence is it to virtue, or how is she at all concerned about it, whether Sir Simon, or Dapperwit, steal away Miss Martha; or who is the father of Lord Froth's, or Sir Paul Pliant's children?

The whole is a passing pageant, where we should sit as unconcerned at the issues, for life or death, as at a battle of the frogs and mice. But, like Don Quixote, we take part against the puppets, and quite as impertinently. We dare not contemplate an Atlantis, a scheme out of which our coxcombical moral sense is for a little transitory ease excluded. We have not the courage to imagine a state of things for which there is neither reward nor punishment. We cling to the painful necessities of shame and blame. We would indict our very dreams.

Amidst the mortifying circumstances attendant upon growing old, it is something to have seen the School for Scandal in its glory. This comedy grew out of Congreve and Wycherley, but gathered some allays of the sentimental comedy which followed theirs. It is impossible that it should be now *acted*, though it continues, at long intervals, to be announced in the bills. Its hero, when Palmer played it at least, was Joseph Surface. When I remember the gay boldness, the graceful solemn plausibility, the measured step, the insinuating voice—to express it in a word—the downright *acted* villany of the part, so different from the pressure of conscious actual wickedness,—the hypocritical assumption of hypocrisy,—which made Jack so deservedly a favourite in that character, I must needs conclude the present generation of play-goers more virtuous than myself, or more dense. I freely confess that he divided the palm with me with his better brother; that, in fact, I liked him quite as well. Not but there are passages, —like that, for instance, where Joseph is made to refuse a pittance to a poor relation,—incongruities which Sheridan was forced upon by the attempt to join the artificial with the sentimental comedy, either of which must destroy the other—but over these obstructions Jack's manner floated him so lightly, that a refusal from him no more shocked you, than the easy compliance of Charles gave you in reality any pleasure; you got over the paltry question as quickly as you could, to get back into the regions of pure comedy, where no cold moral reigns. The highly artificial manner of Palmer in this character counteracted every disagreeable impression which you might have received from the contrast, supposing them real, between the two brothers. You did not believe in Joseph with the same faith with which you believed in Charles. The latter was a pleasant reality, the former a no less pleasant poetical foil to it. The comedy, I have said, is incongruous; a mixture of Congreve with sentimental incompatibilities: the gaiety upon the whole is buoyant; but it required the consummate art of Palmer to reconcile the discordant elements.

A player with Jack's talents, if we had one now, would not dare to do the part in the same manner. He would instinctively avoid every turn which might tend to unrealise, and so to make the character fascinating. He must take his cue from his spectators, who would expect a bad man and a good man as rigidly opposed to each other as the death-beds of those geniuses are contrasted in the prints, which I am sorry to say have disappeared from the windows of my old friend Carrington Bowles, of St. Paul's Church-yard memory,—(an exhibition as venerable as the adjacent cathedral, and almost coeval) of the bad and good man at the hour of death; where the ghastly apprehensions of the former,—and truly the grim phantom with his reality of a toasting fork is not to be despised,—so finely contrast with the meek complacent kissing of the rod,—taking it in like honey and butter,—with which the latter submits to the scythe of the gentle bleeder, Time, who wields his lancet with the apprehensive finger of a popular young ladies' surgeon. What flesh, like loving grass, would not covet to meet half-way the stroke of such a delicate mower?—John Palmer was twice an actor in this exquisite part. He was playing to you all the while that he was playing upon Sir Peter and his lady. You had the first intimation of a sentiment before it was on his lips. His altered voice was meant to you, and you were to suppose that his fictitious co-flutterers on the stage perceived nothing at all of it. What was it to you if that half-reality, the husband, was over-reached by the puppetry—or the thin thing (Lady Teazle's reputation) was persuaded it was dying of a plethory? The fortunes of Othello and Desdemona were not concerned in it. Poor Jack has past from the stage in good time, that he did not live to this our age of seriousness. The pleasant old Teazle *King*, too, is gone in good time. His manner would scarce have past current in our day. We must love or hate—acquit or condemn—censure or pity—exert our detestable coxcombry of moral judgment upon everything. Joseph Surface, to go down now, must be a down-right revolting villain—no compromise—his first appearance must shock and give horror—his specious plausibilities, which the pleasurable faculties of our fathers welcomed with such hearty greetings, knowing that no harm (dramatic harm even) could come, or was meant to come of them, must inspire a cold and killing aversion. Charles (the real canting person of the scene—for the hypocrisy of Joseph has its ulterior legitimate ends, but his brother's professions of a good heart centre in down-right self-satisfaction) must be *loved*, and Joseph *hated*. To balance one disagreeable reality with another, Sir Peter Teazle must be no longer the comic idea of a fretful old bachelor bridegroom, whose teasings (while King acted it) were evidently as much played off at you, as they were meant to concern any body on the stage,—he must be a real person, capable in law of sustaining an injury—a person towards whom duties are to be acknowledged—the genuine crim-con antagonist of the villainous seducer Joseph. To realise him more, his sufferings under his unfortunate match must have the downright pungency of life—must (or should) make you not mirthful but uncomfortable, just as the same predicament would move you in a neighbour or old friend. The delicious scenes which give the play its name and zest, must affect you in the same serious manner as if you heard the reputation of a dear female friend attacked in your real presence. Crabtree, and Sir Benjamin—those poor snakes that live but in the sunshine of your mirth—must be ripened by this hot-bed process of realization into asps or amphisbænas; and Mrs. Candour—O! frightful! become a hooded serpent. O!—who that remembers Parsons and Dodd—the wasp and butterfly of the School for Scandal—in those two characters; and charming natural Miss Pope, the perfect gentlewoman as distinguished from the fine lady of comedy, in this latter part—would forego the true scenic delight—the escape from life—the oblivion of consequences—the holiday barring out of the pedant Reflection—those Saturnalia of two or three brief hours, well won from the world—to sit instead at one of our modern plays—to have his coward conscience (that forsooth must not be left for a moment) stimulated with perpetual appeals—dulled rather, and blunted, as a faculty without repose must be—and his moral vanity pampered with images of notional justice, notional beneficence, lives saved without the spectator's risk, and fortunes given away that cost the author nothing?

No piece was, perhaps, ever so completely cast in all its parts as this *manager's comedy*. Miss Farren had succeeded to Mrs. Abington in Lady Teazle; and Smith, the original Charles, had retired, when I first saw it. The rest of the characters, with very slight exceptions, remained. I remember it was then the fashion to cry down John Kemble, who took the part of Charles after Smith; but, I thought, very unjustly. Smith, I fancy, was more airy, and took the eye with a certain gaiety of person. He brought with him no sombre recollections of tragedy. He had not to expiate the fault of having pleased beforehand in lofty declamation. He had no sins of Hamlet or of Richard to atone for. His failure in these parts was a passport to success in one of so opposite a tendency. But, as far as I could judge, the weighty sense of Kemble made up for more personal incapacity than he had to answer for. His harshest tones in this part came steeped and dulcified in good humour. He made his defects a grace. His exact declamatory manner, as he managed it, only served to convey the points of his dialogue with more precision. It seemed to head the shafts to carry them deeper. Not one of his sparkling sentences was lost. I remember minutely how he delivered each in succession, and cannot by any effort imagine how any of them could be altered for the better. No man could deliver brilliant dialogue—the dialogue of Congreve or of Wycherley—because none understood it—half so well as John Kemble. His Valentine, in Love for Love, was to my recollection, faultless. He flagged sometimes in the intervals of tragic passion. He would slumber over the level parts of an heroic character. His Macbeth has been known to nod. But he always seemed to me to be particularly alive to pointed and witty dialogue. The relaxing levities of tragedy have not been touched by any since him—the playful court-bred spirit in which he condescended to the players in Hamlet—the sportive relief which he threw into the darker shades of

Richard—disappeared with him. He had his sluggish moods, his torpors—but they were the halting-stones and resting-places of his tragedy—politic savings, and fetches of the breath—husbandry of the lungs, where nature pointed him to be an economist—rather, I think, than errors of the judgment. They were, at worst, less painful than the eternal tormenting unappeasable vigilance, the 'lidless dragon eyes', of present fashionable tragedy.

CHARLES LAMB: *Elia*, 1823

PHELPS AT SADLER'S WELLS

October 15 1853.—Every reader of Shakespeare is disposed to regard the *Midsummer Night's Dream* as the most essentially unactable of all his plays. It is a dramatic poem of the utmost grace and delicacy; its characters are creatures of the poet's fancy that no flesh and blood can properly present—fairies who 'creep into acorn-cups', or mortals who are but dim abstractions, persons of a dream. The words they speak are so completely spiritual that they are best felt when they are not spoken. Their exquisite beauty is like that of sunset colours which no mortal artist can intrepret faithfully. The device of the clowns in the play to present Moonshine seems but a fair expression of the kind of success that might be achieved by the best actors who should attempt to present the *Midsummer Night's Dream* on the stage. It was, therefore, properly avoided by managers as lying beside and above their art; nor was there reason to be disappointed when the play some years ago furnished Madame Vestris with a spectacle that altogether wanted the Shakespearean spirit.

In some measure there is reason for a different opinion on these matters in the *Midsummer Night's Dream* as produced at SADLER'S WELLS by Mr. Phelps. Though stage-fairies cannot ride on bluebells, and the members of no theatrical company now in existence can speak such poetry as that of the *Midsummer Night's Dream* otherwise than most imperfectly, yet it is proved that there remains in the power of the manager who goes with pure taste and right feeling to his work, enough for the establishment of this play as a most charming entertainment of the stage.

Mr. Phelps has never for a minute lost sight of the main idea which governs the whole play, and this is the great secret of his success in the presentation of it. He knew that he was to present merely shadows; that spectators, as Puck reminds them in the epilogue, are to think they have slumbered on their seats, and that what appeared before them have been visions. Everything has been subdued as far as possible at SADLER'S WELLS to this ruling idea. The scenery is very beautiful, but wholly free from the meretricious glitter now in favour; it is not so remarkable for costliness as for the pure taste in which it and all the stage-arrangements have been planned. There is no ordinary scene-shifting; but, as in dreams, one scene is made to glide insensibly into another. We follow the lovers and the fairies through the wood from glade to glade, now among trees, now with a broad view of the sea and Athens in the distance, carefully but not at all obtrusively set forth. And not only do the scenes melt dream-like one into another, but over all the fairy portion of the play there is a haze thrown by a curtain of green gauze placed between the actors and the audience, and maintained there during the whole of the second, third, and fourth acts. This gauze curtain is so well spread that there are very few parts of the house from which its presence can be detected, but its influence is everywhere felt; it subdues the flesh and blood of the actors into something more nearly resembling dream-figures, and incorporates more completely the actors with the scenes, throwing the same green fairy tinge, and the same mist over all. A like idea has also dictated certain contrivances of dress, especially in the case of the fairies.

Very good taste has been shown in the establishment of a harmony between the scenery and the poem. The main feature—the Midsummer Night—was marked by one scene so elaborated as to impress it upon all as the central picture of the group. The moon was just so much exaggerated as to give it the required prominence. The change, again, of this Midsummer Night into morning, when Theseus and Hippolyta come to the wood with horn and hound, was exquisitely presented. And in the last scene, when the fairies, coming at night into the hall of Theseus, 'each several chamber bless', the Midsummer moon is again seen shining on the palace as the curtains are drawn that admit the fairy throng. Ten times as much money might have been spent on a very much worse setting of the *Midsummer Night's Dream*. It is the poetical feeling prompting a judicious but not extravagant outlay, by aid of which Mr. Phelps has produced a stage-spectacle more refined and intellectual, and far more absolutely satisfactory, than anything I can remember to have seen since Mr. Macready was a manager.

That the flesh and blood presentments of the dream-figures which constitute the persons of the play should be always in harmony with this true feeling, was scarcely to be expected. A great deal of the poetry is injured in the speaking. Unless each actor were a man who combined with elocutionary power a very high degree of sensibility and genius, it could hardly be otherwise. Yet it cannot be said even here that the poet's effects entirely failed. The *Midsummer Night's Dream* abounds in the most delicate passages of Shakespeare's verse; the SADLER's

WELLS pit has a keen enjoyment for them; and pit and gallery were crowded to the farthest wall on Saturday night with a most earnest audience, among whom many a subdued hush arose, not during but just before, the delivery of the most charming passages. If the crowd at DRURY LANE is a gross discredit to the public taste, the crowd at SADLER'S WELLS more than neutralises any ill opinion that may on that score be formed of playgoers. The SADLER'S WELLS gallery, indeed, appeared to be not wholly unconscious of the contrast, for, when Bottom volunteered to roar high or roar low, a voice from the gallery desired to know whether he could 'roar like Brooke'. Even the gallery at this theatre, however, resents an interruption, and the unexpected sally was not well received.

A remarkably quick-witted little boy, Master F. Artis, plays Puck, and really plays it with faithfulness and spirit as it has been conceived for him by Mr. Phelps. His training has evidently been most elaborate. We see at once that his acts and gestures are too perfect and mature to be his own imaginings, but he has been quick-witted enough to adopt them as his own, and give them not a little of the charm of independent and spontaneous production. By this thoughtfulness there is secured for the character on the stage something of the same prominence that it has in the mind of the closet-readers of the play.

Of Miss Cooper's Helena we cannot honestly say very much. In that as in most of the other characters the spirit of the play was missed, because the arguing and quarrelling and blundering that should have been playful, dreamlike, and poetical, was much too loud and real. The men and women could not fancy themselves shadows. Were it possible so far to subdue the energy of the whole body of actors as to soften the tones of the scenes between Theseus, Hippolyta, Lysander, Demetrius, Hermia, and Helena, the latter character even on the stage might surely have something of the effect intended by the poem. It is an exquisite abstraction, a pitiful and moving picture of a gentle maid forlorn, playfully developed as beseems the fantastic texture of the poem, but not at all meant to excite mirth; and there was a very great mistake made when the dream was so worked out into hard literalness as to create constant laughter during those scenes in which Helena, bewildered by the change of mood among the lovers, shrinks and complains, 'Wherefore was I to this keen mockery born?' The merriment which Shakespeare connected with those scenes was but a little of the poet's sunlight meant to glitter among tears.

It remains for us only to speak of the success of Mr. Phelps as Bottom, whom he presented from the first with remarkable subtlety and spirit, as a man seen in a dream. In his first scene, before we know what his conception is, or in what spirit he means the whole play to be received, we are puzzled by it. We miss the humour, and get a strange, elaborate, and uncouth dream-figure, a clown restless with vanity, marked by a score of little movements, and speaking ponderously with the uncouth gesticulation of an unreal thing, a grotesque nightmare character. But that, we find, is precisely what the actor had intended to present, and we soon perceive that he was right. Throughout the fairy scenes there is a mist thrown over Bottom by the actor's art. The violent gesticulation becomes stillness, and the hands are fixed on the breast. They are busy with the unperceived business of managing the movements of the ass's head, but it is not for that reason they are so perfectly still. The change of manner is a part of the conception. The dream-figure is dreaming, there is dream within dream, Bottom is quiet, his humour becomes more unctuous, but Bottom is translated. He accepts all that happens, quietly as dreamers do; and the ass's head we also accept quietly, for we too are in the middle of our dream, and it does not create surprise. Not a touch of comedy was missed in this capital piece of acting, yet Bottom was completely incorporated with the *Midsummer Night's Dream*, made an essential part of it, as unsubstantial, as airy and refined as all the rest. Quite masterly was the delivery by Mr. Phelps of the speech of Bottom on awakening. He was still a man subdued, but subdued by the sudden plunge into a state of unfathomable wonder. His dream clings about him, he cannot sever the real from the unreal, and still we are made to feel that his reality itself is but a fiction. The pre-occupation continues to be manifest during his next scene with the players, and his parting 'No more words; away; go away', was in the tone of a man who had lived with spirits and was not yet perfectly returned into the flesh. Nor did the refinement of this conception, if we except the first scene, abate a jot of the laughter that the character of Bottom was intended to excite. The mock-play at the end was intensely ludicrous in the presentment, yet nowhere farcical. It was the dream. Bottom as Pyramus was more perfectly a dream-figure than ever. The contrast between the shadowy actor and his part, between Bottom and Pyramus, was marked intensely; and the result was as quaint a phantom as could easily be figured by real flesh. Mr. Ray's Quince was very good indeed, and all the other clowns were reasonably well presented.

It is very doubtful whether the *Midsummer Night's Dream* has yet, since it was first written, been put upon the stage with so nice an interpretation of its meaning. It is pleasant beyond measure to think that an entertainment so refined can draw such a throng of playgoers as I saw last Saturday sitting before it silent and reverent at SADLER'S WELLS.

HENRY MORLEY: *The Journal of a London Playgoer from 1851-1866,* 1891

AT THE PANTOMIME

I AM going to tell you what I was thinking on Friday evening last, in Covent Garden Theatre, as I was looking, and not laughing, at the pantomime of *Ali Baba and the Forty Thieves*. . . . The forty thieves were girls. The forty thieves had forty companions, who were girls. The forty thieves and their forty companions were in some way mixed up with about four hundred and forty fairies, who were girls. There was an Oxford and Cambridge boat-race, in which the Oxford and Cambridge men were girls. There was a transformation scene, with a forest, in which the flowers were girls, and a great rainbow which was all of girls.

Mingled incongruously with these seraphic, and, as far as my boyish experience extends, novel, elements of pantomime, there were yet some of its old and fast-expiring elements. There were, in speciality, two thoroughly good pantomime actors— Mr. W. H. Payne and Mr. Frederick Payne. All that these two did, was done admirably. There were two subordinate actors, who played, subordinately well, the fore and hind legs of a donkey. And there was a little actress of whom I have chiefly to speak, who played exquisitely the little part she had to play. The scene in which she appeared was the only one in the whole pantomime in which there was any dramatic effort, or, with a few rare exceptions, any dramatic possibility. It was the home scene, in which Ali Baba's wife, on washing day, is called upon by butcher, baker, and milkman, with unpaid bills; and in the extremity of her distress hears her husband's knock at the door, and opens it for him to drive in his donkey, laden with gold. The children who have been beaten instead of getting breakfast, presently share in the raptures of their father and mother; and the little lady I spoke of, eight or nine years old,—dances a *pas-de-deux* with the donkey.

She did it beautifully and simply, as a child ought to dance. She was not an infant prodigy; there was no evidence, in the finish or strength of her motion, that she had been put to continual torture through half her eight or nine years. She did nothing more than any child, well taught, but painlessly, might easily do. She caricatured no older person,— attempted no curious or fantastic skill. She was dressed decently—she moved decently,—she looked and behaved innocently,—and she danced her joyful dance with perfect grace, spirit, sweetness, and self-forgetfulness. And through all the vast theatre, full of English fathers and mothers and children, there was not one hand lifted to give her sign of praise but mine.

Presently after this, came on the forty thieves, who, as I told you, were girls; and, there being no thieving to be presently done, and time hanging heavy on their hands, arms, and legs, the forty thief-girls proceeded to light forty cigars. Whereupon the British public gave them a round of applause. Whereupon I fell a thinking; and saw little more of the piece, except as an ugly and disturbing dream.

JOHN RUSKIN: *Time and Tide* (Letter V, 25 February 1867)

'CASTE'

Prince of Wales's Theatre, 10 April 1867

MR. T. W. ROBERTSON'S new comedy, entitled *Caste*, belongs exactly to the class of drama, of which we have already had specimens in *Society* and *Ours*, and which the experience of two years has led us to associate with one particular author and one particular theatre. The 'sensational' melodrama called *Shadow Tree Shaft*, recently brought out at another house, though likewise written by Mr. Robertson, was no type of his manner, and might be regarded as an interruption to the series, which began at the Prince of Wales's with *Society*, and which is now continued in *Caste*. An epigrammatic tendency, which not only shows itself in the dialogue, but points the entire fable; a predilection for domestic pathos, which is ever kept in check by a native abhorrence of twaddling sentimentality; a firm, steady hand, and a freedom from convention in the delineations of character; an eye to picturesque effects, that arise less from the employment of accessories than from the arrangement of groups that are the natural result of the action, and a connexion with the realities, which, perhaps, must not be too closely scrutinized, but which, to a certain extent, makes the stage reflect the world with more than usual accuracy —these are the characteristics which distinguish the best works of Mr. T. W. Robertson, and which have made each of them one of the leading pieces of its season. Nor is there any reason to surmise that the success of *Caste* will prove inferior to that of *Ours*.

As might be inferred from its title, the comedy *Caste* treats of that distinction between various grades of society which, among the Brahmins, is marked by express law, and which among the more western representatives of the great Aryan race, is drawn by a prejudice which has scarcely less than legal force. Since all modern plays must have some reference to love, the question of *mésalliance* naturally presents itself as offering the ground on which the social battle is to be fought. King Cophetua must marry his beggar girl, and the point for artistic discussion is how far he is right and how far wrong.

A play being a work of art addressed to a very mixed assembly the debate will of necessity take a somewhat democratic turn. The brutal way of handling the subject is boldly to revert to what the French call the principles of '89, and to declare that the beggar girl, *qua* beggar girl, was quite as good, if not better, than his Ethiopian Majesty. A more 'shirky' method is to clothe the beggar girl with all the exceptional attributes proper to birth and cultivation, and then dexterously to insinuate that she is a fair average type of mendicity in general. But Mr. Robertson, while impelled by the theatrical Parcæ towards a democratic goal, which he is likewise forced to reach, provides himself with a good conservative snaffle, and is scrupulously careful that his audience shall not mistake a sentiment for a principle. The Hon. George d'Alroy, with the commingled blood of French and English aristocracy in his veins, and with infinite pecuniary resources, marries the Columbine of a minor theatre, and the union proves to be one which gods might sanction, as they did the nuptials of Peleus and Thetis, but he is anxious to show that the example of George d'Alroy

is not to be followed without a vast deal of circum-
spection. Even the model condition of *mésalliance*
which is presented in his history is fraught with
obstacles which cannot be regarded as exceptional,
and which constantly threaten to destroy every
chance of felicity. If Columbine is one of nature's
ladies, she has a father whom nature, as well as
convention, would shrink from acknowledging as a
gentleman, and he is sure to be manifest when his
appearance is least desirable.

The plot is excellently constructed for the purpose
of exhibiting and grasping the various characters.
The Hon. George d'Alroy (Mr. Frederick Younge),
son of the Marquise de Saint-Maur (Miss Larkin),
an English lady of high birth, married to a French
nobleman, has fallen in love with Esther (Miss Lydia
Foote), daughter of Eccles (Mr. George Honey), a
dissipated specimen of the working man, who does
no work, and during the absence of his mother on
the Continent visits the humble residence of the
plebeian in the character of an honourable suitor.
He is accompanied by his friend Captain Hawtree
(Mr. Sydney Bancroft), who lectures him from a
worldly point of view on the danger he is encountering
by entering into a family so much below him in rank.
Old Eccles is simply detestable, his two daughters
support themselves and him by dancing at the
'Theatre Royal Lambeth' (wherever that may be),
and, though Esther, the object of his choice, is a girl
of superior manners, the same cannot be said of her
sister, Polly (Miss Marie Wilton), who is a damsel
of very blunt manners, engaged to Sam Gerridge
(Mr. Hare), a worthy gasfitter, who neither tries nor
even desires to elevate himself above his order. The
reasoning of Captain Hawtree, specious as it is, has

no effect on his fascinated friend, who to prevent his beloved Esther from accepting an engagement at Manchester proposes a speedy marriage, leaving to the destinies the office of settling difficulties with his mother as best they may.

When the second act begins the union has taken place, and eight months have elapsed. The scene of action is now removed from the 'little house in Stangate' to an elegant apartment in Mayfair, the residence of George d' Alroy and his young wife. A gloom is on the brow of the husband, which, however, arises not from regret at the matrimonial step he has taken, but from the fact that the regiment to which he and his friend Hawtree are attached is ordered to India on account of the Sepoy mutiny. This fact he has feared to communicate to Esther, thinking that the shock may be too great for her, and he would gladly transfer the unpleasant office to Hawtree, who in his turn is of opinion that the task of breaking the ice had best be confided to Polly, whose opportune call seems to promise a solution of the difficulty. But in a few moments another visit of a more portentous kind is paid. The formidable Marquise has returned unexpectedly from the Continent, totally ignorant of her son's marriage, and comes prepared to take leave of him prior to his departure for the wars. The announcement of her arrival is a signal for the two sisters to conceal themselves in an ante-room, and the Marquise finding herself alone with George commences a maternal lecture. As becomes an unquestionable daughter of the Plantagenets, whom, with lofty pedantry, she prefers to call the 'Plantagenistæ', the favourite author of the good old lady is Froissart, whole passages from whose chronicles she pours into her

son's ear, who finds himself pelted by their aristocratic tendency, and 'bored' by their length. At
last there is a beam of sunshine. The old lady, after
exhorting her boy to distinguish himself by the most
chivalrous valour, changes the topic, and preaches
in eloquent terms against the sin of seduction,
extolling the love of a woman as something that soars
high above all social distinctions. Poor George begins
to fancy that this is just the right moment to confess
his *mésalliance*, but unfortunately his mother's words
have conveyed the first intimation of his approaching
departure to the sisters hidden in the adjoining room,
and a scream from Esther, who has fainted, causes
the truth to be revealed without due preparation.
The Marquise is not a little displeased so suddenly to
find herself the mother-in-law of a young person of
whose existence she was not aware a minute before,
and the conduct of Polly, who has a rough spirit of
independence, does not tend towards conciliation.
Still, as Esther is a most presentable person, and
Polly is tolerably free from offence when her temper
is not ruffled, matters would not be altogether
desperate, did not the horrible old Eccles stagger
into the room sodden with drink, accompanied by
Sam Gerridge, who, though gifted with every virtue,
has been niggardly in his worship of the Graces, and
who in his best clothes looks even more plebeian than
in his working attire. Horrified at the company by
which she is surrounded, the Marquise seizes the
arm of Captain Hawtree and sails from the room,
while poor Esther takes leave of her husband and
falls senseless to the ground. We may here pause to
remark that this second act is a masterpiece of con-
structive skill. Every movement that takes place
occurs naturally, and answers a definite purpose, the

whole act being, indeed, one situation gradually developed till it reaches its highest point of effectiveness.

Eighteen months have elapsed, and when the third act begins Esther is again at the 'little house in Stangate', her father having lost all her money by low gambling. She wears a widow's dress, for news has arrived of the death of George in India, and at the back of the room is a crib, containing an infant to whom she had given birth since her husband's departure, and who, while the delight of his mother and aunt, is execrated by his hateful grandfather as an oppressive young aristocrat. The chief tyranny of the child consists in wearing a gold coral during a period of distress, when spiritous liquor is scarce in the establishment, and old Eccles thinks that he does but assert the rights of man when he detaches the 'gaud' from the baby's neck, with the intent to convert it into ready cash at the nearest pawnbrokers. The little operation is prevented by Esther, who immediately becomes a Goneril in the eyes of her father, and she has presently another battle to fight with the Marquise, who, hearing of her distressed condition, calls upon her, offering to take upon herself the care of the child, and who, indignantly repulsed, indignantly retires, much to the disgust of old Eccles, whose democratic proclivities have entirely vanished, and who now jumps at an alliance which promises to be lucrative as well as aristocratic. Captain Hawtree, who has returned from India, proves a kind friend to Esther, and at last happiness is restored by the reappearance of George d'Alroy, who, of course, was not really dead, but escaped from the Sepoys, and who is amazed to find his wife a widow and himself a father. The joy felt by the Marquise at her son's return is too great to allow her to retain any feeling of resentment against Esther, and the curtain drops on a general condition of happiness, the long duration of which may be surmised from the fact that old Eccles, in consideration of an annuity, promises to live in Jersey, and there, liquor being cheap, to do his best to drink himself to death.

As a specimen of construction the third act is not to be compared with the second. We feel that George is killed and brought to life again just as his death or life happens to be useful, and that the change in the temper of the Marquise is due rather to the necessity of bringing the story to a happy close than to the operation of any moral law. A little compression, too, might be effected with advantage.

Nevertheless, the defects of the third act are more than compensated by the admirable character of old Eccles, which here reaches its fullest development. It is not impossible that the hint of this character was taken from the father of the 'Dolls' dressmaker' in Mr. Charles Dickens's *Mutual Friend*, but Mr. Robertson by endowing the sot with political attributes has given him an aspect which is peculiarly significant at the present time. Eccles is a degraded mortal, who is always howling about the rights of labour, but who has scarcely been known to do a 'stroke of work' within the memory of his best friends. He hates the aristocracy in theory, but is ready to lick the shoe of a person of quality if anything is to be made by the degradation. That democratic claptrap which is among the leading nuisances of the day is satirized in this character with the most unsparing severity, and the moral effect of the part is heightened by the contrast of Eccles with Sam

Gerridge, intended as a good specimen of the operative class. A less conservative writer would have found
an opportunity for putting a little claptrap into the
mouth of honest Sam, but such operations are not
to the taste of Mr. Robertson. Sam is not at all
idealized, nor are his uncouth appearance or the
vulgar Terpsichorean feats which he performs under
the influence of excessive joy accompanied by the
possession of lofty sentiments. He is honest, indus-
trious, and good-natured, has an eye ever directed
to the main chance, and respects his own 'caste'
without less respecting that of others. He has a
fitting partner in Polly Eccles, whose character is in
the main similar to his own, though a tinge of
feminine coquetry gives her somewhat the tone of a
fine lady. These three parts are as well played as
they can possibly be by Mr. George Honey, Mr. Hare,
and Miss Marie Wilton.

In the treatment of those of his personages who
belong to the other 'caste' Mr. Robertson still
preserves his independence. The reader of the plot
given above will probably imagine that George is a
romantic youth intended to charm all the young
ladies in the stalls—a noble creature with a soul too
big for conventional bondage. He is nothing of the
sort, but a slow, 'spooney' youth, with a thickness of
utterance which, totally distinct from a fashionable
lisp, suggests a density of intellect. Luck, not wisdom,
has guided him to the choice of such an excellent
person as Esther. Had Fortune been less kindly his
career might have been similar to that of the young
man whose eccentricities proved so profitable a
few years since to the members of the legal profession.
He has an excellent heart and a high spirit, but these
can only show themselves under the influence of

some pressure from without, the general manner being stolid and heavy. Let us add that he is intrusted to an essentially comic actor, Mr. F. Younge, who thoroughly understands his qualities, as Mr. Bancroft does those of the more decided 'swell', Captain Hawtree, who is marked by an ungainliness of another kind, and who is intended to show that a man is not necessarily hateful, even though he becomes almost boorish in his desire to be aristocratically exclusive. Neither is the loftiness of the Marquise to be rebuked with a scowl. She is not raised on a pedestal to be knocked down, but represents a social principle, and is to be respected accordingly. This is a part exactly in the line of Miss Larkin, and is represented to the life by Miss Larkin.

The one ideal personage of the play is Esther, who is entirely distinct from her sister Polly, and in whom the boundary marks of 'caste' vanish, though it is on her account that the battle of 'caste' is fought. The author has even given her an aristocratic tinge, and when her spirit is roused she does not assert plebeian independence like Polly, but speaks as Mrs. George d'Alroy, mother of a child of ancient lineage. To Esther belong the strong situations, and generally what may be called the hard work of the piece. The part is most efficiently filled by Miss Lydia Foote.

The success of *Caste* is indubitable, and there is one fact to which we would draw attention before bringing our somewhat lengthy notice to a close. Not only are the characters typical of a lower 'caste', entirely free from claptrap, as we have already remarked, but Old Eccles, with his humbug Jacobinism, would be a positive offence to an audience composed of fanatical levellers, nor would the solid unshining virtues of Sam Gerridge be much more acceptable. Nevertheless, the occupants of the gallery, who are numerous, sanction the author's work, regarding Eccles as a proper object of derision and Sam as a person to be respected. Let it be remembered, too, that the Prince of Wales's Theatre, though it has been fashionable for two years, is by no means in a fashionable neighbourhood, and that the gallery must be peopled by many of those working men who patronized it when it was the humble 'Queen's'. That such an assembly is pleased with an exhibition which is of a most anti-demogogic kind is a fact worth noting by those who take an interest in the study of the real operative of London.

THE TIMES, 11 April 1867

ON NATURAL ACTING

It has commonly been held to be a dexterous and delicate compliment to Garrick's acting that Fielding has paid through the humorous criticisms of Partridge, who saw nothing admirable in 'the terror of the little man', but thought the actor who played the king was deserving of great praise. 'He speaks all his words distinctly, half as loud again as the other. Anybody may see he is an actor.' I cannot say what truth there was in Partridge's appreciation of Garrick, but if his language is to be interpreted as Fielding seems to imply, the intended compliment is a sarcasm. Partridge says, with a contemptuous sneer, 'He the best player! Why, I could act as well as he myself. I am sure if I had seen a ghost, I should have looked in the very same manner, and done just as he did.'

Now assuming this to be tolerably near the truth, it implies that Garrick's acting was what is called 'natural'; but *not* the natural presentation of a Hamlet. The melancholy sceptical prince in the presence of his father's ghost must have felt a tremulous and solemn awe, but cannot have felt the vulgar terror of a vulgar nature; yet Partridge says, 'If that little man upon the stage is not frightened, I never saw any man frightened in my life.' The manner of a frightened Partridge can never have been at all like the manner of Hamlet. Let us turn to Colley Cibber's remarks on Betterton, if we would see how a great actor represented the emotion: 'You have seen a Hamlet, perhaps, who on the first appearance of his father's spirit has thrown himself into all the straining vociferation requisite to express rage and fury, and the house has thundered with applause, though the misguided actor was all the while tearing a passion into rags. I am the more bold to offer you this particular instance because the late Mr. Addison, while I sate by him to see this scene acted, made the same observation, asking me, with some surprise, if I thought Hamlet should be in so violent a passion with the ghost, which, though it might have astonished, it had not provoked him. For you may observe that in this beautiful speech the passion never rises beyond an almost breathless astonishment, or an impatience limited by filial reverence to enquire into the suspected wrongs that may have raised him from his peaceful tomb, and a desire to know what a spirit so seemingly distressed might wish or enjoin a sorrowful son to execute towards his future quiet in the grave. This was the light into which Betterton threw this scene; which he opened with a pause of mute amazement, then slowly rising to a solemn trembling voice he made the ghost equally terrible to the spectator as to himself. And in the descriptive part of the natural emotions which the ghastly visions gave him, the boldness of his expostulation was still governed by decency, manly but not braving; his voice never rising to that seeming outrage or wild defiance of what he naturally revered. But, alas! to preserve this medium between mouthing and meaning too little, to keep the attention more pleasantly awake by a tempered spirit than by mere vehemence of voice, is of all the master-strokes of an actor the most difficult to reach.'

It is obvious that the naturalness required from Hamlet is very different from the naturalness of a Partridge; and Fielding made a great mistake in assimilating the representation of Garrick to the nature of a serving-man. We are not necessarily to believe that Garrick made this mistake; but on the showing of his eulogist he fell into an error quite as reprehensible as the error of the actor who played the king, and whose stilted declamation was recognised by Partridge as something like acting. That player had at least a sense of the *optique du théâtre* which demanded a more elevated style than would have suited the familiarity of daily intercourse. He knew he was there to act, to represent a king, to impress an idealised image on the spectator's mind, and he could not succeed by the naturalness of his own manner. That he failed in his attempt proves that he was an imperfect artist; but the attempt was an attempt at art. Garrick (assuming the accuracy of Fielding's description) failed no less egregiously, though in a different way. He was afraid of being stilted, and he relapsed into vulgarity. He tried to be natural, without duly considering the kind of nature that was to be represented. The supreme difficulty of an actor is to represent ideal character with such truthfulness that it shall affect us as real, not to drag down ideal character to the vulgar level. His art is one of representation, not of illusion. He has to use natural expressions, but he must sublimate them; the symbols must be such as we can sympathetically interpret, and for this purpose they must be the expressions of real human feeling; but just as the language is poetry, or choice prose, purified from the hesitancies, incoherences, and imperfection of careless daily speech, so must his utterances be measured, musical and incisive—his manner typical and pictorial. If the language depart too widely from the logic of passion and truthfulness, we call it bombast; if the elevation of the actor's style be not sustained by natural feeling, we call it mouthing and rant; and if the language fall below the passion we call it prosaic and flat; as we call the actor tame if he cannot present the character so as to interest us. The most general error of authors, and of actors, is turgidity rather than flatness. The striving to be effective easily leads into the error of exaggeration. But it by no means follows, as some persons seem to imply, that because exaggeration is a fault, tameness is a merit. Exaggeration is a fault because it is an untruth; but in art it is as easy to be untrue by falling below as by rising above naturalness.

The acting of Mr. Horace Wigan, as the pious banker in 'The Settling Day', which suggested these remarks, is quite as much below the truth of nature in its tameness and absence of individuality, as it would have been above the truth had he represented the conventional stage hypocrite. He did not by exaggeration shock our common sense; but neither did he delight our artistic sense by his art. If his performance was without offence, it was also without charm. Some of the audience were doubtless gratified to notice the absence of conventionalism; but I suspect that the majority were tepid in their admiration; and critics would ask whether Mr. Horace Wigan could have given a strongly-marked individuality to the character, and at the same time have preserved the ease and naturalness which the representation demanded. Is he not like some novelists, who can be tolerably natural so long as they are creeping on the level of everyday incident and talk, but who become absurdly unnatural the instant they have to rise to the 'height of their high argument' either in character or passion? Miss

Austen's novels are marvels of art, because they are exquisitely true, and interesting in their truth. Miss Austen's imitators fondly imagine that to be quiet and prosaic—in pages which might as well have been left unwritten—is all that the simplicity of art demands. But in art, simplicity is economy, not meagreness: it is the absence of superfluities, not the suppression of essentials; it arises from an ideal generalisation of real and essential qualities, guided by an exquisite sense of proportion.

If we once understand that naturalness in acting means truthful presentation of the character indicated by the author, and not the foisting of commonplace manner on the stage, there will be a ready recognition of each artist's skill, whether he represent the naturalness of a Falstaff, or the naturalness of a Sir Peter Teazle, the naturalness of a Hamlet, or the naturalness of Coriolanus. Kean in Shylock was natural; Bouffé in Père Grandet. Rachel in Phèdre was natural; Farren in Grandfather Whitehead. Keeley in Waddilove was natural; Charles Mathews in Affable Hawk, and Got in Maître Guérin. Naturalness being truthfulness, it is obvious that a coat-and-waistcoat realism demands a manner, delivery, and gesture wholly unlike the poetic realism of tragedy and comedy; and it has been the great mistake of actors that they have too often brought with them into the drama of ordinary life the style they have been accustomed to in the drama of ideal life.

The modern French actors have seen the error; and some English actors have followed their example, and aimed at greater quietness and 'naturalness'. At the Olympic this is attended with some success. But even French actors, when not excellent, carry the reaction too far; and in the attempt to be natural forget the *optique du théâtre*, and the demands of art. They will sit upon side sofas, and speak with their faces turned away from the audience, so that half their words are lost; and they will lounge upon tables, and generally comport themselves in a manner which is not only easy, but free and easy. The art of acting is not shown in giving a conversational tone and a drawing-room quietness, but in vividly presenting character, while never violating the proportions demanded on the one hand by the *optique du théâtre*, and on the other by what the audience will recognise as truth.

This judgment, and the principles on which it was based, appear to have found little favour in certain quarters; and a writer in the *Reader* has attacked me in two columns of sarcasm and argument. He says, in reference to my article, that 'few things are more painful than the nonsense which an exceedingly clever man may write about an art with which he has no real sympathy, to which he has ceased to give any serious thought'. I leave it to my readers to appreciate my imperfect sympathy and want of serious thought; as to the nonsense I may have written, everyone knows how easily a man may set down nonsense, and believe it to be sense. The point which most pressingly forces itself upon me is, that a writer who has given such prolonged and serious thought to the art of acting as my critic may be supposed to have given, should nevertheless have not yet mastered the initial principles on which that art rests. It is to me amazing how any man writing *ex professo*, could cite Kean and Emil Devrient among natural actors, belonging to a 'school of acting in which nature is carefully and closely followed, and

in which small attention is paid to idealised impressions'. I cannot explain how this writer's 'serious
thought' should have left him still in the condition of
innocence which supposes that Art is delusion, not
illusion; and that the nearer the approach to every-
day vulgarity of detail the more consummate is the
artistic effect.

In trying to disengage the question of 'naturalness'
from its ambiguities, I referred to the criticism of
Garrick's Hamlet which Fielding conveys through
the verdict of Partridge, my object being to discriminate between the nature of Hamlet and the
nature of Partridge; and I said that if Fielding were
to be understood as correctly indicating Garrick's
manner, that manner must have been false to nature
and therefore bad art. On this my critic observes:—

'The reasons for this remarkable opinion are very
shortly given. The melancholy sceptical prince in
the presence of his father's ghost must have felt a
tremulous and solemn awe, but cannot have felt the
vulgar terror of a vulgar nature. "The manner of a
frightened Partridge can never have been at all like the
manner of Hamlet. . . . It is obvious that the naturalness required from Hamlet is very different from the
naturalness of a Partridge; and Fielding made a great
mistake in assimilating the representation of Garrick
to the nature of a serving-man." Ordinary people
might find some difficulty in attaining the certainty
which "L" has on this subject. Very few men are
so fortunate as to know a prince; fewer still have
had the advantage of meeting ghosts; it is therefore
difficult for most of us to realise so definitely as "L"
does what the manner of a prince towards a ghost
would be. But the rather positive critic may be
assumed to be right. Probably, if a ghost walked into

Marlborough House, the manner of the Prince of Wales towards the intruder would be very different from that of the footman.'

The answer to this is very simple. The manner of Hamlet must be the manner consistent with that of an ideal prince, and not the manner of a serving-man, nor of one real prince, in Marlborough House or elsewhere. Had Shakespeare conceived a prince stupid, feeble, weak-eyed, weak-chested, or bold, coarse, and sensual, the actor would have been called upon to represent the ideals of these. But having conceived a *princely* Hamlet, i.e. an accomplished, thoughtful, dreamy young man—to represent him as frightened at the ghost and behaving as a serving-man would behave, was not natural, consequently not ideal, for ideal treatment means treatment which is *true to the nature of the character represented under the technical conditions of the representation.*

This leads me to the main point at issue. I have always emphatically insisted on the necessity of actors being true to nature in the expression of natural emotions, although the technical conditions of the art forbid the expressions being exactly those of real life; but my critic, not understanding this, says:—

'In justice to "L.", however, it should be stated that he does not altogether object to natural acting, but only to acting which follows nature very closely. Being a writer who constructs as well as destroys, he explains what real dramatic art is. An actor should impress an idealised image on the spectator's mind; he should "use natural expressions, but he must sublimate them", whatever that may mean; his utterance must be "measured, musical, and incisive; his manner typical and pictorial".'

It is clear not only from this passage, but from the examples afterwards cited, that my critic considers the perfection of art to lie in the closest reproduction of everyday experience. That an actor should raise the natural expressions into ideal expressions—that he should 'sublimate' them is so little understood by my critic, that he professes not to know what sublimating 'may mean'. I will not insult him by supposing that it is the word which puzzles him, or that he does not understand Dryden's verses:—

> As his actions rose, so raise they still their vein,
> In words whose weight best suits a sublimated strain.

But I will ask him if he supposes that an actor, having to represent a character in situations altogether exceptional, and speaking a language very widely departing from the language of ordinary life, would be *true* to the nature of that character and that language, by servilely reproducing the manners, expression, and intonations of ordinary life? The poet is not closely following nature; the poet is ideal in his treatment; is the actor to be less so? I am presumed to have been guilty of talking nonsense in requiring that the musical verse of the poet should be spoken musically, or the elaborate prose of the prose dramatist should be spoken with measured cadence and incisive effect. I cannot be supposed to approve of measured 'mouthing', or to wish for turgidity in wishing for music and precision; would the critic have verse declaimed like prose (naturally, as it is falsely called), and prose gabbled with little reference to cadence and emphasis, like ordinary talk? When he objects to the manner being typical, would he have it not to be recognisable? When he objects to the manner being pictorial, would he have it careless, ungraceful, the slouching of club-rooms and London streets carried into Verona or the Ardennes? Obviously, the pictorial manner which would be natural (ideal) to Romeo or Rosalind, would be unnatural in Charles Surface or Lady Teazle.

But so little does this writer discriminate between music and mouthing that he says:—

'The performers may not come up to his standard, but it is satisfactory to think that their aim is in the right direction. No one will ever accuse Mr. Phelps or Mr. Creswick, or Miss Helen Faucit, of being too natural. These artists certainly have a highly idealised style. Their utterance may not be musical, but it is measured and incisive—with a vengeance. On the French stage things are less satisfactory. Many of the leading actors there have a foolish hankering after nature. The silly people who think that French acting is sometimes admirable, and that English acting is generally execrable, should correct their opinions by studying the canons of a higher criticism; for the Paris actors have essentially shallow views of their art. Got, in that marvellous passage in "Le Duc Job," which has made grey-haired men cry like children, is much in error. He merely behaves just as a warm-hearted man would behave on suddenly receiving the news of a dear friend's death; and this has been thought to make his performance so intensely touching. But it is quite wrong; his language is not "measured, musical, and incisive", his manner decidedly not "typical and pictorial". Sanson, with his satirical *bonhomie* in "Le Fils de Giboyer", has been much admired, because, having to act the Marquis d'Auberive, he was so precisely like a French nobleman of the old *régime*. His business, he should have learnt, was not to resemble a real marquis, but to "impress the idealised image" of a marquis upon the spectator's mind. The terrible reality of Delaunay's acting in the last scene of "On ne Badine pas avec l'Amour" has made many spectators shudder; but then it is so perfectly natural, the expressions are not the least "sublimated".'

If he knew more of the French stage, he would, I think, have paused before writing such a passage. He would know that Rachel was supreme in virtue of those very qualities which he asserts the French actors to have relinquished in their hankering after nature; he would know that Mdme. Plessy is the most musical, the most measured, the most incisive speaker (whether of verse or prose) now on the stage; he would know that Got, Sanson, and Regnier are great actors, because they represent types, and the types are recognised as true.

When we are told that Got 'merely behaves just as a warm-hearted man would behave on suddenly receiving the news of a dear friend's death,' we ask *what* warm-hearted man? A hundred different men would behave in a hundred different ways on such an occasion, would say different things, would express their emotions with different looks and gestures. The actor has to select. He must be typical. His expressions must be those which, while they belong to the recognised symbols of our common nature, have also the peculiar individual impress of the character represented. It is obvious, to anyone who reflects for a moment, that nature is often so reticent —that men and women express so little in their faces and gestures, or in their tones of what is tearing their hearts—that a perfect copy of almost any man's expressions would be utterly ineffective on the stage.

It is the actor's art to express in well-known symbols what an individual man may be supposed to feel, and we, the spectators recognising these expressions, are thrown into a state of sympathy. Unless the actor follows nature sufficiently to select symbols that are recognised as natural, he fails to touch us, but as to any minute fidelity in copying the actual manner of murderers, misers, avengers, broken-hearted fathers, &c., we really have had so little experience of such characters, that we cannot estimate the fidelity; hence the actor is forced to be as typical as the poet is. Neither pretends closely to copy nature, but only to represent nature sublimated into the ideal. The nearer the approach to every-day reality implied by the author in his characters and language—the closer the coat-and-waistcoat realism of the drama—the closer must be the actor's imitation of every-day manner; but even then he must idealise, *i.e.* select and heighten—and it is for his tact to determine how much.

G. H. LEWES: *On Actors and the Art of Acting,* 1875

ELLEN TERRY[1]

The Merchant of Venice: Prince of Wales's Theatre,
April 1875

MISS ELLEN TERRY, who in her early childhood
served an apprenticeship at the Princess's Theatre
under the rule of Mr. and Mrs. Charles Kean, is
now an artist of real distinction. With all the charms
of aspect and graces of manner indispensable to the
impersonation of the heiress of Belmont, Miss Terry
is gifted with a voice of silvery and sympathetic
tone, while her elocutionary method should be
prized by her fellow-actors. Portia has been presented
now with tragedy-queen airs, and now with vivacity
of the soubrette sort—as when in Garrick's time Mrs.
Clive played the part and made a point of mimicking
the more famous barristers of her time; indeed, a
nice combination of stateliness, animation, sentiment,
archness, poetry, tenderness, and humour is required
of the actress intrusted with the character. Miss
Terry's Portia leaves little to be desired; she is
singularly skilled in the business of the scene, and
assists the action of the drama by great care and
inventiveness in regard to details. There is something
of passion in the anxiety with which she watches
Bassanio's choice of the leaden casket; while the
confession of her love, which follows upon that
incident is delivered with a depth of feeling such as
only a mistress of her art could accomplish. Thus it
chanced that, probably for the first time, the portions
of the play that relate to the loves of Portia and

[1] Passages extracted from Dutton Cook's extended
notices of plays in which Ellen Terry appeared.

Bassanio became of more importance and interest than the scenes in which Shylock appears.

Olivia, by W. G. Wills (founded on *The Vicar of Wakefield*), Court Theatre, April 1878

In the hands of Miss Ellen Terry Olivia becomes a character of rare dramatic value, more nearly allied, perhaps, to the Clarissa of Richardson than to the heroine of Goldsmith. The actress's singular command of pathetic expression obtains further manifestation. The scenes of Olivia's farewell to her family, all unconscious of the impending blow her flight is to inflict upon them, is curiously affecting in its subtle and subdued tenderness; while her indignation and remorse upon discovering the perfidy of Thornhill are rendered with a vehemence of emotion and tragic passion such as the modern theatre has seldom exhibited. Only an artist of distinct genius could have ventured upon the impulsive abrupt movements by means of which she thrusts from her the villain who has betrayed her, and denotes the intensity of her scorn of him, the completeness of her change from loving to loathing. Miss Terry is no less successful in the quieter passages of the drama, while her graces of aspect and manner enable her to appear as Olivia even to the full satisfaction of those most prepossessed concerning the personal charms of that heroine,—so beloved of painters and illustrators,—to whom have been dedicated so many acres of canvas, so many square feet of boxwood.

Hamlet: Lyceum Theatre, January 1879

From Miss Ellen Terry Mr. Irving receives invaluable support. An Ophelia so tender, so graceful,

so picturesque, and so pathetic has not been seen
in the theatre since Macready's Hamlet many years
ago found his Ophelia in the person of Miss Priscilla
Horton. In characters of this class, the heroines
of genuine poetry, Miss Terry is now without a rival,
is indeed unapproached by any other actress upon
our stage. Her personal graces and endowments, her
elocutionary skill, her musical speech, and, above all,
her singular power of depicting intensity of feeling,
are most happily combined, as the audience were
quick to discover and applaud in this very exquisite
presentment of Ophelia.

The Lady of Lyons, by Lord Lytton: Lyceum
Theatre, April 1879

[As played by Irving, Claude Melnotte's] crimin-
ality certainly gained in intensity by contrast with
the singular delicacy and refinement of Miss Ellen
Terry's Pauline, who really points the moral of the
play when she demands—

> What was the slight of a poor powerless girl
> To the deep wrong of this most vile revenge?

But there have been Paulines not fairly describable
as poor or powerless, but almost vixenish in their
attributes, repaying their lover's perjury with infinite
scorn, and uttering very fierce tirades in reply to
his rather long-winded explanations. With curious
art Miss Terry passes over the artificial quality of
Pauline's harangues, and lays stress on her more
amiable characteristics—shows that her pride is
rather matter of education than of nature—that she
is in truth tender, gentle, trusting, loving, and
altogether womanly. To some, no doubt, the part
will seem under-played, particularly with reference

to the intentions of the author and the traditions of representation. Miss Terry's performance, however, takes high rank among contemporary efforts, in right of its poetic sensibility, its girlish grace, its simplicity, its subtlety, its exquisite elocution, and that surprising picturesqueness of aspect, pose, and movement which seem to be the peculiar and exclusive possession of the actress. The costumes of the Directory period Miss Terry invests with an artistic elegance which scarcely belongs to them as a matter of right.

The Merchant of Venice: Lyceum Theatre,
November 1879

Happily the Portia of 1875—who rendered memorable a revival that was otherwise rather ill-starred, for all the taste and refinement of its scenic decorations—Miss Ellen Terry, lends her invaluable assistance to Mr. Irving at the Lyceum; and a more admirable Portia there could scarcely be. Nervous at first, and weighed down possibly by the difficulty of equalling herself and of renewing her former triumph, the lady played uncertainly, and at times with some insufficiency of force; but as the drama proceeded her courage increased and her genius asserted itself. Radiantly beautiful in her Venetian robes of gold-coloured brocaded satin, with the look of a picture by Giorgione, her emotional acting in the casket-scene with Bassanio; her spirited resolve, confided to Nerissa, to prove 'the prettier fellow of the two'; her exquisite management of the most melodious of voices in the trial before the Doge; the high comedy of the last act—these left nothing to be desired, and obtained, as they deserved, the most enthusiastic applause.

Othello: Lyceum Theatre, May 1881

As Desdemona, Miss Ellen Terry was very charming of aspect, as, indeed, she never fails to be: she was, moreover, graceful, tender, and pathetic. But she suffered, I think, from the nervousness of the occasion, and seemed sometimes less completely absorbed in the character she personated than she is usually. And she should be cautioned against permitting her Desdemona, even in her moments of severest suffering, to fling herself upon the bosom of Iago,[1] and to accept the consolation of his embraces and caresses. The wives of commanding officers are not, or should not be, wont thus to accept comfort at the hands of subalterns; for it must be remembered that Iago is only an ensign, and but twenty-eight years old, as he himself announces.

The Desdemona of Miss Ellen Terry is now one of her most charming performances; very sympathetic, graceful, and picturesque. And I note that when Mr. Booth is her Iago, Miss Terry's Desdemona does not permit herself to fall weeping upon his bosom or to find consolation in his soothing endearments.

DUTTON COOK: *Nights at the Play*, 1883

---

[1] Irving was Iago and Edwin Booth Othello. After the third performance they alternated in these parts. See *post*, pp. 178–81.

ELLEN TERRY

THE performance, at the Princess's,[1] by Miss Ellen Terry, of the character of Pauline, in *The Lady of Lyons*, gives to an entertainment intended for one night only, and appealing to a limited section of the public, an interest a similar occasion has seldom claimed. Its effect is to set the seal upon a growing reputation, and to make evident the fact that an actress of a high, if not the highest, order has arisen in our midst. One of the pleasantest, in as much as it is one of the rarest tasks the critic is called upon to discharge is that of heralding to the world the advent of genius. So vast a space separates, ordinarily, aspiration from accomplishment, the critic's duty becomes merged in that of the censor, and the public comes to regard him as one whose sole function is to point out irregularities of workmanship and failure of effort. In the case of things dramatic and histrionic it is rarely indeed the critic can do more than suggest some promise of talent behind crude performance— some glimpse of meaning or intention in a commonplace rendering. There is, accordingly, a pleasure of no ordinary kind in announcing a fact Miss Terry's recent performances have fully established, viz. that an actress has developed in whom there is that perception of analogies, that insight into mysteries and that power of interpretation, on which the world has bestowed the name of genius. Circumstances took Miss Terry from the stage at a time[2] when men dimly perceived in her the promise which has since been realized. It is probable that some

[1] 14 August 1875.   [2] From 1868 to 1874.—ED.

delay in that maturity of style indispensable to perfection in histrionic art has resulted from this break in her career. The interval can scarcely have been misspent, however, since Miss Terry reappeared on the stage with improved powers and with improved method. After one or two attractive performances in parts which showed one side only of her talent, Miss Terry went to the Prince of Wales's Theatre, and played Portia in *The Merchant of Venice*, and Clara Douglas in *Money*. To these *rôles* is now added a third, the result of the three being to prove Miss Terry a subtle interpreter of poetic character, and an admirable exponent of various phases of passion.

Physical advantages are, of course, an all-important portion of the stock-in-trade of an actress. The long, tender lines of a singularly graceful figure add wonderful picturesqueness to the illustrations Miss Terry affords. Her presentation of Pauline comprised a series of pictures each more graceful than the preceding, and all too good for the lackadaisical play in which she appeared. They would have been perfectly in place as illustrations to some border ballad or legend of the 'Round Table'. More important, however, than this gift of picturesqueness, magical as is its effect in illustrating art, is the power of getting inside the character and revealing it to the public. This, in the case of Portia, Miss Terry does, showing one of the loveliest of Shaksperian creations in colours in which few among students even had dressed it, flooding it, so to speak, with a light of illumination. As interpretation, her Pauline is less successful. Pride, which in the character of Pauline divides the empire with love, in the interpretation makes scarcely a fight. Conceding, however, that the conception is wrong to this extent, the impersonation is singularly fine. A score of natural and artistic touches reveal the tenderness and longing of the woman's heart, while the rendering of the fourth act, in which Pauline seeks to force herself from the environing arms of her parents and join her departing lover, whose words of farewell sting her to madness, is one of those pieces of electrical acting that produce upon the mind an effect of which art in other developments seems scarcely capable. It is too early yet to gauge fully the talent which has revealed itself. It seems probable that Miss Terry's powers will be restrained to depicting the grace, tenderness, and passion of love. In the short scene in the third act, in which Pauline chides her lover for treachery, the actress scarcely rises to the requisite indignation. Limiting, however, what is to be hoped from her within the bounds indicated, what chance is there not afforded? Juliet in the stronger scenes would be, we should fancy, outside the physical resources of the artist. Beatrice, Rosalind, Viola, Imogen, Miranda, and a score other characters of the most delicate and fragrant beauty are, however, all within what appears to be her range. In the present state of public feeling respecting the Shakspearian drama, it will be strange indeed if some manager does not take the opportunity of mounting some of those plays for which her talent is so eminently adapted. The period during which an actress can play such parts with effect is brief; and a portion of Miss Terry's career has already been lost so far as the stage is concerned. There will be regrettable waste if talent so specially suited to the Shakspearian drama is confined to Lord Lytton's facile sentiment and sparkling rhetoric.

JOSEPH KNIGHT: *Theatrical Notes,* 1893

IRVING IN SHAKESPEARE[1]

Hamlet: Lyceum Theatre, November 1874

ALTHOUGH Mr. Irving has on several occasions
played Hamlet in the provinces, he has now assumed
the part for the first time in London. His performance
attracted a very large audience, and, it may be said
at once, secured every evidence of complete success.
Mr. Irving was applauded as though he were another
Garrick; he was recalled at every opportunity, and
rewarded with as many crowns of laurel wreaths
and bouquets of flowers as though he had been
Mdme. Patti herself. This enthusiasm was no
doubt excessive, but it may not be condemned as
spurious, although certainly containing a suspicious
element. Mr. Irving's Hamlet is the conscientious
effort of an intelligent and experienced player, and
presents just claims to respectful consideration and
a fair measure of approval. It seemed, however,
that the audience were predisposed to form an exaggerated estimate of the merits of the performance.
In truth, the difficulty of winning favour in such a
part as Hamlet is less great than is generally supposed. The character is well known among players
to be secure of applause to any representative
possessed of certain physical qualifications, some
knowledge of the stage, and thorough acquaintance
with the words of the play. Indeed, it is difficult to
call to mind any representation of *Hamlet* which did
not elicit abundance of applause for its leading
player: the actor of Hamlet is so helped by the nature

[1] Extracts from Dutton Cook's extended notices of these
productions.

of the speeches he is charged to deliver, by the incidents in which he takes part as the central figure, by the support he receives of necessity from the other characters, even when these are but indifferently personated. Mr. Irving, who invariably acts with extreme painstaking, was not likely to play Hamlet without careful study of the text. His rendering of the part, however, does not, perhaps could not, differ much from that adopted by preceding Hamlets. Such change of aspect as the part assumes is mainly to be attributed to the marked physical qualities of the actor. Some few new readings he has adopted, and here and there he has varied the traditional business of the scene; but substantially his Hamlet is the ordinary Hamlet of the stage, supplemented by the peculiarities of manner of his latest representative. A marked manner, it may be noted, has been possessed by every actor of distinction, and no charge can therefore be levelled against Mr. Irving on this account. Still, a certain heaviness of movement, an occasional subsidence of interest which marked the progress of the performance, may be accounted for by Mr. Irving's limited compass of voice and lack of strength to sustain fully so arduous a character. Mr. Irving is far from a robust Hamlet, and is not one of those tragedians skilled in rumbling out soliloquies in deep chest notes. His voice seems sometimes artificially treble in quality and to be jerked out with effort. His movements are angular, and his bearing is deficient in dignity and courtliness, though not without a certain refinement of its own. There are artistic qualities in the representation, indeed, which are not to be denied; and if Mr. Irving scarcely impresses us so completely as did some earlier interpreters, he yet rarely fails to interest

and but for an unfortunate choice of costume of a
strangely docked and confined kind, might always
present a picturesque appearance upon the scene.
In any case, for those who care to see *Hamlet*
played at all, here is a Hamlet who is always
zealous and thoughtful; often very adroit; who
spares no pains to please: who has at command a
certain feverish impetuosity, which, if it makes his
passion sometimes too petulant, is yet surprisingly
effective on the stage; and who is, in short, as complete a representative of the part as the modern
theatre can furnish.

Othello: Lyceum Theatre, February 1876

Mr. Irving's Othello has been enthusiastically
applauded and as sharply condemned. There has
never, we may note, been perfect unanimity in regard
to the achievements of the actor; but on the present
occasion the party of dissent has gained strength,
and ventured upon more distinct assertion of its
opinions. Something of this may probably be due to
the fact that Othello is Mr. Irving's third Shakspearian assumption. His histrionic system has become a
more familiar matter than it was two seasons ago,
and thus defects of style that escaped remark, if
they did not win favour in his Hamlet, now incur
grave rebuke. The personal peculiarities and shortcomings of an actor of any force are speedily forgiven
him. The playgoers of the past soon learned to
forget that low stature of Garrick and the 'foggy
throat' of John Kemble. It is understood now that
every delineation presented by Mr. Irving must
suffer in some degree from the irremediable physical
characteristics of the actor. But it has, perhaps, been
insufficiently taken into account that there exist

strong preconceptions concerning the character of Othello which almost attach exceptional conditions to its representation upon the stage, and what are known as Mr. Irving's 'mannerisms', in this regard, acquire a curious prominence, and place him at an unforeseen disadvantage. In effect, Othello has long enjoyed popular admiration for the very qualities that Mr. Irving is least enabled to impart to his stage portraitures. This should, perhaps, have withheld the actor from the part; but it should not induce unmindfulness of much that is worthy and distinguished in his performance; for the 'mannerisms' notwithstanding—and the many blemishes of a far more serious kind—there remain passages of Mr. Irving's Othello marked by rare artistic beauty, and meriting cordial recognition.

It is not only nature and continued habit of manner that separate his Othello from previous Othellos. The costume is different, for one thing. Othello has usually worn robes of an Oriental texture and device; but Mr. Irving will none of these. His Othello follows the counsel given years ago by Mr. Disraeli in *Vivian Grey*, and appears 'in the full dress of a Venetian magnifico of the middle Ages; a fit companion for Cornaro, or Grimani, or Barberigo, or Foscari'. No loss of picturesqueness is thus incurred, however. The absence of Othello's wonted dignity and repose of bearing is far more seriously felt. In the first two acts Mr. Irving is feverish and sensitive, but does not aim apparently at making any great impression. 'Keep up your bright swords' is spoken petulantly; the address to the Senate is delivered with considerable art, although an almost tearful sentiment attends the description of the wooing of Desdemona. Othello is without chivalric bearing; he becomes curiously effeminate in the presence of his bride; there is evidence of moral weakness in his obsequious uxoriousness. 'Silence that dreadful bell' is properly spoken as a command, and without due display of wrath. The dismissal of Cassio is well delivered. But it is not until the third act that there is either pronounced failure or consummate success in the performance. Mr. Irving's play of face and skilful application of tone when jealousy first stirs in the mind of Othello are very admirable; for although Coleridge and others have maintained that the passion of Othello is not jealousy, but that his suffering arises from 'the dire necessity of loving without limit one whom his heart pronounces to be unworthy of that love', it is clear that at the outset the Moor is troubled by the most ignoble and degrading suspicions. Mr. Irving discriminates finely between Othello's consideration of feminine frailty as an abstract if painful proposition, and his gradual perception that Iago's hints apply to Desdemona, and that the wreck of his happiness is imminent. But the mine of passion is sprung too soon and too suddenly, and there is absolute waste of force in the wild utterance of the line beginning, 'I had rather be a toad'. After this the merits and demerits of the representation become scarcely divisible. We may note, however, the acute plaintiveness of 'No, not much moved'; the acute and distressing air of shame which marks the delivery of the direction, 'Set on your wife to observe'; the sense of mystery conveyed by the description of the handkerchief; and the declamatory force of the passage, 'Like to the Pontic sea', &c. The 'Farewell' necessarily lacked music of voice; and other speeches suffered severely from the impetuosity of the speaker. One of Hazlitt's descriptions of Kean is indeed peculiarly applicable to Mr. Irving: 'He is too often in the highest key of passion, *too uniformly on the verge of extravagance*, too constantly on the rack.' He wearies the eye with his incessant changes of posture, his excessive and graceless movements of head and hands; while he offends the ear by too frequently permitting the fervour of his speech to degenerate into unintelligible and inarticulate rant. Yet it is fair to state that there are redeeming touches even in his worst and coarsest painting; that there are grand moments even in the very uncouthness and grotesqueness of his frenzy, and that the sense of an aberrant and diseased brain accompanied by exceeding physical prostration after the epileptic seizure of the fourth act, is conveyed with great artistic force and singular regard for natural truth. The fifth act is weirdly pathetic and impressive, with recourse to melodramatic terrors or literal interpretation of the stage directions. Mr. Irving's acting here abounds in emotion and passion, with grateful intervals of desperate calm, as when Othello stands petrified and aghast at his own most miserable folly and crime, resembling, it must be confessed, as he folds round him his robe, one of the late Mr. Fenimore Cooper's Mohawk braves draped in his blanket. The death scene avoids the conceits of Signor Salvini and Mr. Fechter, and is well contrived: Othello stabs himself, falls, drags himself beside the bed of Desdemona, and there sinks dead.

As a first essay, the performance is certainly remarkable, but, as we have shown, its imperfections are many and grave. Certain of these, no doubt, Mr. Irving has power to amend, and his Othello will probably mellow and sober under the wholesome influences of time and experience. But there will always remain defects and blemishes inseparable from the actor which in this character the public may find it very difficult altogether to forgive and forget.

Richard III: Lyceum Theatre, February 1877

The revival greatly interested the audience; but it must be confessed that the assumption of a new and arduous part by Mr. Irving was generally viewed as a matter of still more importance. Of late there has been a measure of decline in the fervour of the reception awarded to Mr. Irving's performances of Shakspeare. It is, of course, difficult to maintain enthusiasm at its first fever-heat, and reaction is apt to follow upon emotional excesses. But if there has been any failure on the part of the actor, some fickleness should certainly be charged against his public. The ardent admirers of his Hamlet should certainly have shown themselves more content than they confessed themselves with both his Macbeth and his Othello, seeing that all three impersonations were closely united by similarity of intellectual view and histrionic method. But the charm of novelty perhaps made its absence seriously felt; and the frequent performance, nightly wear and tear, seemed to affect the tragedian injuriously, heightening the defects and extravagances of his manner of art. As Richard, however, it is likely that Mr. Irving may regain any favour he has forfeited, and even attach to himself a section of critical opinion that has held itself unsympathetically aloof from his Shakspearian efforts. Those confirmed habits or tricks of accent or pronunciation, of gesture, of gait, of facial expression, hitherto denounced as disfiguring 'mannerisms', are not out of harmony with the individuality of

Richard; for Richard is very much of what actors call a 'character part', and permits of the minute and special rendering of personal and physical traits and peculiarities. Gloster enters immediately upon the rising of the curtain; there is no need to prepare the minds of the spectators in regard to him, for his character had been sufficiently exhibited and developed in the Second and Third parts of *King Henry VI*. Mr. Irving, looking very like Louis XI, is content to represent the deformity of 'hard-favoured' Richard by means merely of rounded shoulders and a halting walk. In the earlier scenes there is some want of repose and repression. Richard, who has proclaimed, 'I am myself alone', and avowed that he has 'neither pity, love, nor fear', seems deficient in mental fortitude, in self-confidence and sufficiency. But the actor is assuredly to be excused for any nervousness that may have interfered with his intentions, or led to an unequal expenditure of his resources. At present his impersonation suffers from over-emphasis and excess of elaboration; and yet these defects are really merits, in so far as they indicate his devoted study of his text, his desire that no line or point of it should fail in effect through lack of zeal or painstaking on his part. The incredible scene of the wooing of Lady Anne is skilfully represented, and admirable art is displayed in Gloster's dealings with the kinsfolk of the Queen and in his encounter with Margaret of Anjou. It is to be noted that Richard, in right of the intensity and thoroughness of his villainy, always commands the favour, admiration, and even a measure of the sympathy of his audience; they are carried away by his superb force of character; they perceive that the other *dramatis personæ* are but puppets in his hands, and that he is very fully possessed of the kingly attributes of sagacity, energy, indomitable courage, and signal power of command, the while he is endowed with an appreciation of humour that is even in advance of Iago's sense of jocosity. Mr. Irving capitally depicts Richard's enjoyment of his own villainy, and of the mocks and jibes and insults he heaps upon friends and foes alike. Hypocrisy has always been a comic leaven upon the stage, and Richard's powers of dissimulation, his ability to 'wet his cheeks with artificial tears and frame his face to all occasions', his affectation of religion and piety—notably in the scene with the Lord Mayor—are represented with extraordinary fulness and force, and win very cordial applause. The rebuke of Buckingham is no longer delivered as a wild burst of passion, but, much more judiciously, is spoken with considerable calmness, and yet with a malignant, bitter, and menacing contempt that is extremely effective. Throughout the play, indeed, the desire of the actor appears to be to depict Richard not as the petulant, vapouring, capering, detonating creature he has so long been represented in the theatre, but as an arch and polished dissembler, the grimmest of jesters, the most subtle and the most merciless of assassins and conspirators, aiming directly at the crown, and ridding himself one by one of every obstacle appearing on his path thitherward— 'hewing his way out with a bloody axe', smiling and 'murthering while he smiles'—and gifted or afflicted with a certain diabolical delight in his own enormities. At the same time it should be stated that the scenes really demanding passionate interpretation, such as the arrest and condemnation of Hastings, the bearing of Richard on the interception of his march, and his treatment of the messengers bringing tidings of the successful advance of Richmond, were rendered with sufficient force. Exhaustion of voice and a rather hysterical display of remorse weakened the effect of the tent-scene. Here Richard seemed embarrassed with the velvet and ermined robes he had carried with him from Westminster to Bosworth Field, and too much disposed to make strange attitude and curious gesticulation serve as means of depicting anguish of mind and the pangs of a guilty conscience. The performance will without doubt gain by the further consideration the artist can now bring to his undertaking; experience will teach him to economise his forces, to reduce the inequalities of his portraiture, and to rid himself of the minor defects of redundant action and excessive play of face. But as it stands, this representation of Shakespeare's Richard may surely take its place among the most remarkable of histrionic achievements. As an actor's first impersonation of a part entirely new to him, it is startling in its originality, its power, and completeness.

Hamlet: Lyceum Theatre, January 1879

Mr. Irving's managerial career has commenced most auspiciously. The opening representation was, indeed, from first to last simply triumphant. A distinguished audience filled to overflowing the redecorated Lyceum Theatre, and the new *impresario* was received with unbounded enthusiasm. These gratifying evidences of goodwill were scarcely required, however, to convince Mr. Irving that his enterprise carried with it very general sympathy. His proved devotion to his art, his determination to uphold the national drama to his utmost, have secured for him the suffrages of all classes of society. And it is recognized that he has become a manager,

not to enhance his position as an actor—for already
he stands in the front rank of his profession—but the
better to promote the interests of the whole stage, and
to serve more fully, to gratify more absolutely, the
public, his patrons. Let it be added as a minor matter,
that he has followed the good examples set by Mr.
Hollingshead and Mrs. Bancroft, and has been careful of the comfort of the audience, neither permitting
them to be pinched for room, nor subjecting them to
those petty imposts which, like so many turnpike dues,
have so persistently impeded the visitor on his passage
from the street to his seat within the theatre.

The tragedy of *Hamlet* was well chosen for the first
performance under the new management: as Hamlet
Mr. Irving has obtained his greatest success. It has
been said that no actor has ever been known to fail
as Hamlet; it may be added that no actor has ever
as Hamlet satisfied critical opinion. To many the
play is a metaphysical study wholly unsuited for
theatrical exhibition: 'an enigmatic work', as Schlegel
says, 'resembling those irrational equations in which
a fraction of unknown magnitude always remains
that will in no way admit of solution'. To many
Hamlet is a mysterious and complex character,
beyond the power of histrionic art adequately to
interpret. Mr. Irving can at any rate point to the
fact that, four years ago, for two hundred nights in
succession he played Hamlet to delighted crowds at
the Lyceum. Weighed against popular success so
consummate and prodigious, objections of whatever
kind are but as feathers in the scale; and even those
least disposed to accept this latest stage portraiture
of Hamlet can afford to admit that the picture is
in itself consistent and harmonious, the work of
an ingenious and intellectual artist. Mr. Irving's

Hamlet is very much now what it was in 1874; the colouring somewhat sobered perhaps, with here and there further elaboration of detail. There have been more princely Hamlets and more passionate; for it is not given to Mr. Irving to be graceful, and his physical means limit his expression of fury or frenzy; his voice lacks sonority, is usually, indeed, rather flat in tone, and he has to practise what Lamb called 'politic savings and fetches of the breath, husbandry of the lungs', to induce his light tenor organ to perform baritone duties. For this reason he is more effective in colloquy than in soliloquy; his longer passages are without the music of sustained elocution, and to secure variety of tone he seems compelled to resort to incoherences of speech, and rapid changes of key, as it were, high falsetto alternating with notes of bass quality. His Hamlet is less intolerant of Polonius than formerly, if still exceedingly splenetic with Rosencrantz and Guildenstern; proceeding even to brutal violence in the scene of his destroying the inoffensive recorder borrowed from the musicians simply to illustrate his censure of his friends—the student Hamlet would surely have treated more tenderly the little instrument of art. In modern regard, however, Hamlet is not the amiable character he was once deemed. Schlegel dissented from Goethe's too favourable judgement of him; and a later critic has laboured to show that Hamlet was wholly unworthy of admiration or sympathy, that he 'basely and persistently shirked his duty, and made mean subterfuges to excuse himself'. But with these opinions theatrical audiences have not much concerned themselves. The Hamlet of the stage retains his popularity in right of the opportunities for display he affords his impersonator; and perhaps also in right of his youth and picturesqueness, his inky cloak and black silk stockings. In like manner, according to Macaulay, Charles I obtained a larger share of compassion than was strictly his due because of 'his Vandyke dress, his handsome face, and his peaked beard'.

Mr. Irving always interests and succeeds in impressing, for he is an original actor; he has invented a histrionic method of his own, and he brings to his every performance, not merely stage adroitness of a special sort, but much refined intelligence. The restlessness of expression and gesture which seems natural to him, or not perfectly controllable, is of real service in representing Hamlet's exacerbated nervous condition, which the visitation of his father's spirit inflames and intensifies almost to madness; for in Mr. Irving's Hamlet it is to be noted that a simulated insanity keeps pace with, and yet is distinct from a mental excitement near akin to absolute disease of brain. At the suggestion, possibly, of the late G. H. Lewes, certain passages usually suppressed of Hamlet's semi-jocose converse with the Ghost 'in the cellarage' at the close of the first act have been restored to the stage. The gain is not very apparent, however, and curtailment being absolutely necessary, this portion of the play could better have been spared than some others: for instance, Hamlet's interview with Claudius in the fourth act. The total exclusion of Hamlet from the fourth act is, indeed, a grave defect in the acting version of the play adopted at the Lyceum. Mr. Irving's best successes are obtained in his difficult scenes with Ophelia, and, presently, with the Queen. Here with subtle art he suggests the presence of an extreme tenderness beneath the veil of all his bitterness and vehemence. With the players he is familiar almost to flippancy, while permitting himself to be unduly indignant at the harmless foppery of Osric. His modes of pronunciation and elocution Mr. Irving cannot now, perhaps, be expected to amend; genius makes laws for itself, and its aberrations must be tolerated; otherwise it might be worth while to inquire, among other matters, why Mr. Irving's Hamlet, meditating the murder of Claudius at his prayers, waves about a lighted torch within a few feet of him, as though expressly to rouse him to a sense of his peril, as a danger-signal warns a coming train of a possible accident? Or why, in his duel with Laertes, Hamlet is cumbered with a bonnet and Mephistophelian plumes of a caricature kind? Or why, bidding good-night to his mother, Hamlet so involves himself with the chamber candlesticks? It may be thought, perhaps, that the scene thus becomes more real; but these details tend to vulgarize poetic tragedy, which should occupy ground removed from the trivialities and the homeliness of ordinary life. Moreover, such small effects and artifices of stage management may oftentimes deserve censure fully as much as the interpolations of the clowns, and for the same reason, that they divert attention from its proper object, and are apt to set on barren spectators to laugh when some necessary question of the play has to be considered. While Hamlet is so busy with torch or candle, Shakspeare is forgotten in the thought that misadventure of an incendiary sort may possibly occur upon the stage with serious consequences.

The Merchant of Venice: Lyceum Theatre, November 1879

It had seemed to me, from the time of Mr. Irving's first experiments with the Shakspearian repertory,

that, in the part of Shylock, he would find peculiar
opportunities for the employment of his art; his power
as an actor greatly consisting in the portrayal of
definite character and special individuality as
opposed to the more abstract and ideal creations.
His best successes, to my thinking, have arisen from
his presentment of strong personalities in which the
prosaic element has prevailed over the poetic.
His Richard I have always accounted his most
complete achievement, and I am now much disposed
to rank his Shylock with his Richard. No doubt
Shylock, as a stage figure, has long worn the impress
of Edmund Kean's genius; but there is a sort of
natural Statute of Limitations in regard to histrionic
traditions and prescriptions; and the lapse of nearly
half a century has a good deal blunted, so to say,
Kean's points, and rendered nugatory the old conventions of performance. Mr. Irving's Shylock, I may
say at once, is not the Shylock of the patent theatres;
nor must the violence of tone, the fierceness of
gesture, the explosions of passion, so long associated
with the part, be looked for at the Lyceum. I have
known Shylocks who have seemed from first to last
in a frenzy of malignancy, whose every speech had a
certain detonating quality, and with whom ranting
and raving were as close and continuous habits
of life; and I must own that very cordial applause
was wont to wait upon those excesses of representation. It is not only that Mr. Irving has not sufficient
physical force for such clamorous exhibitions, but
his conception and treatment of the character are
altogether more subdued. He plays in a minor key,
as it were; sufferance appears genuinely the badge of
his tribe; long oppression and the custom of submission have tamed and cowed him until intolerable

wrong blows the grey ashes of his wrath red-hot
again; he is veritably 'old Shylock', as he describes
himself and as the Doge addresses him: the years
weigh upon him, he is infirm of gait, his face manifests
the furrows of care and the pallors of sickness; and
if he has stinted Launcelot Gobbo, his servant, in
the matter of food, he has not been more liberal to
himself. Mr. Irving is always picturesque. His Shylock is carefully arrayed, if without the traditional
red cap which Venetian law compelled the Jews to
wear, and by no means fails in artistic qualities of
expression, line, and colour. The performance is
altogether consistent and harmonious, and displays
anew that power of self-control which has come to
Mr. Irving this season as a fresh possession. Every
temptation to extravagance or eccentricity of action
was resolutely resisted, and with the happiest results.
I never saw a Shylock that obtained more commisera-
tion from the audience; for usually, I think, Shylock
is so robustly vindictive and energetically defiant, as
to compel the spectators to withhold from him their
sympathies. But Mr. Irving's Shylock, old, haggard,
halting, sordid, represents the dignity and intellect
of the play; beside him, the Christians, for all their
graces of aspect and gallantry of apparel, seem but
poor creatures. His hatred of them finds justification
in his race and his religion, and in the fact that they,
his mental inferiors, are his tyrants; and when he is
plundered by them alike of his child and his gold,
his detestation turns naturally not so much to blind
fury as to a deadly purpose of revenge. There is
something grandly pathetic in the fixed calm of the
Jew as he stands in the judgement-hall, a figure of
Fate inexorably persistent, demanding the penalty
of his bond; he is no mere usurer punishing a

bankrupt debtor; if he avenges private injuries, he also represents a nation seeking atonement for centuries of wrong. By what a technical quibble is he denied justice, and tricked out of both penalty and principal! What a pitiful cur is Gratiano to yelp at his heels! One's sympathies follow the baffled and persecuted Jew as he slowly withdraws from the court; it is impossible to feel much interest in the release from peril of that very dull personage Antonio.

This was Mr. Irving's best scene, as it is of course the climax of the play. In the earlier passages he seemed bent, I thought, upon varying his tones too frequently, dropping into a colloquial manner too suddenly; while his interview with Tubal suffered somewhat from an accidental failure of memory on the part of his playfellow. But the representation was upon the whole singularly complete; the success of Mr. Irving's new venture was, indeed, never questionable for a moment.

Othello: Lyceum Theatre, May 1881

Mr. Irving's exertions as Iago were very favourably received by the audience; his success, indeed, was quite beyond question. And yet, it seems to me, that in some respects his manner of performance will bear revision. Something too much I found of the strut and swagger, the attitudinizing of melodrama, with a confirmed restlessness of deportment that was certainly disturbing to the spectators. As Verges would be talking, so Mr. Irving's Iago would be doing and moving. He could not—at any rate he did not—stand still for a moment: his hands were ever busy, now with this 'property', now with that. Of course these are minor defects, which the actor is very likely to amend in his future performances.

Nor need much stress be laid upon the eccentricity which has marked his choice of dress. So far as I know, there is no warrant discoverable for attiring Iago as something between a Spanish bull-fighter and an Italian bandit. These objections admitted, Mr. Irving is to be heartily congratulated: his Iago is one of his happiest impersonations; vigorous, subtle, ingenious, individual, an altogether impressive histrionic achievement. By and by his Iago may be accounted as his most complete Shakspearian assumption.

[Othello: Edwin Booth; Desdemona: Ellen Terry[1]]

After three performances of *Othello*, with Mr. Booth as the Moor and Mr. Irving as Iago, the cast has been changed or reversed, without, however, much abatement of public interest or curiosity in the matter. Mr. Booth has appeared as Iago and Mr. Irving as Othello. . . . As Othello, Mr. Irving has not, I think, been seen in London since the year 1876, when his impersonation obtained only a qualified sort of success. For he seemed at that time to have but an incomplete control over his resources, was often carried away by his own vehemence, was at times tempted to tear his passion to tatters, to very rags, and lapsed into curious excesses of manner and speech. In the interval, however, Mr. Irving has become a practised interpreter of Shakspeare; he is now a far more disciplined performer than he was five years ago; his art has been tempered and chastened; he is able to concentrate his forces, and to endow his efforts with a completer sense of climax. That his Othello is wholly satisfying I do not pretend to say; but certainly his performance exhibits fewer defects, is altogether more sustained and even than

[1] See *ante*, p. 158, footnote.

once it was. His chief success was obtained in the earlier scenes, when, if he betrayed a disposition too frequently to 'take the stage', as the technical term has it, and paced and promenaded about over-much, as though he liked to hear the rustling behind him of his gorgeous silk robes, he was yet impressive, self-contained, and stately. His love for Desdemona struck me as rather sentimentally expressed, his uxoriousness was of a very pronounced sort: in a very public manner, heedless of the opinions and the presence of bystanders, he lavished the most rap-turous and doting of embraces and caresses upon his young bride, hurried to meet her ere she entered the council-chamber—as though she were a dan-gerous witness against him, and he desired to school her as to the evidence she should give the court—and afterwards held her veil for her with rather an effeminate air of affection and obsequiousness the while she delivered her first speech to her father. But he declaimed well, addressed the senate with excellent art, bore with dignity the charges and the wrath of Brabantio, and afterwards acquitted himself with distinction in the scene of Cassio's brawling and degradation at Cyprus. Nor could fault fairly be found with his manner of listening to the first insinuations and temptations of Iago. He was careful to avoid that eagerness to suspect the fidelity of Desdemona, to which the tragedians of the past were prone; he finely exhibited Othello's reluctance to doubt, his struggles with his own misgivings and alarms. In later passages of the play, I missed the poetic grandeur and profundity of Othello's passion, his extremity of perplexity, his leonine fury, his demoniac frenzy, his exquisite pathos and dreadful despair: the outward forms, modes, and shows of grief, anguish, and abandonment were present, but something of the terrible inward and mental suffering seemed but imperfectly suggested. At times, too, in his anxiety to avoid the inarticulateness of rant, the actor fell into the opposite error of drawling, adopted an artificial system of speech, and doled out his words with a sort of sepulchral monotony of effect, as though he were striving to imitate a pulpit manner of the worst kind. But throughout he played intelligently, anxiously, artistically, with indeed the utmost desire to spare himself in no way, to render every justice he possibly could to the part he had undertaken; and his exertions were rewarded, as they deserved to be, by cordial and prolonged applause. His method of costume, it may be noted, has undergone revision. He now appears arrayed in much magnificence of a barbaric sort: jewels sparkle in his turban and depend from his ears, strings of pearls circle his dusky throat, he is abundantly possessed of gold and silver ornaments, and his richly-brocaded robes fall about him in the most lustrous and ample folds. He is blacker of face than the Othello of the stage has ventured to be since the times of Macready, and altogether he presents as superb an appearance as an Eastern king pictured by Paolo Veronese. It may be, indeed, that the actor has laid too much stress both upon the luxury and gorgeousness, as upon the Orientalism, of his apparel. As a naturalized Venetian in the employment of the State, it may be urged that Othello was more likely to assume the dress of his adopted country, to appear clothed as a civilized European of the sixteenth century.

DUTTON COOK: *Nights at the Play*, 1883

'GHOSTS'

Royalty Theatre, 13 March 1891

GHOSTS has been talked about; *Ghosts* has been advertised; *Ghosts* has been trumpeted into unnecessary and spurious notoriety; and at last *Ghosts* has been acted. The 'Independent Theatre', as it is called, though it depends for its existence on the guineas of the faithful and the charitable mercy of the Lord Chamberlain, has been duly inaugurated by a special performance. The Ibensites have attended in full force, full of enthusiasm, full of fervour, and tyrannical enough to cough or hush down anyone prepared to laugh at the dramatic importance and ludicrous amateurishness of the 'master'. It was a great night. Here were gathered together the faithful and the sceptical; the cynical and the curious. The audience was mainly composed of the rougher sex, who were supposed to know something of the theme that had been selected for dramatic illustration, and were entitled to discuss the licentiousness of Chamberlain Alving, his curious adventure in the dining-room with the attractive parlour-maid, and the echo of his amorous enterprise as repeated in his 'worm-eaten' son. But, strange to say, women were present in goodly numbers, women of education, women of refinement, no doubt women of curiosity, who will take away to afternoon teas and social gatherings, the news of the sensation play that deals with subjects that hitherto have been to most men horrible and to all pure women loathsome. Possibly, nay probably, they were all disappointed. They expected to find something indescribably shocking, and only met

that which was deplorably dull. There was little to
offend the ear directly. On the Ibsen stage their
nastiness is inferential, not actual. They call a spade
a spade in a roundabout and circumlocutory fashion.
Those who, actuated by curiosity, expected to find a
frankness and direct exposition of fact only equalled
by the sensation trials by judge and jury at the Cider
Cellars in the days of Baron Nicholson, only found
a dull, undramatic, verbose, tedious, and utterly
uninteresting play.

But in one respect the ground was completely cut
from under the feet of the Ibsenite faction, who will
applaud everything in the world that is unconventional, even to a scene played in the dark, merely
because the humble and prosaic gas had gone out.
It was open to the worthy admirers of the 'master' to
lay the whole blame on the actors. This is an old
dodge. Supposing that the play were found dull,
undramatic, and inconsequent, as it ever must be,
and the playing had been incomplete, we can see
the Ibsenites shrugging their shoulders and saying,
'What could you expect with such acting as that?
You have not seen the play. The master has been
outraged.' But last night again, as has always occurred
before, it was the acting, and the acting alone, that
created the whole interest that existed. *A Doll's
House* was remarkably well acted. It was the acting
which gave it even a temporary success. The
Pillars of Society has more than once been cleverly
acted. *Rosmersholm* the other day was very fairly
acted indeed. But having seen all these plays, we
can recall no part in any of them that was played
with such distinction, such tact, such taste, and such
high comedy finish as was the part of Mrs. Alving
by Mrs. Theodore Wright last night. The lady is

unknown to us. It is rumoured that she has played as an amateur—some say occasionally as a professional —but we defy any connoisseur of acting not to have been struck by the delicacy, the thoughtfulness, and the humanity of this very remarkable performance. Possibly Mrs. Theodore Wright may be an Ibsenite enthusiast; we know not. It is within the bounds of probability that the ardour of her faith may have inspired her to represent Mrs. Alving as few more experienced artists might have done. But we defy Ibsen and all his disciples to get a better Mrs. Alving than this lady, who, quite apart from her Ibsenite profession of faith, even if it exists, acted with that peculiar breadth, womanliness, and tenderness which must have reminded many of our own Mrs. Stirling in her sunniest days of comedy. And here we come to our great point, and it is this—that it is only the human scenes of Ibsen that are worth a brass button. There was scarcely a spark of interest in the play of *Ghosts*, last night, except when Mrs. Alving was on the scene. Why? Because Mrs. Alving is a human creature, and because Mrs. Theodore Wright touched everyone with her infinite womanliness. Who in their hearts cared for this 'worm-eaten' prig of a boy, moaning and whining and blubbering about his fate, and heartlessly saying to his mother, 'Of course I know how fond you are of me, and I can't but be grateful to you—and you can be so useful to me now that I am ill'? Oswald is a conceited, sensual and unnatural cub. But the 'one touch of nature' comes out in the character of Mrs. Alving, and it was struck hard and with melodious results by Mrs. Theodore Wright.

It is a wretched, deplorable, loathsome history, as all must admit. It might have been a tragedy had it been treated by a man of genius. Handled by an egotist and a bungler, it is only a deplorably dull play. There are ideas in *Ghosts* that would have inspired a tragic poet. They are vulgarised and debased by the suburban Ibsen. You want a Shakespeare, or a Byron, or a Browning to attack the subject-matter of *Ghosts* as it ought to be attacked. It might be a noble theme. Here it is a nasty and a vulgar one.

But out of all this mass of vulgarity, egotism, coarseness and absurdity we can at least select one character, if not for our sympathy, at least for our pity. Mrs. Alving stands out from the rest because she is human. This is the one conventional character in the play. We are attracted to her because she is not an egotist, because she is not always whining about herself, because she suffers nobly in silence and with dignity. Ibsen makes an attempt to convert Mrs. Alving to Ibsenism, but he soon gives it up. There is a wild idea of making her a mouthpiece of freethinking, but the master thinks better of it. The others preach; Mrs. Alving acts.

What human being can fail to pity this wretched and heroic woman? She has married a bad man and done her duty by a bad man. What she swore to do, that she did. She caught him taking liberties with her servant and overlooked the insult. She has humoured him up in the study with curious conversation. She has adopted his illegitimate child; and sooner than split upon him when he is dead or destroy his reputation as a 'good fellow', she has erected an orphanage to his memory after his decease. This Mrs. Alving does, and what noble woman could do more? She is rewarded for her unselfishness and self-sacrifice by being told by her cub of a son, whom she adores, that he would sooner be nursed by his sister, whom he incestuously adores, than by her mother, because she will have to die and leave the unnatural little monster.

It was Mrs. Alving, and Mrs. Alving alone, who held the audience last night, because she was a bit of human nature, and not a monstrosity. The story of her life was told by Mrs. Theodore Wright with exquisite simplicity and truth. There was no posing, no egotism; it was true and natural. The misery of this woman's life had been locked up in her own heart, and when the overcharged heart was unlocked it was done simply, deliberately, without effort, and like a woman. Hateful as the play is as a whole, we can recall few scenes made so impressive by an artist as that one scene where Mrs. Alving, so delightfully and naturally rendered by Mrs. Theodore Wright, tells the story of her life to the worldly and Scripture-wise Pastor Manders. But one scene and one human touch of character does not make a play, nor is even Mrs. Alving exploited with any dramatic skill. They all preach, and lecture, and proclaim their views with wearisome iteration. There was a time when brilliant French dramatists such as Dumas and Augier were considered too argumentative and blamed as being talky-talky. But, ye gods! only hear Ibsen talk. He never leaves off. It is one incessant stream of talk, and not very good talk either. Suddenly he discovers that he must bring down the curtain, which he does on some ludicrous anti-climax, as with the silly remark, 'And uninsured, too!' that closes the second act. But, for the most part, it is all dull, undramatic, uninteresting verbosity—formless, objectless, pointless. It is an essay on heredity and contagious disease, and probable incest, cut into lengths—not a play at all. Acting of a very remarkable character alone saved it from speedy condemnation, which, even as matters stood, it would have received at the hands of an 'independent' audience.

The next best-played part to that of Mrs. Alving was the Pastor Manders of Mr. Leonard Outram— a most conscientious, well-observed, and admirable study of puritanical egotism. It may be that Norwegian pastors are like our English parsons, but many must have recognised an English friend in the argumentative and suave Manders. Mr. Outram and Mrs. Wright held many a scene which otherwise would have been wearisome and intolerable. But, indeed, we fail to see what fault could be found with the acting. Mr. Sydney Howard as Jacob Engstrand and Miss Edith Kenward as the selfish Regina were equally admirable, and Mr. Frank Lindo could do little more than make Oswald Alving a mean, contemptible and loathsome cad. If he is 'worm-eaten' in his body, he certainly is in his 'manners', and far worse than his heredited disease from the father who once 'made him sick' is the sublimated egotism, exaggerated selfishness, and pestilent pessimism that makes a healthy audience equally sick.

When the much-vaunted play had at last dragged its slow length along, and the curtain had fallen on a very mixed verdict, indeed notwithstanding the presence of the shrine worshippers, Mr. J. T. Grein, the founder and sole manager of the Independent Theatre in London, came forward and, fairly inoculated with the true spirit of Ibsen egotism, took the British drama under his gracious patronage. He naturally asked for support from the faithful to secure the independence of his establishment, delightfully oblivious of the Act of Parliament that can only be strained to admit of the Independent Theatre at all.

But Mr. Grein, an estimable foreigner, who has taken the British drama under his sheltering wing, seems to be labouring under the impression, not only that England has no drama of its own, but never had one. Such names as Shakespeare and Sheridan could not possibly be household words to this educated Dutchman, but, passing over the disputed period of Sheridan Knowles, Boucicault, Westland Marston, and Robertson, the egotistical Ibsen faith would not permit the founder and sole manager of the Independent Theatre to recognise such humble and insignificant individuals as Pinero, Wills, Gilbert, Grundy, and H. A. Jones. The tenour of the speech of Mr. Grein was that the Continental stage was far ahead of our own in literary production. We imagined that exactly the contrary was the fact. We suppose there never was a time in the memory of man when the literary production of England was so prolific as compared to other countries than it is now. Why, scarcely a day passes that we do not hear of English plays being acted on stages that, apart from Shakespeare, never heard of the English drama before. And this is the time, forsooth, to tell us that our literary drama is making no progress, and wants an 'Independent Theatre' and an Ibsen to foster it into growth! God forbid! 'If there be any young dramatist here present,' virtually contended Mr. Grein, with sublime assurance, 'let him come to me, or to some other discreet and learned minister of the Ibsen religion, and we will turn his erring footsteps into the right paths.' We advise him to do nothing of the kind if he would study his fortune or his fame. The last state of that man would be worse than the first. Our literary drama may be as bare as Mother Hubbard's cupboard. But we would sooner have none than any feeble imitation of *Ghosts* under the direction of the founder, manager, and combined fellows of the Independent Theatre.

DAILY TELEGRAPH,[1] 14 March 1891

---

[1] Clement Scott's authorship of this article is well known through Bernard Shaw's references to it in *The Quintessence of Ibsenism*.

'ARMS AND THE MAN'

Avenue Theatre, 21 April 1894

No one with even a rudimentary knowledge of human nature will expect me to deal impartially with a play by Mr. George Bernard Shaw. 'Jones write a book!' cried Smith, in the familiar anecdote— 'Jones write a book! Impossible! Absurd! Why, *I knew his father*!' By the same cogent process of reasoning, I have long ago satisfied myself that Mr. Shaw cannot write a play. I had not the advantage of knowing his father (except through the filial reminiscences with which he now and then favours us), but—what is more fatal still—I know himself. He is not only my esteemed and religiously-studied colleague, but my old and intimate and valued friend. We have tried our best to quarrel many a time. We have said and done such things that would have sufficed to set up a dozen lifelong vendettas between normal and rightly-constituted people, but all without the slightest success, without engendering so much as a temporary coolness. Even now, when he has had the deplorable ill-taste to falsify my frequently and freely expressed prediction by writing a successful play, which kept an audience hugely entertained from the rise to the fall of the curtain, I vow I cannot work up a healthy hatred for him. Of course I shall criticise it with prejudice, malice, and acerbity; but I have not the faintest hope of ruffling his temper or disturbing his self-complacency. The situation is really exasperating. If only I could induce him to cut me and scowl at me, like an ordinary human dramatist, there would be some chance of his writing better plays—or none at all. But one might as well attempt 'to bully the Monument'.

There is not the least doubt that *Arms and the Man* is one of the most amusing entertainments at present before the public. It is quite as funny as *Charley's Aunt* or *The New Boy*; we laughed at it wildly, hysterically; and I exhort the reader to go and do likewise. But he must not expect a humdrum, rational, steady-going farce, like *Charley's Aunt*, bearing a well-understood conventional relation to real life. Let him rather look for a fantastic, psychological extravaganza, in which drama, farce, and Gilbertian irony keep flashing past the bewildered eye, as in a sort of merry-go-round, so quickly that one gives up the attempt to discriminate between them, and resigns oneself to indiscriminating laughter. The author (if he will pardon my dabbling in musical metaphor) is always jumping from key to key, without an attempt at modulation, and nine times out of ten he does not himself know what key he is writing in. Here, indeed, lies the whole trouble. If one could think that Mr. Shaw had consciously and deliberately invented a new species of prose extravaganza, one could unreservedly applaud the invention, while begging him in future to apply it with a little more depth and delicacy. But I more than suspect that he conceives himself to have written a serious comedy, a reproduction of life as it really is, with men and women thinking, feeling, speaking, and acting as they really do think, feel, speak, and act. Instead of presenting an episode in the great war between the realms of Grünewald and Gerolstein, or in the historic conflict between Paphlagonia and Crim Tartary, he places his scene in the (more or less) real principality of Bulgaria, dates his action to the year and day

(6th March 1886), and has been at immense pains to work-in Bulgarian local colour in the dialogue, and to procure (regardless of expense—to the management) correct Bulgarian costumes and genuine Balkan scenery. It is an open secret, I believe, that Mr. Shaw held counsel on these matters with a Bulgarian Admiral,—a Bohemian Admiral would scarcely be more unexpected,—and that this gallant horse-marine gave him the hints as to the anti-saponaceous prejudices of the Bulgarians, their domestic architecture, their unfamiliarity with electric bells, and the mushroom growth of their aristocracy, which he has so religiously, and in some cares amusingly, utilised. But all this topographical pedantry proves, oddly enough, that ''e dunno where 'e are'. By attempting to fix his action down to the solid earth he simply emphasises its unreality. He is like the young man in *Pickwick*, who, having to write an essay on 'Chinese Metaphysics', read up the articles 'China' and 'Metaphysics' in the Encyclopaedia, and combined the two. Mr. Shaw went to his Admiral for 'Bulgaria', and to his inner consciousness for 'Psychology', and combined the two in an essay on 'Bulgarian Psychology'. Why confound the issues in this way, my dear G. B. S.? Some critics have assumed, quite excusably, that the play was meant as a satire upon Bulgaria, and I should not be in the least surprised if it were to lead to a 'diplomatic incident' like that which arose from the introduction of the Sultan in *Don Juan*. Of course you really know and care no more about Bulgaria than I do. Your satire is directed against humanity in general, and English humanity in particular. Your Saranoff and Bluntschli and Raïna and Louka have their prototypes, or rather their antitypes, not in the

Balkan Principalities, but in that romantic valley which nestles between the cloud-capped summits of Hampstead and Sydenham. Why not confess as much by making your scene fantastic, and have done with it?

Having now disentangled 'Bulgaria' and 'Psychology', I put the former article aside as irrelevant, and turn to the latter. Mr. Shaw is by nature and habit one of those philosophers who concentrate their attention upon the seamy side of the human mind. Against that practice, in itself, I have not a word to say. By all means let us see, examine, realise, remember the seamy side. You will never find me using the word 'cynic' as a term of moral reproach. But to say of a man that he is habitually and persistently cynical is undoubtedly to imply an artistic limitation. To look at nothing but the seamy side may be to see life steadily, but is not to see it whole. As an artist, Mr. Shaw suffers from this limitation; and to this negative fault, if I may call it so, he superadds a positive vice of style. He not only dwells on the seamy side to the exclusion of all else, but he makes his characters turn their moral garments inside out and go about with the linings displayed, flaunting the seams and raw edges and stiffenings and paddings. Now this simply does not occur in real life, or only to a very limited extent; and the artist who makes it his main method of character-presentation at once converts his comedy into extravaganza. It is not Mr. Shaw's sole method, but he is far too much addicted to it. His first act is genuine fantastic comedy, sparkling and delightful. Here he has set himself to knock the stuffing, so to speak, out of war: to contrast a romantic girl's ideal of battle and its heroic raptures, with the sordid reality as it appears to a professional soldier. He has evidently 'documents' to go upon, and he has seized with inimitable humour upon the commonplace and ludicrous aspects of warfare. Of course Bluntschli's picture is not the whole truth any more than Raïna's, but it presents a real and important side of the matter, the side which chiefly appeals to Mr. Shaw's sceptical imagination. The great and serious artists—Tolstoi, Zola (for I am impenitent in my admiration for *La Débâcle*), Whitman in his *Specimen Days*, Stendhal (I am told) in *La Chartreuse de Parme*—give us both sides of the case, its prose and its poetry. Even Mr. Kipling, who also has his 'documents', has found in them a thing or two beyond Mr. Shaw's ken. But for the nonce, and in its way, Mr. Shaw's persiflage is not only vastly amusing, but acceptable, apposite. So far good. At the end of the first act we do not quite know where the play is coming in, for it is obvious that even Mr. Shaw cannot go on through two more acts mowing down military ideals with volleys of chocolate-creams. But there are evident possibilities in this generous, romantic girl and her genially cynical instructor in the art of war; and we hope for the best. Observe that as yet we have not got upon the ground of general psychology, so to speak; we have had nothing but a humorous analysis of one special phase of mental experience—the sensations of a soldier in battle and in flight. In the second act all is changed. Bluntschli, in whom the author practically speaks in his own person, without any effort at dramatization, has almost disappeared from the scene, and the really dramatic effort commences in the characterization of the Byronic swaggerer, Sergius Saranoff, and the working out of his relation to Raïna. At once Mr. Shaw's ease and lightness of touch desert him,

and we find ourselves in Mr. Gilbert's Palace of
Truth. The romantic girl is romantic no longer, but
a deliberate humbug, without a single genuine or
even self-deluding emotion in her bloodless frame.
Sergius the Sublime has no sort of belief in his own
sublimity, but sets to work before he has been ten
minutes on the stage to analyse himself for the entertainment of the maid-servant, and enlarge on the
difficulty of distinguishing between the six or seven
Sergiuses whom he discovers in his composition.
Petkoff and his wife are mere cheap grotesques,
both more or less under the influence of the Palace of
Truth. The major-domo, under the same magic
spell, affords a vehicle for some of the author's
theories as to the evils engendered on both sides by
the relation of master and servant. And the most
wonderful character of all, perhaps, is the maid
Louka, who seems to have wandered in from one of
the obscurer of Mr. Meredith's novels, so keen is her
perception, and so subtle her appreciation, of
character and motive. All this crude and contorted
psychology, too, is further dehumanised by Mr.
Shaw's peculiar habit of straining all the red cor-
puscles out of the blood of his personages. They have
nothing of human nature except its pettinesses; they
are devoid alike of its spiritual and its sensual
instincts. It is all very well for Mr. Shaw to be
sceptical as to the reality of much of the emotion
which passes by the name of love, and over which so
much fuss is made both in fiction and in life. For my
part, I quite agree with him that a great deal of
foolish and useless unhappiness is caused by our habit
of idealising and eternalising this emotion, under all
circumstances and at all hazards. But it is one thing
to argue that the exultations and agonies of love are

apt to be morbid, factitious, deliberately exaggerated and overwrought, and quite another to represent life as if these exultations and agonies had no existence whatever. Here we have a girl who, in the course of some six hours transfers her affections (save the mark!) from a man whom she thought she had adored for years, to one whom she has only once before set eyes on, and a young man who, in the same space of time, quarrels with the mistress about nothing at all, and, for no conceivable reason, makes up his mind to marry the maid. Such instantaneous *chassés croisés* used to be common enough in Elizabethan drama, and are quite the order of the day in Gilbertian extravaganza. In any more serious form of drama they would be not only preposterous but nauseous.

It is impossible, in short, to accept the second and third acts of *Arms and the Man* as either 'romantic comedy' or coherent farce. They are bright, clever, superficially cynical extravaganza. In the second act, there are some, not many, intervals of dullness; but with the reappearance of Captain Bernard Bluntschli-Shaw the fun fully revives, and in the third act there are even some patches of comedy, in the author's finer vein. Pray do not suppose, moreover, from my dwelling on the pettiness and sordidness of motive which reign throughout, that the whole effect of the play is unpleasant. Mr. Shaw's cynicism is not in the least splenetic; on the contrary it is imperturbably good-humoured and almost amiable. And amid all his irresponsible nonsense, he has contrived, generally in defiance of all dramatic consistency, to drag in a great deal of incidental good sense. I begin positively to believe that he may one day write a serious and even an artistic play, if only he will repress his irrelevant whimsicality, try to clothe his character-conceptions in flesh and blood, and realise the difference between knowingness and knowledge.

The acting was good from first to last. Mr. Yorke Stephens seemed to have cultivated that ironic twist of his lip for the special purpose of creating the 'chocolate-cream soldier'; Mr. Bernard Gould played the 'bounder' with humour and picturesqueness; Miss Alma Murray lent her seriousness and charm (invaluable qualities both, as it happened) to the part of Raïna; Miss Florence Farr made a memorable figure of the enigmatic Louka; and Mr. Welch, Mrs. Charles Calvert, and Mr. Orlando Barnett were all as good as need be.

WILLIAM ARCHER: *The World,* 25 April 1894

'TRILBY'

Haymarket Theatre, 30 October 1895
To readers of Mr. Du Maurier's novel, the most
striking feature of the play *Trilby* (brought last night
to the Haymarket Theatre by Mr. Tree from the
provinces) is the fidelity with which the leading
characters of the story are reproduced on the stage—
a result seldom attained in the case of adaptations.
Trilby and Svengali, in particular, live again. For
the former character the management have had the
good fortune to find an admirable exponent in Miss
Dorothea Baird, a young provincial actress, who so
far as face and bust go might have been cut out by
Nature herself for the now famous heroine of the
Latin Quarter. Trilby, by dint of Mr. Du Maurier's
graphic portraiture, may almost be said to have
become a living acquaintance, and in Miss Dorothea
Baird she will be recognized at a glance. Not that
the figure here shown is absolutely perfect. The
famous Trilby foot is still to seek. In its place we
have a fair English substitute, of which due exhibition
is made when Trilby, released from her labours as a
model, visits the studio of the 'trois Anglisch',
Taffy, the Laird, and Little Billee, and kicks off her
slippers from her naked feet in token of her return
to freedom. The detail is, perhaps, of less importance
on the stage than readers of the novel would suppose,
since the Trilby foot is at the best indistinctly seen
from the auditorium. Even a daub on the wall of the
studio passes muster for Little Billee's inspired sketch
of that member. Of much greater moment is the
faithful reproduction of the Trilby face and physique

and the fresh, full, rich Trilby voice, and in this respect Miss Dorothea Baird's embodiment leaves nothing to be desired. The play opens with the interior of the studio, and the 'three musketeers of the brush' are brought before us in Mr. Edmund Maurice, a stalwart, flaxen-haired and bearded Taffy; Mr. Lionel Brough, a canny laird, sparing of speech, but prodigal in resource; and Mr. Patrick Evans, a highly emotional Little Billee. Of Svengali, who is but a sketch in the novel, we see and hear a great deal in the play, for this is the character which in the present adaptation becomes the pivot of the action, overshadowing the winsome Trilby herself. In Mr. Tree's hands it naturally assumes a dominating aspect. Never before, we will venture to say, has the actor's genius for make-up been exercised with such remarkable effect. The stage Svengali, with his long, matted black hair and beard, his hooked nose, his unwholesome, sallow face, his piercing eye, and his lazy, octopus-like limbs is positively demoniac, the veritable evil genius of poor Trilby, over whom from the first act he casts his hypnotic spell. If this were not a stage romance, to inquire into the realism of which were to inquire too curiously, exception might be taken on scientific grounds to the hypnotism of which Svengali is the exponent. Doubtless many strange effects are attributed to hypnotism by the specialists, who are by no means agreed among themselves as to the limits of the influence that may be exercised over a highly susceptible subject. The novel leaves the question in an agreeable obscurity, except in so far as we are asked to believe that the terrible Svengali, as an accomplished musician, is able to make the wholly uneducated grisette, who in her waking state is 'tone-deaf', outsing the operatic celebrities of her day by force of 'suggestion'. Mr. Tree performs feats which, we suspect, even the 'Nancy school' would repudiate. He hypnotizes Trilby from behind without her knowledge; in obedience to the wave of his long, spider-like arm he fetches her from a room, 'off', where, presumably, she can neither see nor hear him. And most assuredly the stage Svengali theorizes incorrectly as to the nature of his powers. He believes, what was effectually disproved a hundred years ago, that a certain virtue, an 'odic force' of some kind, passes from the hypnotizer to his patient. 'It is my genius', he explains, 'passing into Trilby, and if I don't take care it will kill me.' On another occasion he observes, 'Every note she sings is killing both her and me.' And, indeed, it is on this hypothesis that the story is worked in its dramatic form, for which an American playwright, Mr. Paul Potter, appears to be responsible, since Trilby's success as a singer in a hypnotized condition has by the third act reduced Svengali to his last gasp, besides shattering her own nervous system so completely that in the end, like Marguerite Gautier, she dies of a decline, the centre of a pathetic group of her old studio friends and admirers.

That the public are in any mood to question such details of the drama we do not say. It is a romance passing in the far-off world of the Latin Quarter in the early sixties, and whatever realistic asperities it might reveal to the realist who searched for them with a lantern, they are ingeniously obscured by the artistic atmosphere around the characters of this fable. The life of the studio is agreeably diversified by a plentiful introduction of music and dance. There is an after-dinner *divertissement* of students and grisettes in the second act which is more suggestive of the Carnival than of the 'Vie de Bohême', as known to Henri Murger and his contemporaries; but the effect upon the house is exhilarating, and will appreciably contribute to the popularity which is doubtless in store for *Trilby* on the boards of the Haymarket. Nor are the purely dramatic points of the story neglected. Indeed, the wonder of the novel-reader will be that Mr. Paul Potter should have gathered them all up so effectively within the com pass of four acts, each of which is full of movement and colour. The abduction of Trilby by Svengali, on the eve of her wedding with Little Billee, is elevated by the dramatist into a striking and highly melodramatic situation, and the episodes of her successful singing at the concert-hall and her lament-able breakdown the moment that Svengali's illness deprives her of his 'influence' are ingeniously sug-gested; all this dangerous business being conducted in the wings, with the spectators of the supposed scene occupying the stage. Svengali's death on the stage, his body falling back over a table, with his pallid and distorted face hanging downwards in full view of the house, is one of the most graphic scenes that Mr. Tree has given us; and highly impressive is the final scene in which the moribund Trilby is hypnotized by the portrait of her evil genius in her death-throes.

Through the introduction of grisettes, students, officers, and other minor characters that go to the making of local colour, including an admirable *concierge* by Miss Rosina Filippi, the stage is pic-turesquely filled; while here and there a true note of observation is struck in the acting. One such note which caught the attention and won the applause of the house last night was Mr. Charles Allan's portrayal of the stern and puritanical father of Little

Billee, who suddenly finds himself in the midst of an orgie of the Latin Quarter. But the impressions of the spectator will be mainly concerned with the weird, spectral, Satanic figure of Mr. Tree's Svengali, the winsomeness of Miss Dorothea Baird's Trilby, and the admirable contrast of character in the Taffy, the Laird, and the Little Billee of Messrs. Maurice, Brough, and Evans. Few first nights at the Haymarket have given more pleasure or promised a longer or more prosperous run than that of *Trilby*.

THE TIMES: 31 October 1895

DONKEY RACES

ENGLISH acting had for some time past still been
making a feint of running the race that wins. The
retort, the interruption, the call, the reply, the surprise, had yet kept a spoilt tradition of suddenness
and life. You had, indeed, to wait for an interruption
in dialogue—it is true you had to wait for it; so had
the interrupted speaker on the stage. But when the
interruption came, it had still a false air of vivacity;
and the waiting of the interrupted one was so ill
done, with so roving an eye and such an arrest and
failure of convention, such a confession of a blank, as
to prove that there remained a kind of reluctant and
inexpert sense of movement. It still seemed as though
the actor and the actress acknowledged some forward
tendency.

Not so now. The serious stage is openly the scene
of the race that loses. The donkey race is candidly
the model of the talk in every tragedy that has a
chance of popular success. Who shall be last? The
hands of the public are for him, or for her. A certain
actress who has 'come to the front of her profession'
holds, for a time, the record of delay. 'Come to the
front', do they say? Surely the front of her profession
must have moved in retreat, to gain upon her tardi-
ness. It must have become the back of her profession
before ever it came up with her.

It should rejoice those who enter for this kind of
racing that the record need never finally be beaten.
The possibilities of success are incalculable. The play
has perforce to be finished in a night, it is true, but
the minor characters, the subordinate actors, can

be made to bear the burden of that necessity. The principals, or those who have come 'to the front of their profession', have an almost unlimited opportunity and liberty of lagging.

Besides, the competitor in a donkey race is not, let it be borne in mind, limited to the practice of his own tediousness. Part of his victory is to be ascribed to his influence upon others. It may be that a determined actor—a man of more than common strength of will—may so cause his colleague to get on (let us say 'get on', for everything in this world is relative); may so, then, compel the other actor, with whom he is in conversation, to get on, as to secure his own final triumph by indirect means as well as by direct. To be plain, for the sake of those unfamiliar with the sports of the village, the rider in a donkey race may, and does, cudgel the mounts of his rivals.

Consider, therefore, how encouraging the prospect really is. The individual actor may fail—in fact, he must. Where two people ride together on horseback, the married have ever been warned, one must ride behind. And when two people are speaking slowly one must needs be the slowest. Comparative success implies the comparative failure. But where this actor or that actress fails, the great cause of slowness profits, obviously. The record is advanced. Pshaw! the word 'advanced' comes unadvised to the pen. It is difficult to remember in what a fatuous theatrical Royal Presence one is doing this criticism, and how one's words should go backwards, without exception, in homage to this symbol of a throne.

It is not long since there took place upon the principal stage in London the most important event in donkey-racing ever known until that first night. A tragedian and a secondary actor of renown had a duet together. It was in 'The Dead Heart'. No one who heard it can possibly have yet forgotten it. The two men used echoes of one another's voice, then outpaused each other. It was a contest so determined, so unrelaxed, so deadly, so inveterate that you might have slept between its encounters. You did sleep. These men were strong men, and knew what they wanted. It is tremendous to watch the struggle of such resolves. They had their purpose in their grasp, their teeth were set, their will was iron. They were foot to foot.

And next morning you saw by the papers that the secondary, but still renowned, actor, had succeeded in sharing the principal honours of the piece. So uncommonly well had he done, even for him. Then you understood that, though you had not known it, the tragedian must have been beaten in that dialogue. He had suffered himself in an instant of weakness, to be stimulated; he had for a moment—only a moment—got on.

That night was influential. We may see its results everywhere, and especially in Shakespeare. Our tragic stage was always—well, different, let us say—different from the tragic stage of Italy and France. It is now quite unlike, and frankly so. The spoilt tradition of vitality has been explicitly abandoned. The interrupted one waits, no longer with a roving eye, but with something almost of dignity, as though he were fulfilling ritual.

Benvolio and Mercutio outlag one another in hunting after the leaping Romeo. They call without the slightest impetus. One can imagine how the true Mercutio called—certainly not by rote. There must have been pauses indeed, brief and short-breath'd pauses of listening for an answer, between every nickname. But the nicknames were quick work. At the Lyceum they were quite an effort of memory: 'Romeo! Humours! Madman! Passion! Lover!'

The actress of Juliet, speaking the words of haste, makes her audience wait to hear them. Nothing more incongruous than Juliet's hurry of phrase and the actress's leisure of phrasing. None act, none speak, as though there were such a thing as impulse in a play.

To drop behind is the only idea of arriving. The nurse ceases to be absurd, for there is no one readier with a reply than she. Or, rather, her delays are so altered by exaggeration as to lose touch with Nature. If it is ill enough to hear haste drawled out, it is ill, too, to hear slowness out-tarried. The true nurse of Shakespeare lags with her news because her ignorant wits are easily astray, as lightly caught as though they were light, which they are not; but the nurse of the stage is never simply astray: she knows beforehand how long she means to be, and never, never forgets what kind of race is the race she is riding. The Juliet of the stage seems to consider that there is plenty of time for her to discover which is slain—Tybalt or her husband; she is sure to know some time; it can wait.

A London success, when you know where it lies, is not difficult to achieve. Of all things that can be gained by men or women about their business, there is one thing that can be gained without fear of failure. This is time. To gain time requires so little wit that, except for competition, every one could be first at the game. In fact, time gains itself. The actor is really not called upon to do anything. There is nothing, accordingly, for which our actors and actresses do not rely upon time. For humour even, when the humour occurs in tragedy, they appeal to time. They give blanks to their audiences to be filled up.

It might be possible to have tragedies written from beginning to end for the service of the present kind of 'art'. But the tragedies we have are not so written. And being what they are, it is not vivacity that they lose by their length of pause, this length of phrasing, this illimitable tiresomeness; it is life itself. For the life of a scene conceived directly is its directness; the life of a scene created simply is its simplicity. And simplicity, directness, impetus, emotion, nature fall out of the trailing, loose, long dialogue, like fish from the loose meshes of a net—they fall out, they drift off, they are lost.

The universal slowness, moreover, is not good for metre. Even when an actress speaks her lines as lines, and does not drop into prose by slipping here and there a syllable, she spoils the *tempo* by inordinate length of pronunciation. Verse cannot keep upon the wing without a certain measure in the movement of the pinion. Verse is a flight.[1]

ALICE MEYNELL: *The Colour of Life*, 1896

[1] See *post*, p. 260, footnote.

FORBES ROBERTSON'S HAMLET

2 October 1897

THE Forbes Robertson Hamlet at the Lyceum is,
very unexpectedly at that address, really not at all
unlike Shakespear's play of the same name. I am
quite certain I saw Reynaldo in it for a moment;
and possibly I may have seen Voltimand and Cor-
nelius; but just as the time for their scene arrived,
my eye fell on the word 'Fortinbras' in the program,
which so amazed me that I hardly know what I saw
for the next ten minutes. Ophelia, instead of being a
strenuously earnest and self-possessed young lady
giving a concert and recitation for all she was worth,
was mad—actually mad. The story of the play
was perfectly intelligible, and quite took the attention
of the audience off the principal actor at moments.
What is the Lyceum coming to? Is it for this that
Sir Henry Irving has invented a whole series of
original romantic dramas, and given the credit of
them without a murmur to the immortal bard whose
profundity (as exemplified in the remark that good
and evil are mingled in our natures) he has just
been pointing out to the inhabitants of Cardiff, and
whose works have been no more to him than the
word-quarry from which he has hewn and blasted
the lines and titles of masterpieces which are really
all his own? And now, when he has created by these
means a reputation for Shakespear, he no sooner
turns his back for a moment on London than Mr.
Forbes Robertson competes with him on the boards
of his own theatre by actually playing off against
him the authentic Swan of Avon. Now if the result

had been the utter exposure and collapse of that impostor, poetic justice must have proclaimed that it served Mr. Forbes Robertson right. But alas! the wily William, by literary tricks which our simple Sir Henry has never quite understood, has played into Mr. Forbes Robertson's hands so artfully that the scheme is a prodigious success. The effect of this success, coming after that of Mr. Alexander's experiment with a Shakespearean version of As You Like It, makes it almost probable that we shall presently find managers vying with each other in offering the public as much of the original Shakespearean stuff as possible, instead of, as heretofore, doing their utmost to reassure us that everything that the most modern resources can do to relieve the irreducible minimum of tedium inseparable from even the most heavily cut acting version will be lavished on their revivals. It is true that Mr. Beerbohm Tree still holds to the old scepticism, and calmly proposes to insult us by offering us Garrick's puerile and horribly caddish knockabout farce of Katharine and Petruchio for Shakespear's Taming of the Shrew; but Mr. Tree, like all romantic actors, is incorrigible on the subject of Shakespear.

Mr. Forbes Robertson is essentially a classical actor, the only one, with the exception of Mr. Alexander, now established in London management. What I mean by classical is that he can present a dramatic hero as a man whose passions are those which have produced the philosophy, the poetry, the art, and the statecraft of the world, and not merely those which have produced its weddings, coroners' inquests, and executions. And that is just the sort of actor that Hamlet requires. A Hamlet who only understands his love for Ophelia, his grief for his father, his vindictive hatred of his uncle, his impulse to snub Rosencrantz and Guildenstern, and the sportsman's excitement with which he lays the 'mousetrap' for Claudius, can, with sufficient force or virtuosity of execution, get a great reputation in the part, even though the very intensity of his obsession by these sentiments (which are common not only to all men but to many animals) shews that the characteristic side of Hamlet, the side that differentiates him from Fortinbras, is absolutely outside the actor's consciousness. Such a reputation is the actor's, not Hamlet's. Hamlet is not a man in whom 'common humanity' is raised by great vital energy to a heroic pitch, like Coriolanus or Othello. On the contrary, he is a man in whom the common personal passions are so superseded by wider and rarer interests, and so discouraged by a degree of critical self-consciousness which makes the practical efficiency of the instinctive man on the lower plane impossible to him, that he finds the duties dictated by conventional revenge and ambition as disagreeable a burden as commerce is to a poet. Even his instinctive sexual impulses offend his intellect; so that when he meets the woman who excites them he invites her to join him in a bitter and scornful criticism of their joint absurdity, demanding 'What should such fellows as I do crawling between heaven and earth?' 'Why wouldst thou be a breeder of sinners?' and so forth, all of which is so completely beyond the poor girl that she naturally thinks him mad. And, indeed, there is a sense in which Hamlet is insane; for he trips over the mistake which lies on the threshold of intellectual self-consciousness: that of bringing life to utilitarian or Hedonistic tests, thus treating it as a means instead of an end. Because Polonius is

'a foolish prating knave', because Rosencrantz and
Guildenstern are snobs, he kills them as remorselessly
as he might kill a flea, shewing that he has no real
belief in the superstitious reason which he gives for
not killing himself, and in fact anticipating exactly
the whole course of the intellectual history of Western
Europe until Schopenhauer found the clue that
Shakespear missed. But to call Hamlet mad because
he did not anticipate Schopenhauer is like calling
Marcellus mad because he did not refer the Ghost to
the Psychical Society. It is in fact not possible for
any actor to represent Hamlet as mad. He may (and
generally does) combine some notion of his own of a
man who is the creature of affectionate sentiment
with the figure drawn by the lines of Shakespear; but
the result is not a madman, but simply one of those
monsters produced by the imaginary combination of
two normal species, such as sphinxes, mermaids, or
centaurs. And this is the invariable resource of the
instinctive, imaginative, romantic actor. You will see
him weeping bucketsful of tears over Ophelia, and
treating the players, the gravedigger, Horatio,
Rosencrantz, and Guildenstern as if they were mutes
at his own funeral. But go and watch Mr. Forbes
Robertson's Hamlet seizing delightedly on every
opportunity for a bit of philosophic discussion or
artistic recreation to escape from the 'cursed spite' of
revenge and love and other common troubles; see
how he brightens up when the players come; how he
tries to talk philosophy with Rosencrantz and
Guildenstern the moment they come into the room;
how he stops on his country walk with Horatio to lean
over the churchyard wall and draw out the grave-
digger whom he sees singing at his trade; how even
his fits of excitement find expression in declaiming

scraps of poetry; how the shock of Ophelia's death relieves itself in the fiercest intellectual contempt for Laertes's ranting, whilst an hour afterwards, when Laertes stabs him, he bears no malice for that at all, but embraces him gallantly and comradely; and how he dies as we forgive everything to Charles II for dying, and makes 'the rest is silence' a touchingly humorous apology for not being able to finish his business. See all that; and you have seen a true classical Hamlet. Nothing half so charming has been seen by this generation. It will bear seeing again and again.

And please observe that this is not a cold Hamlet. He is none of your logicians who reason their way through the world because they cannot feel their way through it: his intellect is the organ of his passion: his eternal self-criticism is as alive and thrilling as it can possibly be. The great soliloquy— no: I do NOT mean 'To be or not to be': I mean the dramatic one, 'O what a rogue and peasant slave am I!'—is as passionate in its scorn of brute passion as the most bull-necked affirmation or sentimental dilution of it could be. It comes out so without violence: Mr. Forbes Robertson takes the part quite easily and spontaneously. There is none of that strange Lyceum intensity which comes from the perpetual struggle between Sir Henry Irving and Shakespear. The lines help Mr. Forbes Robertson instead of getting in his way at every turn, because he wants to play Hamlet, and not to slip into his inky cloak a changeling of quite another race. We may miss the craft, the skill double-distilled by constant peril, the subtlety, the dark rays of heat generated by intense friction, the relentless parental tenacity and cunning with which Sir Henry nurses his own pet creations on Shakespearean food like a fox rearing its litter in the den of a lioness; but we get light, freedom, naturalness, credibility, and Shakespear. It is wonderful how easily everything comes right when you have the right man with the right mind for it—how the story tells itself, how the characters come to life, how even the failures in the cast cannot confuse you, though they may disappoint you. And Mr. Forbes Robertson has certainly not escaped such failures, even in his own family. I strongly urge him to take a hint from Claudius and make a real ghost of Mr. Ian Robertson at once; for there is no sort of use in going through that scene night after night with a Ghost so solidly, comfortably, and dogmatically alive as his brother. The voice is not a bad voice; but it is the voice of a man who does not believe in ghosts. Moreover, it is a hungry voice, not that of one who is past eating. There is an indescribable little complacent drop at the end of every line which no sooner calls up the image of purgatory by its words than by its smug elocution it convinces us that this particular penitent is cosily warming his shins and toasting his muffin at the flames instead of expiating his bad acting in the midst of them. His aspect and bearing are worse than his recitation. He beckons Hamlet away like a beadle summoning a timid candidate for the post of junior footman to the presence of the Lord Mayor. If I were Mr. Forbes Robertson I would not stand that from any brother; I would cleave the general ear with horrid speech at him first. It is a pity; for the Ghost's part is one of the wonders of the play. And yet, until Mr. Courtenay Thorpe divined it the other day, nobody seems to have had a glimpse of the reason why Shakespear would not trust anyone else with it, and played it himself. The weird music of that long speech which should be the spectral wail of a soul's bitter wrong crying from one world to another in the extremity of its torment, is invariably handed over to the most squaretoed member of the company, who makes it sound, not like Rossetti's Sister Helen, or even, to suggest a possible heavy treatment, like Mozart's statue-ghost, but like Chambers's Information for the People.

Still, I can understand Mr. Ian Robertson, by sheer force of a certain quality of sententiousness in him, overbearing the management into casting him for the Ghost. What I cannot understand is why Miss Granville was cast for the Queen. It is like setting a fashionable modern mandolinist to play Haydn's sonatas. She does her best under the circumstances; but she would have been more fortunate had she been in a position to refuse the part.

On the other hand, several of the impersonations are conspicuously successful. Mrs. Patrick Campbell's Ophelia is a surprise. The part is one which has hitherto seemed incapable of progress. From generation to generation actresses have, in the mad scene, exhausted their musical skill, their ingenuity in devising fantasias in the language of flowers, and their intensest powers of portraying anxiously earnest sanity. Mrs. Patrick Campbell, with that complacent audacity of hers which is so exasperating when she is doing the wrong thing, this time does the right thing by making Ophelia really mad. The resentment of the audience at this outrage is hardly to be described. They long for the strenuous mental grasp and attentive coherence of Miss Lily Hanbury's conception of maiden lunacy; and this wandering, silly, vague Ophelia, who no sooner catches an emotional impulse than it drifts away from her again, emptying her voice of its tone in a way that makes one shiver, makes them horribly uncomfortable. But the effect on the play is conclusive. The shrinking discomfort of the King and Queen, the rankling grief of Laertes, are created by it at once; and the scene, instead of being a pretty interlude coming in just when a little relief from the inky cloak is welcome, touches us with a chill of the blood that gives it its right tragic power and dramatic significance. Playgoers naturally murmur when something that has always been pretty becomes painful; but the pain is good for them, good for the theatre, and good for the play. I doubt whether Mrs. Patrick Campbell fully appreciates the dramatic value of her quite simple and original sketch—it is only a sketch—of the part; but in spite of the occasional triviality of its execution and the petulance with which it has been received, it seems to me to settle finally in her favour the question of her right to the very important place which Mr. Forbes Robertson has assigned to her in his enterprises.

I did not see Mr. Bernard Gould play Laertes: he was indisposed when I returned to town and hastened to the Lyceum; but he was replaced very creditably by Mr. Frank Dyall. Mr. Martin Harvey is the best Osric I have seen: he plays Osric from Osric's own point of view, which is, that Osric is a gallant and distinguished courtier, and not, as usual, from Hamlet's, which is that Osric is a 'waterfly'. Mr. Harrison Hunter hits off the modest, honest Horatio capitally; and Mr. Willes is so good a Gravedigger that I venture to suggest to him that he should carry his work a little further, and not virtually cease to concern himself with the play when he has spoken his last line and handed Hamlet the skull. Mr. Cooper Cliffe is not exactly a subtle Claudius; but he looks as if he had stepped out of a picture by Madox Brown, and plays straightforwardly on his very successful appearance. Mr. Barnes makes Polonius robust and elderly instead of aged and garrulous. He is good in the scenes where Polonius appears as a man of character and experience; but the senile exhibitions of courtierly tact do not match these, and so seem forced and farcical.

Mr. Forbes Robertson's own performance has a continuous charm, interest, and variety which are the result not only of his well-known grace and accomplishment as an actor, but of a genuine delight —the rarest thing on our stage—in Shakespear's art, and a natural familiarity with the plane of his imagination. He does not superstitiously worship William; he enjoys him and understands his methods of expression. Instead of cutting every line that can possibly be spared, he retains every gem, in his own part or anyone else's, that he can make time for in a spiritedly brisk performance lasting three hours and a half with very short intervals. He does not utter half a line; then stop to act; then go on with another half line; and then stop to act again, with the clock running away with Shakespear's chances all the time. He plays as Shakespear should be played, on the line and to the line, with the utterance and acting simultaneous, inseparable and in fact identical. Not for a moment is he solemnly conscious of Shakespear's reputation, or of Hamlet's momentousness in literary history: on the contrary, he delivers us from all these boredoms instead of heaping them on us. We forgive him the platitudes, so engagingly are they delivered. His novel and astonishingly effective and touching treatment of the final scene is an inspiration, from the fencing match onward. If only Fortinbras could also be inspired with sufficient force and brilliancy to rise to the warlike splendor of his helmet, and make straight for that throne like a man who intended to keep it against all comers, he would leave nothing to be desired. How many generations of Hamlets, all thirsting to outshine their competitors in effect and originality, have regarded Fortinbras, and the clue he gives to this kingly death for Hamlet, as a wildly unpresentable blunder of the poor foolish old Swan, than whom they all knew so much better! How sweetly they have died in that faith to slow music, like Little Nell in The Old Curiosity Shop! And now how completely Mr. Forbes Robertson has bowled them all out by being clever enough to be simple.

By the way, talking of slow music, the sooner Mr. Hamilton Clarke's romantic Irving music is stopped, the better. Its effect in this Shakespearean version of the play is absurd. The four Offenbachian young women in tights should also be abolished, and the part of the player-queen given to a man. The courtiers should be taught how flatteringly courtiers listen when a king shews off his wisdom in wise speeches to his nephew. And that nice wooden beach on which the ghost walks would be the better for a seaweedy looking cloth on it, with a handful of shrimps and a pennorth of silver sand.

BERNARD SHAW: *The Saturday Review,*
2 October 1897[1]

[1] Reprinted in *Our Theatres in the Nineties*, Vol. III, 1931.

'TRELAWNY OF THE "WELLS"'

January 1898

MR. PINERO, with a modesty bordering on humility, calls this delightful play a comedietta. He wants us, therefore, to take it lightly, and not to consider it as a finished picture of some theatrical and non-theatrical folk of the crinoline and horse-hair sofa days. But however light his touch, however sketchy his characters, however thin the thread of plot that strings the four acts together, there is far more depth in this little work than in many volumes of bulky proportions.

The question is, will the large world of playgoers see and understand the play as it ought to be seen and understood? Mr. Pinero has oftentimes done things which enchanted the few and bewildered the many: *The Times* is an example; the memorable *Cabinet Minister* is another; yet another is *The Amazons*; and all of these, for which he has been sparsely praised, are of his later and glorious days. Earlier, when he had not yet 'arrived', and wrote in that same half satirical, half pathetic style which is all his own, he was roundly abused. No man has encountered more treacherous nails and splinters upon the ladder of fame than our Pinero. And even now, while we hail him as the premier playwright of the English-speaking world, it would seem that the public is slow to appreciate Pinero at his best; it would have little of the fascinating *Princess and the Butterfly*, and it is by no means certain whether it will enjoy to the full the exquisite charm of *Trelawny*. For our author leads us into a sphere which is foreign to most, even though their memory reaches back to the period when the eccentric theatre—i.e. the theatre on the fringe of West London—was in the lowest water.

Yet what a field of humour and of true comedy, what a treasure-trove for an observant man! And Pinero, whose eyes dwell as keenly on the past as they do on modern society, has drawn a wonderfully vivid picture of the simple-minded, kind-hearted, rough and ready *cabotins* who flourished at the 'Wells', and of the fossilized gentlefolk who lived in cold monotony in fashionable squares. This Rose, who, like 'bon chien chasse de race', is not happy when she is taken from the stage to the noble mansion of her fiancé's grandfather, to see how she would acclimatize; this Tom Wrench, sick of stiltedness and convention, and yearning to give something of his simple, natural self in a play of unconventional form; this Avonia, common little creature, wants to please the lowly crowd with her freaks and funny little ways, yet warm-blooded and kind of heart as the best of women; these mummers all, whose H's rise and fall like the tide, are no mere puppets of the author's conceit. No; they are sketched from life, and, perhaps, a little rouged and made up for the purpose of the stage; but, if we try to understand them, we can feel for them, and live with them. The author is not quite so happy in his portraiture of the non-theatrical folk; here the satirist is uppermost, and, if young Gower, who wooed Rose, is a normal type of a young gentleman of the sixties, the Vice-Chancellor, Sir William Gower, his sister, and his friends, are more or less caricatures, obviously overdrawn for the purpose of contrast, but, for this reason, the weaker part of the play.

However, it matters little that the collateral

characters are more fanciful than real; I would even venture to say that the very exaggeration enhances the charm of the play. It is from beginning to end highly diverting; it is episodically deeply interesting, and, to those who are intimate with the world behind the footlights, it is a conceit of amazing cleverness.

As usual Mr. Pinero has the good fortune to be well interpreted. I have but to take exception to two impersonations. Mr. Dion Boucicault is undoubtedly clever, but he seems to forget that our London palate is more sensitive to the condiment of 'overdoing' than colonial taste. His performance as the old Vice-Chancellor constantly reminded us that a comparatively young man endeavoured to embody old age; it reminded us also of how great a loss the Court Theatre sustained in Arthur Cecil. And in the abundantly paragraphed Mr. James Erskine, however painstaking he was, I discovered none of those qualifications which justified his being preferred to one of the many tried and hard-working actors who appear to be 'resting' just now. Acting in 'thinking parts' and a thorough training in elocution and deportment, would, I submit, be of greater service to Mr. Erskine than his present occupation. Miss Irene Vanbrugh was a charming Rose; the part is long, difficult, and somewhat unsuited to her delicate style, but she conquered the obstacle with flying colours. Miss Hilda Spong had to do what would have been a fitting task for Marie Wilton; that she did not altogether fail is to her credit. Mr. Athol Forde as the old actor, Mr. Robson as the funny little Colroys, and Mr. Paul Arthur as Wrench, the yearning author, were an admirable triumvirate. But smaller parts were equally well done by Miss

Bateman, Miss Le Thière, Miss Eva Williams, Mr. du Maurier—in fact, I should like to transcribe the whole cast with a menu of fitting adjectives, for Mr. Pinero always chooses the right people. On purpose I have not yet named Miss Pattie Browne, who was the joy of the evening as Avonia. True, the part plays itself, as it were; but Miss Pattie Brown endowed it with so much vivacity, so much *savoir faire*, engendered by vast experience, that the character, which is only secondary, stood out in brilliant prominence.

All things considered, *Trelawny of the 'Wells'* will hold its own in the record of Mr. Pinero, and if London is to be taken by charm, it will assuredly capitulate.

J. T. GREIN: *Dramatic Criticism*, 1899

F. R. BENSON'S RICHARD II

Manchester, December 1899

MR. BENSON, whom nothing seems to tire, played Richard II on Saturday afternoon and Petruchio in the evening. Of the latter one need not at this time of day say much. Like his Hamlet—of which by a misprint we were made to say the other day that it was one of his 'least known' instead of one of his 'best known' pieces of acting,—it is familiar to every Manchester playgoer. It is unconventional, and in that sense contentious; when it was seen in London ten years ago those of the critics who hold a brief for the conventions of the moment were scandalised at the notion that anything Shaksperean or partly Shaksperean should be played in a vein so boisterous. By this time one would hope that Mr. Benson must have brought it home to everybody that the play is itself a roaring extravanganza, only to be carried off at all upon the stage by a sustained rush of high spirits that leaves no time to think. Is is full of legible notices to this effect—the burlesque bidding for Bianca, for instance, and the 'my horse, my ox, my ass' speech, and endless others. Mr. Benson's gusty and tearing Petruchio, with a lyrical touch of romance in the voice and look here and there in his delivery of lines like

> Such wind as scatters young men through the world,
> To seek their fortunes further than at home,
> Where small experience grows,

strikes us as not only the best Petruchio we have seen but the only reading of the part that will hold water.

The play, too, furnishes Mrs. Benson with, we think, her best part in Katharine and Mr. Weir with a very good one in Grumio, both played in the same key of vehement and fantastical humour as Mr. Benson's Petruchio. It does one good to see a play so well understood and so courageously and consistently played on that understanding. It was played with infinite zest and spirit on Saturday night to a very full house, which it kept in almost continuous laughter.

The chief interest of the day, however, attached to Mr. Benson's Richard II., a piece of acting which is much less known here, and to whose chief interest we do not think that critical justice has ever been done. An actor faulty in some other ways, but always picturesque, romantic, and inventive, with a fine sensibility to beauty in words and situations and a voice that gives this sensibility its due, Mr. Benson brings out admirably that half of the character which criticism seems almost always to have taken pains to obscure—the capable and faithful artist in the same skin as the incapable and unfaithful King. With a quite choice and pointed infelicity, Professor Dowden has called Shakspere's Richard II. 'an amateur in living, not an artist'; Mr. Boas, generally one of the most suggestive of recent writers on Shakspere, has called his grace of fancy 'puerile' and its products 'pseudo-poetic'. The general judgment on the play reads as if the critics felt they would be 'only encouraging' kings like the Richard of this play if they did not assure him throughout the ages that his poetry was sad stuff at the best. 'It's no excuse', one seems to hear them say, and 'Serve you right, you and your poetry.' It is our critical way to fall thus upon the wicked or weak in books and leave him half-dead, after taking from him even the good side that he hath. Still it is well to see what Shakspere meant us to, and we wonder whether any one who hears Mr. Benson in this part with an open mind can doubt that Shakspere meant to draw in Richard not only a rake and muff on a throne and falling off it but, in the same person, an exquisite poet: to show with one hand how kingdoms are lost and with the other how the creative imagination goes about its work; to fill the same man with the attributes of a feckless wastrel in high place and with the quite distinct but not incompatible attributes of a typical, a consummate artist.

'But', it will be asked by persons justly tired of sloppy talk about art, 'What *is* an artist; what, exactly, is it in a man that makes an artist of him?' Well, first a proneness in his mind to revel and bask in its own sense of fact; not in the use of fact—that is for the men of affairs, the Bolingbrokes; nor in the explanation of fact—that is for the men of science; but simply in his own quick and glowing apprehension of what is about him, of all that is done on the earth or goes on in the sky, of dying and being born, of the sun, clouds, and storms, of great deeds and failures, the changes of the seasons, and the strange events of men's lives. To mix with the day's diet of gifts and sounds the man of this type seems to bring a wine of his own that lights a fire in his blood while he takes the meal. What the finest minds of other types eschew he does, and takes pains to do. To shun the dry light, to drench all he sees with himself, his own temperament, the humours of his own moods—this is not his dread but his wish, as well as his bent. 'The eye sees what the eye brings the means of seeing.' 'A fool sees not the same tree that a wise man sees.' 'You shall see the world in a grain of sand and heaven in a wild flower.' This heightened and delighted personal sense of fact, a knack of seeing visions at the instance of seen things, is the basis of art.

Only the basis, though. For that art may come a man must add to it a veritable passion for arresting and defining in words or lines and colours or notes of music, not each or any thing that he sees, nor anybody else's sense of that thing, nor yet the greatest common measure of many trained or untrained minds' senses of it, but his own unique sense of it, the precise quality and degree of emotion that the spectacle of it breeds in him and nobody else, the net result of its contact with whatever in his own temperament he has not in common with other men. That is the truth of art, to be true less to facts without you than to yourself as stirred by facts. And truth it must be with a vengeance. To find a glove-fit of words for your sense of 'the glory and the freshness of a dream', to model the very form and pressure of an inward vision to the millionth of a hair's breadth— the vocabulary of mensuration ludicrously fails to describe those infinitesimal niceties of adjustment between the inward feeling and the means of its presentment. And indeed it is only half true to speak as if feeling and its expression were separable at all. In a sense the former implies the latter. The simplest feeling is itself changed by issuing in a cry. Attaining a kind of completeness, given, as it were, its rights, it is not the same feeling after the cry that it was before. It has become not merely feeling interpreted by something outside it and separable from it, but fuller feeling, a feeling with more in it, feeling pushed one stage further in definiteness and intensity, an arch of feeling crowned at last. So, too, all artistic expression, if one thinks the matter out, is seen to be not merely a transcription of the artist's sense of fact but a perfecting of that sense itself; and the experience which never attains expression, the experience which is loosely said to be unexpressed, is really an unfinished, imperfect experience and one which, in the mind of an artist, passionately craves for its own completion through adequate expression. 'There are no beautiful thoughts', a fastidious artist has said, 'without beautiful forms.' The perfect expression *is* the completed emotion. So the artist is incessantly preoccupied in leading his sense of fact up to the point at which it achieves not merely expression but its own completion in the one word, phrase, line, stanza that can make it, simply as a feeling of his own, all that it has in it to be. He may be said to write or paint because there is a point beyond which the joy of tasting the world about him cannot go unless he does so; and his life passes in a series of moments at which thought and expression, the sense of fact and the consummate presentation of that sense, rush together like Blake's 'soul and body united', to be indistinguishably fused together in a whole in which, alone, each can attain its own perfection.

We have drawn out this tedious description of the typical artist because the further it goes the more close a description does it become of the Richard whom Mr. Benson shows us in the last three acts. In him every other feeling is mastered, except at a few passing moments, by a passion of interest in the exercise of his gift of exquisite responsiveness to the appeal made to his artistic sensibility by whatever life throws for the moment in his way. Lamb said it was worth while to have been cheated of the legacy so as not to miss 'the idea of' the rogue who did it. That, on a little scale, is the kind of aesthetic disinterestedness which in Shakspere's Richard, rightly presented by Mr. Benson, passes all bounds. The 'idea of' a King's fall, the 'idea of' a wife and husband torn apart, the 'idea of' a very crucifixion of indignities—as each new idea comes he revels in his own warmed and lighted apprehension of it as freely as in his apprehension of the majesty and mystery of the idea of a kingship by divine right. He runs out to meet the thought of a lower fall or a new shame as a man might go to his door to see a sunset or a storm. It has been called the aim of artistic culture to witness things with appropriate emotions. That is this Richard's aim. Good news or bad news, the first thing with him is to put himself in the right vein for getting the fullest and most poignant sense of its contents. Is ruin the word—his mind runs to steep itself in revelant pathos with which in turn to saturate the object put before it; he will 'talk of graves and epitaphs', 'talk of wills', 'tell sad stories of the death of kings'. Once in the vein, he rejoices like a good artist who has caught the spirit of his subject. The very sense of the loss of hope becomes 'that sweet way I was in to despair'. To his wife at their last meeting he bequeaths, as one imaginative writer might bequeath to another some treasure of possibilities of tragic effect, 'the lamentable tale of me'. And to this intoxicating sense of the beauty or poignancy of what is next him he joins the true passion of concern for its perfect expression. At the height of that preoccupation enmities, fears, mortifications, the very presence of onlookers are as if they were not. At the climax of the agony of the abdication scene

Shakspere, with a magnificent boldness of truth, makes the artist's mind, in travail with the lovely poetical figure of the mirror, snatch at the possibility of help at the birth of the beautiful thing, even from the bitterest enemy,——

> say that again;
> The shadows of my sorrow; ha, let's see.

And nothing in Mr. Benson's performance was finer than the King's air, during the mirror soliloquy, as of a man going about his mind's engrossing business in a solitude of its own making. He gave their full value, again, to all those passages, so enigmatic, if not ludicrous, to strictly prosaic minds, in which Richard's craving for finished expression issues in a joining of words with figurative action to point and eke them out; as where he gives away the crown in the simile of the well, inviting his enemy, with the same artistic neutrality as in the passage of the mirror, to collaborate manually in an effort to give perfect expression to the situation. With Aumerle Richard is full of these little symbolic inventions, turning them over lovingly as a writer fondles a phrase that tells. 'Would not this ill do well', he says of one of them, like a poet showing a threnody to a friend.

There was just one point—perhaps it was a mere slip—at which Mr. Benson seemed to us to fail. In the beginning of the scene at Pomfret what one may call the artistic heroism of this man, so craven in everything but art, reaches its climax. Ruined, weary, with death waiting in the next room, he is shown still toiling at the attainment of a perfect, because perfectly expressed, apprehension of such sad dregs as are left him of life, still following passionately on the old quest of the ideal word, the unique image, the one perfect way of saying the one thing.

> I cannot do it; yet I'll hammer it out.

Everybody knows that cry of the artist wrestling with the angel in the dark for the word it will not give, of Balzac 'plying the pick for dear life, like an entombed miner', of our own Stevenson, of Flaubert 'sick, irritated, the prey a thousand times a day of cruel pain' but 'continuing my labour like a true working man, who, with sleeves turned up, in the sweat of his brow, beats away at his anvil, whether it rain or blow, hail or thunder'. That 'yet I'll hammer it out' is the gem of the whole passage, yet on Saturday Mr. Benson, by some strange mischance, left the words clean out. He made amends with a beautiful little piece of insight at the close, where, after the lines

> Mount, mount, my soul! Thy seat is up on high,
> Whilst my gross flesh sinks downward, here to die,

uttered much as any other man might utter them under the first shock of the imminence of death, he half rises from the ground with a brightened face and repeats the two last words with a sudden return of animation and interest, the eager spirit leaping up, with a last flicker before it goes quite out, to seize on this new 'idea of' the death of the body. Greater love of art could no man have than this, and it was a brilliant thought of Mr. Benson's to end on such a note. But indeed the whole performance, but for the slip we have mentioned, was brilliant in its equal grasp of the two sides of the character, the one which everybody sees well enough and the one which nearly everybody seems to shun seeing, and in the value which it rendered to the almost continuous flow of genuine and magnificent poetry from Richard, to the descant on mortality in kings, for instance, and the exquisite greeting to English soil and the gorgeous rhetoric of the speeches on divine right in kings. Of Mr. Benson's achievements as an actor his Richard II. strikes us as decidedly the most memorable.

C. E. MONTAGUE: *Manchester Guardian,*
4 December 1899

DAN LENO

5 November 1904

So little and frail a lantern could not long harbour so big a flame. Dan Leno was more a spirit than a man. It was inevitable that he, cast into a life so urgent as is the life of a music-hall artist, should die untimely.[1] Before his memory fades into legend, let us try to evaluate his genius. For mourners there is ever a solace in determining what, precisely, they have lost.

Usually, indisputable pre-eminence in any art comes of some great originative force. An artist stands unchallenged above his fellows by reason of some 'new birth' that he has given to his art. Dan Leno, however, was no inaugurator. He did not, like Mr. Albert Chevalier, import into the music-hall a new subject-matter, with a new style. He ended, as he had started, well within the classic tradition. True, he shifted the centre of gravity from song to 'patter'. But, for the rest, he did but hand on the torch. His theme was ever the sordidness of the lower middle class, seen from within. He dealt as his forerunners had dealt, and as his successors are dealing, with the 'two-pair back', the 'pub', the 'general store', the 'peeler', the 'beak', and other such accessories to the life of the all-but-submerged. It was rather a murky torch that he took. Yet, in his hand, how gloriously it blazed, illuminating and warming! All that trite and unlovely material, how new and beautiful it became for us through Dan Leno's genius! Well, where lay the secret of that genius? How came we to be spell-bound?

[1] On 31 October 1904, aged 43.

Partly, without doubt, our delight was in the quality of the things actually said by Dan Leno. No other music-hall artist threw off so many droll sayings—droll in idea as in verbal expression. Partly, again, our delight was in the way that these things were uttered—in the gestures and grimaces and antics that accompanied them; in fact, in Dan Leno's technique. But, above all, our delight was in Dan Leno himself. In every art personality is the paramount thing, and without it artistry goes for little. Especially is this so in the art of acting, where the appeal of personality is so direct. And most especially is it so in the art of acting in a music-hall, where the performer is all by himself upon the stage, with nothing to divert our attention. The moment Dan Leno skipped upon the stage, we were aware that here was a man utterly unlike any one else we had seen. Despite the rusty top hat and broken umbrella and red nose of tradition, here was a creature apart, radiating an ethereal essence all his own. He compelled us not to take our eyes off him, not to miss a word that he said. Not that we needed any compulsion. Dan Leno's was not one of those personalities which dominate us by awe, subjugating us against our will. He was of that other, finer kind: the lovable kind. He had, in a higher degree than any other actor that I have ever seen, the indefinable quality of being sympathetic. I defy any one not to have loved Dan Leno at first sight. The moment he capered on, with that air of wild determination, squirming in every limb with some deep grievance, that must be outpoured, all hearts were his. That face puckered with cares, whether they were the cares of the small shopkeeper, or of the landlady, or of the lodger; that face so tragic, with all the tragedy that is writ on the face of a baby-monkey, yet ever liable to relax its mouth into a sudden wide grin and to screw up its eyes to vanishing point over some little triumph wrested from Fate, the tyrant; that poor little battered personage, so 'put upon', yet so plucky, with his squeaking voice and his sweeping gestures; bent but not broken; faint but pursuing; incarnate of the will to live in a world not at all worth living in—surely all hearts went always out to Dan Leno, with warm corners in them reserved to him for ever and ever.

To the last, long after illness had sapped his powers of actual expression and invention, the power of his personality was unchanged, and irresistible. Even had he not been in his heyday a brilliant actor, and a brilliant wag, he would have thrown all his rivals into the shade. Often, even in his heyday, his acting and his waggishness did not carry him very far. Only mediocrity can be trusted to be always at its best. Genius must always have lapses proportionate to triumphs. A new performance by Dan Leno was almost always a dull thing in itself. He was unable to do himself justice until he had, as it were, collaborated for many nights with the public. He selected and rejected according to how his jokes, and his expression of them 'went'; and his best things came to him always in the course of an actual performance, to be incorporated in all the subsequent performances. When, at last the whole thing had been built up, how perfect a whole it was! Not a gesture, not a grimace, not an inflection of the voice, not a wriggle of the body, but had its significance, and drove its significance sharply, grotesquely, home to us all. Never was a more perfect technique in acting. The technique for acting in a music-hall is of a harder, perhaps finer, kind than is needed for acting in a theatre; inasmuch as the artist must make his effects so much more quickly, and without the aid of any but the slightest 'properties' and scenery, and without the aid of any one else on the stage. It seemed miraculous how Dan Leno contrived to make you see before you the imaginary persons with whom he conversed. He never stepped outside himself, never imitated the voices of his interlocutors. He merely repeated, before making his reply, a few words of what they were supposed to have said to him. Yet there they were, as large as life, before us. Having this perfect independence in his art—being thus all-sufficient to himself—Dan Leno was, of course, seen to much greater advantage in a music-hall than at Drury Lane. He was never 'in the picture' at Drury Lane. He could not play into the hands of other persons on the stage, nor could they play into his. And his art of suggestion or evocation was nullified by them as actualities. Besides, Drury Lane was too big for him. It exactly fitted Herbert Campbell, with his vast size and his vast method. But little Dan Leno, with a technique exactly suited to the size of the average music-hall, had to be taken, as it were, on trust.

Apart from his personality, and his technique, Dan Leno was, as I have said, a sayer of richly grotesque things. He had also a keen insight into human nature. He knew thoroughly, outside and inside, the types that he impersonated. He was always 'in the character', whatever it might be. And yet if you repeat to anyone even the best things that he said, how disappointing is the result! How much they depended on the sayer and the way of saying! I have always thought that the speech over Yorick's skull would have been much more poignant

if Hamlet had given Horatio some specific example
of the way in which the jester had been wont to set
the table on a roar. We ought to have seen Hamlet
convulsed with laughter over what he told, and
Horatio politely trying to conjure up the ghost of a
smile. This would have been good, not merely as
pointing the tragedy of a jester's death, but also as
illustrating the tragic temptation that besets the
jester's contemporaries to keep his memory green.
I suppose we shall, all of us, insist on trying to give
our grand-children some idea of Dan Leno at his
best. We all have our especially cherished recollection of the patter of this or that song. I think I myself
shall ever remember Dan Leno more vividly and
affectionately as the shoemaker than as anything else.
The desperate hopefulness with which he adapted
his manner to his different customers! One of his
customers was a lady with her little boy. Dan Leno,
skipping forward to meet her, with a peculiar skip
invented specially for his performance, suddenly
paused, stepped back several feet in one stride, eyeing
the lady in wild amazement. He had never seen such
a lovely child. *How* old, did the mother say? Three?
He would have guessed seven at least—'except when
I look at you, Ma'am, and then I should say he was
one at most.' Here Dan Leno bent down, one hand
an each knee, and began to talk some unimaginable
kind of baby-language. . . . A little pair of red boots
with white buttons? Dan Leno skipped towards an
imaginary shelf; but, in the middle of his skip, he
paused, looked back, as though drawn by some
irresistible attraction, and again began to talk to
the child. As it turned out, he had no boots of the
kind required. He plied the mother with other
samples, suggested this and that, faintlier and faintlier,

as he bowed her out. For a few moments he stood gazing after her, with blank disappointment, still bowing automatically. Then suddenly he burst out into a volley of deadly criticisms on the child's personal appearance, ceasing as suddenly at the entrance of another customer. . . . I think I see some of my readers—such of them as never saw Dan Leno in this part—raising their eyebrows. Nor do I blame them. Nor do I blame myself for failing to recreate that which no howsoever ingenious literary artist could recreate for you. I can only echo the old heart-cry, 'Si ipsum audissetis!' Some day, no doubt, the phonograph and the bioscope will have been so adjusted to each other that we shall see and hear past actors and singers as well as though they were alive before us. I wish Dan Leno could have been thus immortalised. No actor of our time deserved immortality so well as he.

MAX BEERBOHM: *Around Theatres*, 1924

THE WILD DUCK'[1]

Court Theatre, October 1905
THE performance of *The Wild Duck* at the Court
Theatre was rather disappointing. Though each
part was admirably played, as a whole it was not so
impressive as the performance of Herr Andresen's
company at the German Theatre last winter. This
was due firstly to the actors taking some scenes too
fast, and secondly to the peculiarity of Mr. Granville
Barker's rendering of Hialmar, though in itself it
was an accomplished and consistent piece of acting.

His Hialmar Ekdal was a pitiable and ridiculous
figure, instead of a repulsive and ridiculous one; and
though many may deny the harsh impeachment,
Hialmar is a wide shot that hits half the world. But
that he should be represented as insufferable as well
as ridiculous, is absolutely essential if the unity of the
play is to be maintained. If any scene in *The Wild
Duck* is played as simple comedy, if your laughter is
not always on the wrong side of your mouth, the
meaning of the play is obscured, and the suicide of
Hedvig at the end will seem the wilful work of a
morbid pessimist who sets down things in malice.

Ibsen's work seems that of a man who started life
self-distrusting, modest, and ready to admire, and
found out at last that men whom he thought better

[1] This was one of the productions of the famous
Vedrenne-Barker repertory season at the Court Theatre
in Sloane Square, when thirty-two plays were staged for a
total of 988 performances, 701 of these being of eleven
plays by Bernard Shaw. For a full account of the season,
with detailed programmes, see *The Court Theatre: 1904-7*,
by Desmond MacCarthy (1907).—ED.

were in reality worse than himself. There is a kind of hard pity in this play which speaks most distinctly in the mouth of Relling, who has kept alive that modicum of self-respect necessary to life in the poor wrecks of humanity he meets, by fostering in them what he calls their 'life illusions'. Ibsen allows no good nature in art, and the fault we have to find with Mr. Barker's interpretation is that it is too good-natured. He played Hialmar as though he were a creation of the relenting and vivacious satire of Mr. Shaw, who is always careful to let every character state his case, to lend him the brains of a devil's advocate for the occasion, and not only to show the very pulse of the machine but to lecture to the audience upon its working. Though it would be absurd to say that Mr. Barker intentionally took the audience into his confidence, he often emphasized too consciously the ironic intentions of the dramatist. If Hedvig at the end had emerged from the sliding doors of the garret and made an irrefutable little speech, asserting her intention to get a comfortable settlement out of Werle, and explaining that her father did not really care two straws whose child she was, it would not have been very incongruous with the spirit in which some of the scenes were played. No, that is saying too much; but if this statement is taken with a large pinch of salt, readers of the play will get an idea of what was disappointing in the performance in spite of many fine bits of acting.

Mr. George, as old Ekdal, was good, especially in the first act, when Hialmar, Gregars (the idealist), and he are drinking their beer together. His tipsy winks and dark hints that his hunting days are not over, his determination that very night to show the garret, with its strange contents, withered Christmas trees, sleeping fowls and rabbits, and the cherished *wild duck* snug in her basket, all these were admirable. The group round the garret door, the mysterious moonlit peep within, the old man with upraised lamp, his proud chuckling replies to the guests' astonished questions, Hialmar's simulated indifference and the child's eager explanations made up a scene not easy to forget; while in the foreground sat the anxious, silent woman who keeps these creatures fed an housed, hugging her shawl about her with a shiver, feeling—not understanding, the shame and shirking which such substitutes for real life mean.

Miss Agnes Thomas was the best English Gina I remember. The only criticism which can be made upon her interpretation, which was complete in itself, is that it is not the most interesting one possible. She emphasized the impatience which can be read into Gina's replies; but these are most impressive when they are spoken not impatiently but passively in self-defence. The Gina most worth acting is the Gina who, padding about in her felt slippers, never doubts for a moment that she should do everything for those she loves, and, unless she is defending her husband from criticism, which she is quick to scent far off, dimly feels what Relling the philosopher understands; and to act her thus the superficial comedy of her clumsy simplicity must never quite distract attention from the delicacy of her nature, which finds expression in that moving exclamation when Hedvig lies dead, while Hialmar rants over her, and Relling looks down at her with professional detachment, 'The child mustn't lie here for a show'.

One moment Miss Thomas succeeded in stamping on the imagination with a force no actress could have bettered; the moment when she rounds on

Hialmar's petulant, bullying questions about Hedvig's parentage with 'I don't know—how can I tell—a creature like me?' In her voice and gesture you felt indignation, revolt, and shame. This was Hialmar's best scene, too, unless he was as admirable when he repulsed Hedvig, with hysterical gesticulations of abhorrence, and dashed like a maniac from the house. Miss Dorothy Minto's Hedvig was particularly good. But she missed expressing to the full the blank dismay of horror Hedvig must have felt, when her sulky father, looking into the sitting-room the morning after his debauch, tells her to get out, and holds the door open, glowering suddenly at her, without a word. It is the last time she sees her father, and she cannot understand. That walk across the stage to the kitchen is an important incident, if we are to be convinced that Hedvig would have shot herself.

Mr. Lang's Relling could have only been improved in one respect, which was not in his power to remedy. In casting the part of Relling, I believe the important quality to look for in the personality of the actor is his voice. As this may seem a fanciful flight of criticism, it is necessary to explain; for it rests on a conception of the character which may not be shared. Relling has been described by Brandes as a humorous personification of Ibsen himself, and certainly the moral of the piece speaks through his mouth; but this definition of him is far from the truth. He, too, has gone to seed, though he remains a sort of doctor still, and still can help the spiritually sick by hiding their natures from their own eyes; that is his universal remedy. But the secret of his peculiar blend of bitter tenderness and cynical leniency lies in his own character. If you met him you would see in his eyes that he had defrauded his own soul. Now, you cannot get an impression from a person on the stage in that subtle way; but you can hear it in a voice. The actor, then, to play Relling is a man whose voice contrasts oddly, disagreeably, though sometimes the sound of it brings a sense of relief, with the grating things he says. This is a personal impression, of course, and must be taken for what it is worth. You should hear something like despair in his voice, however trenchant and contemptuous his manner of speaking when he pronounces his famous dictum, 'Life would be quite tolerable if only we could get rid of the confounded duns that keep on pestering us in our poverty with the claims of the ideal'.

Many think *The Wild Duck* the best of Ibsen's prose dramas. There is certainly none which shows a completer mastery of stage craft. It must have astonished his admirers when it first appeared; for it looks like a satire on his own philosophy. It is an assault on 'Ibsenites', on men and women who think that to blurt out the truth and destroy everything which has an alloy of compromise and sham in it, is the sure remedy for social and private evils. Nothing Ibsen has written makes us respect him more. He had always declared that, 'What is wanted is a revolution in the spirit of man'; in this play he faces the reformer's worst trial, the conviction of the fundamental weakness of human nature.

DESMOND MacCARTHY: *The Speaker*, October 1905

'THE VOYSEY INHERITANCE'[1]

Yes, decidedly the Court is our 'Shavian' theatre.

Mr. Shaw's own plays are shown there nightly, and in the afternoons they give you new plays by the younger men, all different in essentials, but all alike in the one particular that there clings to them a faint aroma—observe that we resist the temptation of saying the taint—of Mr. Shaw. It is in the air of the Court Theatre, just as a vague odour of patchouli is in the air of the Burlington-arcade or as the ball-room in *La Cagnotte*, when entered by the gentleman who had had his swallow-tail coat cleaned, smelt of benzine. Mr. St. John Hankin's *Return of the Prodigal* had been delicately scented with a Shaw *sachet*, and now *The Voysey Inheritance* of Mr. Granville Barker gratifies your nostrils with *triple extrait de* Shaw. You recognize the subtle perfume whenever the personages fall to giving solemnly nonsensical or nonsensically solemn explanations of life, morality, and one another. Mr. Barker has a story to tell, an interesting story in itself, and so long as he lets the facts speak for themselves all is plain sailing. But at periodical intervals, overcome by the atmosphere of the Court Theatre, he feels compelled to offer you a gloss, a 'Shavian' gloss, on the facts. Then all is confusion, 'new' morality, Nietzschean 'transvaluation', and goodness knows what. It is legitimate enough for Mr. Shaw himself to indulge in this game. He invented it. His dramatic works are so many pretexts for playing it. It would never do for *him* to let his

[1] See *ante*, p. 237, footnote.

facts speak for themselves, because observation of external facts is not his strong point. He never allows himself the chance of looking fairly and squarely at the facts, because of his haste to be evolving a theory from them. In so far as he sees them at all, he sees them only in the light of his preconceived explanation. It is quite otherwise with Mr. Barker, who shows in this play a real gift of keen, minute, relentless observation. If only he had been content with that! If only he had let us enjoy in peace, and without comment, the curious little spectacle of life, or a certain corner of it, which he has had the skill to put before us! But no; he must get to work with the 'Shavian' scent-spray. 'Conventional' morality must be made to stand on its head, and things that need no explanation must be explained all wrong. We venture to commend to him an example from China. When two mandarins are engaged in conversation they pause at intervals to exchange little scraps of paper, inscribed with jokes. Thus they fulfil the recognized duty of mingling grave thoughts with refined pleasantry. In a similar fashion the Court dramatists might serve up that admixture of Shaw which the etiquette of the place demands. The story might go on in a plain way, and at fixed intervals the personages might retire in pairs to the background and converse for a few moments *sotto voce*. We should not be bothered by hearing their remarks; but it would be an understood thing that these were the 'Shavian' explanations. Another recommendation, and we have done with advice. Mr. Barker should remember the French proverb:—*Qui trop embrasse mal étreint*. He sets out to tell not one story but several—the story of old Voysey's rascality, of Edward Voysey's trials, of Hugh Voysey's matrimonial experiences. He sketches for us a round dozen of Voyseys or people allied to the Voysey family by marriage. This is a scheme of almost Balzacian dimensions, a little *Comédie Humaine*. Even with the liberal allowance of five acts and three hours it is hardly possible to handle so much matter without crowding, diffuseness, lack of perspective. At times you can hardly see the wood for the trees.

All this notwithstanding, *The Voysey Inheritance* has great merits. It has fresh and true observation, subtle discrimination of character, sub-acid humour, an agreeable irony, and a general air of *reality*. That is the great thing. We have got miles away from the theatrical. We do genuinely feel that the roof has been lifted off an office in Lincoln's Inn or a suburban mansion and that the people disclosed to view behave and talk ('Shavian' explanations always excepted) in a perfectly natural way. One supremely realistic effect Mr. Barker has adopted from a far greater master than Mr. Shaw We refer to his gradual unfolding of the principal character by leaving parts of it at first enigmatic and then clearing them up by the method of retrospection. You have to piece this and that bit of evidence together till at last you have something like a complete picture of the man and his motives. This, of course,—hats off, please!—is the famous 'Ibsen touch'. When you first hear Mr. Voysey's confession and *apologia*—which he makes to his son almost as soon as the curtain is up—you do not quite know how much of it to believe. Ostensibly a prosperous solicitor, of the highest respectability, a liberal father of a family, a generous parishoner, altogether one of the brightest ornaments of our great middle-class, Voysey is in truth a thief. He has been living all these years on his clients' money, using their trust funds while regularly paying them their interest. But how, asks his horrified son (and newly-made partner) did he come to embark on his frauds. He answers that his own father began it and, like a dutiful son, he took up the burden of the inheritance. Beginning, then, as a martyr he now considers himself something very like a hero. He has played a difficult and dangerous game successfully. It is he, the confessed swindler, who exults while it is his as yet clean-handed son who is abashed—the son who has fed himself on books of ethics ('the kind of garden oats', says the father contemptuously, 'you young men sow nowadays'). Voysey is the Borkman of Lincoln's Inn. But why does the father confess to his son? He says it is because he feels his time is getting short and he hopes his son will take up the Voysey inheritance from him as he took it up from his own father. But is this true? Someone suggests, later, another reason, a generalization of criminal psychology. Men who succeed at the dangerous game played by Voysey, sen., feel an overmastering impulse to disclose their secret—an instance of perverted pride. A further doubt; did the grandfather really begin the swindling? Ultimately the most probable conclusion seems to be that he did, but to an extent so slight that the son in a few years was able to replace the stolen funds, and *after that*, seeing how easy the thing was and eager for wealth, began stealing on his own account and on a large scale.

And now what will the son do? Wash his hands of the dirty business? Or take up the Voysey inheritance? If he takes it up, it shall only be in order to devote his life to restitution. Hardly has he made up his mind to the latter course when the father gets a chill and dies. The son, Edward, tells the truth to the

assembled family as soon as they have come home
from the funeral. Here come in some capital scenes
depicting the several members of the Voysey family
—Booth Voysey, the military fool, who cannot understand, but bullies everybody in a loud voice; Tren-
chard Voysey, a cautious K.C.; Hugh Voysey,
exponent of the unpractical 'artistic temperament';
Honor Voysey, the old maid of the family; and the
several wives or sweethearts of the sons. They are
all shocked by the disclosure (save poor deaf Mrs.
Voysey, who knew something of the truth already,
and now, with the insensibility of age, is unmoved);
but none of them will help Edward. He at first
resolves to publish the truth and take the consequences
—among them prison. His sweetheart dissuades
him, not without 'Shavian' reflections. Then he will
carry on the old game—gradually setting aside the
profits of the business to replacing the smaller sums.
Thus the poorer clients will at any rate be recouped;
the rich ones must wait. But suppose if, in carrying
on the game, he should become demoralized, like
his father, and steal, not from the rich for the poor,
but for himself? His sweetheart says she will take
that risk. But very soon the game is up. One of the
bigger clients comes to withdraw his funds, and has
to be told the truth. 'And now prosecute, do prosecute', says Edward, 'prison would be a rest from this
harassing toil.' The client wavers, finally decides
not to prosecute, but tells other clients. What will be
the end? We never know. Prison perhaps? Then
Edward's sweetheart will be more proud of him than
ever. Anything rather than a life of slavery, in the
hopeless attempt to make restitution. The debate,
nebulous with 'Shawisms', is cut short by the final
curtain. We have an idea that the pair were

discussing a case of conscience from the point of view of an entirely revised system of ethics (perhaps the Nietzschean—on the principle of *omne ignotum pro Nietzscheano*); but we are not sure.

The best things in the play, however, have nothing to do with cases of conscience, or with Nietzsche, or with Mr. Shaw; but with the humours, feuds, tiffs, and daily life of a prosperous suburban family. To describe them in detail would be merely tedious. Nor can we go into particulars of the acting, which is of an all-round excellence. But we must just mention the admirable performance of Mr. Charles Fulton as the military fool, the delightful old man of Mr. O. B. Clarence, and the still more delightful old lady of Miss Florence Haydon.[1]

THE TIMES (*Literary Supplement*), 10 November 1905

[1] Reprinted, with slight amendments and without the last paragraph, in *Drama and Life*, by A. B. Walkley, 1907.

'THE PLAYBOY OF THE WESTERN WORLD'[1]

I

Abbey Theatre, Dublin, January 1907

MR. J. M. SYNGE's new comedy, *The Playboy of the Western World,* was produced in the Abbey Theatre on Saturday night by the National Theatre Society. The theatre was crowded with an audience the majority of whom were prepared to give a friendly reception to the latest work of a playwright who had already proved himself possessed of ability to present an effective stage representation of Irish people. On those who visited the Abbey Theatre on Saturday night for the first time, however, the performance must have produced a strange impression. The majority of theatre-goers are not accustomed to

[1] This first production of what is now generally regarded as Synge's masterpiece provoked one of the most famous rows in theatre history. For several successive nights the audiences refused to listen to the actors, who nevertheless continued to perform amid the turmoil. A number of court cases resulted, and the Dublin papers rocked with controversy. The Abbey management arranged a public debate, held in the theatre on 4 February 1907, at which W. B. Yeats defended the play in face of much further noise and impassioned dissent. Having demonstrated in this way the otherwise commendable Irish habit of taking the theatre seriously, Dublin then went about its normal business and *The Playboy* caused little further trouble. As the files of other Irish newspapers were not accessible in the circumstances prevailing during the compilation of this book I was compelled to draw entirely from the one source available to me. The *Freeman's Journal* of the same period should be consulted for a presentation of the anti-*Playboy* argument.—ED.

'remorseless truth' in characterisation, and after witnessing *The Playboy* they will be rather strengthened than otherwise in their preference for the conventional form of stage representation. Mr. Synge set himself the task of introducing his audience to a realistic picture of peasant life in the far West of Ireland, and he succeeded in accomplishing his purpose with a remarkable degree of success. The roadside publichouse, in which the action of the play takes place, and the peasants who come upon the scene, are true to life; the atmosphere of 'the West' is all around, and the dialogue full and free. There is much to commend in Mr. Synge's work, but it is open to serious question whether he has been well advised in regard to some of the dialogue. While there is not a word or a turn of expression in the play that is not in common use amongst peasants, it is quite another matter to reproduce some of the expressions on a public stage in a large city. People here will not publicly approve of the indiscriminate use of the Holy Name on every possible occasion, nor will they quietly submit to the reproduction of expressions which, to say the least, are offensive to good taste, however true they may be to actual life. A large section of Saturday night's audience very properly resented these indiscretions on the part of the author, and brought what, in other respects, was a brilliant success to an inglorious conclusion. Mr. Synge, we are afraid, must to some extent sacrifice the 'remorseless truth' if his play is to be made acceptable to healthy public opinion. As to the acting of the piece, it was worthy of the highest commendation. Mr. W. G. Fay took the principal part of Christopher Mahon, and gave an admirable representation of the part, and Miss Maire O'Neill was also excellent as Margaret Flaherty. Mr. F. J.

Fay was very good as Shawn Keogh, the rival of Christy Mahon, and the other parts were well filled by Mr. A. Power, Mr. Arthur Sinclair, Mr. J. A. O'Rourke, Mr. J. M. Kerrigan, Mr. U. Wright, Mr. Harry Young, Miss Sara Allgood, Miss Bright O'Dempsey, Miss Alice O'Sullivan, and Miss Mary Craig. *The Playboy* will be repeated each evening during this week.

THE IRISH TIMES, 28 January 1907

II

THE NATIONAL THEATRE COMPANY cannot complain that Dublin's reception of Mr. Synge's play, *The Playboy of the Western World*, at the Abbey Theatre has been lacking in warmth. The play, Mr. Synge tells us, was 'made to amuse'. Perhaps a section of our countrymen can only achieve amusement by working themselves into a violent passion. At any rate they have amused themselves during the last two nights by making such a pandemonium at the Abbey Theatre that the actors have been obliged to go through their parts in dumb show. The charges made against the play in defence of this rowdy conduct are that its plot and characters are an outrageous insult to the West of Ireland and its people, and that some of its language is vulgar, and even indelicate. The hero of the play is a disreputable tramp, who only ceases to be courted by the women of a Western village when they discover that he is not really a parricide. Such an incident would be uncommon in any civilised country. The 'Irish Ireland' critics of Mr. Synge's play have decided that it would be absolutely impossible in Ireland— just as they decided previously, in the case of *Countess*

Cathleen, that it would be impossible for any Irish-woman to sell her soul to the devil, and, in the case of *The Spell*, that it would be impossible for any Irish-woman to believe in the potency of a love-philtre. 'Calumny gone raving mad' is how the *Freeman's Journal* describes *The Playboy of the Western World*, and during the last two nights considerable bodies of apparently intelligent young men have endorsed that verdict by appearing to go raving mad at the Abbey Theatre.

It need hardly be said that no well-balanced mind can defend for a single moment the *Sinn Fein* party's crude and violent methods of dramatic criticism. Let us admit at once that Mr. Synge's play has serious faults. It seems to be granted by his most enthusiastic admirers that some of his language has the material fault of being indelicate and the artistic fault of obscuring the essential realities of the play. An error in taste, however, is not a crime, and the shriekings of an infuriated mob are not the proper method of rebuking it. As to the main incident of the play being impossible, Mr. Synge had produced *prima facie* evidence in favour of its possibility. The idea, he says, was suggested to him by the fact that a few years ago a man who committed a murder was kept hidden by the people on one of the Arran Islands until he could get off to America. Mr. Synge refers us also to the case of Lynchehaun, who was a most brutal murderer of a woman, and yet, by the aid of Irish peasant women, managed to conceal himself from the police for months. The fact is that while, in our opinion, there are aspects of Mr. Synge's play which may be justly and severely criticised, the *Sinn Fein* shouters have ignored these altogether, and have founded their objections on a theory of Celtic

impeccability which is absurd in principle, and
intolerable when it is sought to be rigidly imposed as
a canon of art. Our own criticism of the play is based
solely on artistic considerations. We blame Mr.
Synge, for instance, for not having made his motive
clear to his audience. Hardly any member of the
gathering which witnessed the first production on
Saturday night seems to have been able to guess
what the author was 'driving at'. In another column
that clever writer, 'Pat',[1] evolves an interesting and
plausible theory of what was in Mr. Synge's mind.
Even, however, if it were a true theory Mr. Synge
appears to have failed to give his audience a definite
appreciation of it. But, if Mr. Synge is correctly
represented in an 'interview' which he gave yesterday
to an evening newspaper, 'Pat's' motive was not
really his motive—in fact, he had no serious motive
at all. He is said to have stated that the play is an
extravaganza, that he wrote it to please himself,
and that its Irish setting was a mere accident. If
this can be a true explanation we confess that we
find it hard to defend *The Playboy of the Western World*.
The idle aim of a mere extravaganza does not justify
the grimly realistic treatment of a distinctly unpleasant
theme. A serious purpose, clearly brought home,
would have vindicated the play. If, however, Mr.
Synge was simply a humourist, then he has played
with edged tools, and he can hardly lay claim to
that feeling of self-approval which was the consolation
of the Roman actress when she, too, was hissed from
the stage.

Yet even if the faults of Mr. Synge's play were
much greater than we take them to be, the treatment
which it has received from a section of the public is

[1] See *post*, pp. 254–9.

utterly indefensible. Mr. Synge is an artist, and, as such, not immune from criticism; but it ought to be intelligent criticism. The claim—not now advocated for the first time—that people should be allowed to howl down a play or a book merely because it offends their crude notions of patriotism cannot be tolerated for a moment, if there is ever to be such a thing as independent thought in Ireland. We heartily endorse everything that Mr. W. B. Yeats said yesterday on this subject.

When I was a lad (said Mr. Yeats) Irishmen obeyed a few leaders; but during the last ten years a change has taken place. For leaders we now have societies, clubs, and leagues. Organised opinion of sections and coteries has been put in place of these leaders, one or two of whom were men of genius. . . . There are some exceptions, as heretofore, but the mass only understand conversion by terror, threats, and abuse.

It is high time for thoughtful Irishmen of all parties to make a stand for freedom of thought and speech against bodies which seek to introduce into the world of the mind the methods which the Western branches of the United Irish League have introduced into politics. For this reason we sympathise with the plucky stand which the National Theatre Company is making against the organised tyranny of the clap-trap patriots. We hope, however, that the next battle will be over a play to which, as a work of art, we shall be able to give a more whole-hearted approval than we find it possible to offer to *The Playboy of the Western World*.

THE IRISH TIMES (*Leading Article*), 30 January 1907

III

DUBLIN audiences are said to be very critical, and those at the Abbey Theatre are said to be the most critical of them, but they have not yet permitted themselves to see *The Playboy of the Western World*, and I hope the plucky players will play on until there is a chance to understand, when the screaming has exhausted itself. The screamers do not know what they are missing.

In a way there are two plays, one within another, and unless the inner one is seen, I am not surprised at the screaming about the outer one, which in itself is repellent, and must so remain until seen in the light of the conception out of which it arises, as when we welcome a profane quotation in a sermon, recognising a higher purpose that it is employed to emphasise. *The Playboy of the Western World* is a highly moral play, deriving its motive from sources as pure and lofty as the externals of its setting are necessarily wild and vulgar; and I cannot but admire the moral courage of the man who has shot his dreadful searchlight into the cherished accumulation of social skeletons. He has led our vision through the Abbey-street stage into the heart of Connacht, and revealed to us there truly terrible truths, of our own making, which we dare not face for the present. The merciless accuracy of his revelation is more than we can bear. Our eyes tremble at it. The words chosen are, like the things they express, direct and dreadful, by themselves intolerable to conventional taste, yet full of vital beauty in their truth to the conditions of life, to the character they depict, and to the sympathies they suggest. It is as if we looked into a mirror for the first time, and found ourselves hideous. We fear to face the thing. We shrink at the word for it. We scream.

True, a play ought to explain itself; but then, the audience has not yet permitted it to explain itself. Perhaps the externals are unworkably true to the inherent facts of life behind them; but that is a superficial matter, and though it is hard for an artist to select language less strong than the truth impelling him, I think a working modification may be arrived at without sacrificing anything essential. Mr. Synge must remember the shock was sincere.

'Pegeen' is a lively peasant girl in her father's publichouse on the wild wayside by the Western sea, and it is arranged for her to marry 'Shaneen Keogh', the half idiot, who has a farm, but not enough intelligence to cut his yellow hair. There is no love. Who could think of loving 'Shaneen'? Love could not occur to her through him. He has not enough intelligence to love. He has not enough character to have a single vice in him, and his only apparent virtue is a trembling terror of 'Father Reilly'. Yet there is nothing unusual in the marriage of such a girl to such a person, and it does not occur to her that love ought to have anything to do with the matter.

Why is 'Pegeen' prepared to marry him? 'God made him; therefore let him pass for a man', and in all his unfitness, he is the fittest available! Why? Because the fit ones have fled. He remains because of his cowardice and his idiocy in a region where fear is the first of the virtues, and where the survival of the unfittest is the established law of life. Had he been capable, he would have fled. His lack of character enables him to accept the conditions of his existence, where more character could but make him less acceptable, and, therefore, less happy. Character wants freedom, and so escapes, but the 'Shaneens' remain to reproduce themselves in the social scheme. We see in him how the Irish race die out in Ireland, filling the lunatic asylums more full from a declining population, and selecting for continuance in the future the human specimens most calculated to bring the race lower and lower. 'Shaneen' shows us why Ireland dies while the races around us prosper faster and faster. A woman is interested in the nearest thing to a man that she can find within her reach, and that is why 'Pegeen' is prepared to marry her half idiot with the yellow hair. 'Shaneen' accepts terror as the regular condition of his existence, and there is no need for him to emigrate with the strong and clever ones who insist on freedom for their lives.

Such is the situation into which the 'Playboy' drifts, confessing in callous calmness that he has killed his father, and claiming sanctuary as potboy in the publichouse—not, by the way, a convincing position in which to disguise a murderer. Women do not choose murderers for their husbands, but the 'Playboy' is a real, live man, and the only other choice is the trembling idiot, who would be incapable even to kill his father. Instinctively and immediately, 'Pegeen' prefers the murderer. Besides, there is the story of why he 'stretched his father with the loy'. The father had wanted to force him into a marriage with a woman he hated. The son had protested. The father had raised the scythe, but the son's blow with the spade had fallen first. Murder is not pleasant, but what of the other crime—that of a father forcing his son to marry a woman he hated? Were it not for this crime, the other could not have followed. A real, live man was new and fascinating to 'Pegeen', even a parricide, and the man who had killed his father, rather than marry a woman he hated, might at least be capable of loving sincerely. Then, he was a man who had achieved something, if only murder, and he had achieved the murder obviously because his better character had not been permitted to govern him. When trembling idiotcy tends to be the standard of life, intelligence and courage can easily become criminal, and women do not like trembling men. In their hearts, they prefer murderers. What is a woman to do in conditions of existence that leave her a choice only between the cowardly fool and the courageous criminal?

The choice itself is full of drama, the more tragic because it is the lot of a community. The woman's only alternatives are to be derelict or to be degraded; poor 'Pegeen' personifies a nation in which the 'Shaneens' prevail, and in which strong, healthy men can stay only to be at war with their surroundings. It is the revolt of Human Nature against the terrors ever inflicted on it in Connacht, and in some subtle way of his own the dramatist has succeeded in realising the distinction; so that when even the guilt is confessed, we cannot accept the 'Playboy' quite as a murderer, and we are driven back to the influences of his environment for the origin of his responsibility, feeling that if we do not permit men to grow morally, we are ourselves to blame for the acts by which they shock us. Such are Synge's insights into life and character in Connacht. Can the Western peasantry have a truer friend than the one who exhibits to criticism and to condemnation the forces afflicting their lives?

The peasant women of Connacht are no more partial to murderers than other women in other countries, but we must take the conduct of women anywhere in the light of their environment, and we must take the conduct of men in the same way. The difference between a hero and a murderer is sometimes, in the comparative numbers they have killed, morally in the favour of the murderer; and we all know how the 'pale young curate' loses his drawing-room popularity when the unmarried subaltern returns from his professional blood-spilling. It is not that women love murder; it is that they hate cowardice, and in 'Pegeen's' world it is hard for a man to be much better than a coward. Hence the half-idiot with the yellow hair, who, controlling his share of the nation's land, can inflict his kind on the community generation after generation.

The fierce truth and intensity of the dramatist's insight make strength of expression inevitable, but, confining myself strictly to the artistic interest, I feel that the language is overdone, and that the realism is overdone. They irritate, and, worse still, they are piled up to such excess in the subsidiaries of expression as to make us lose sight in some measure of the dramatic essentials. As to the discussions on feminine underclothing, I have often heard discussions more familiar among the peasantry themselves, without the remotest suggestion of immorality, and if Dublin is shocked in this connection, it is because its mind is less clean than that of the Connacht peasant woman.

In itself, the plot is singularly undramatic by construction, suggesting drama rather than exploiting 'cheap' effect. We have to think down along the shafts of light into Connacht in order to realise the picture at the end of the vista, but when we see it we find it inevitable and fascinating. The play is more a psychological revelation than a dramatic process, but it is both.

I have not said much to suggest 'comedy', which is the official adjective for this play. I have tried to bring out the unseen interests that await criticism and appreciation while the Abbey Street audiences scream. It is a play on which many articles could be written.

There was a large audience last night, mainly there to 'boo', but they must pay to come in, so that the management stands to make money, and to be heard in the end.

PAT [P. D. KENNY]: *The Irish Times*,
30 January 1907

GRANVILLE BARKER'S PRODUCTION OF 'TWELFTH NIGHT'[1]

Savoy Theatre, 15 November 1912

Orsino	. ARTHUR WONTNER
Sebastian	DENIS NEILSON-TERRY
Antonio	. HERBERT HEWETSON
A Sea Captain . . .	. DOUGLAS MUNRO
Valentine	. COWLEY WRIGHT
Curio	. FRANK CONROY
Sir Toby Belch . . .	. ARTHUR WHITBY
Sir Andrew Aguecheek .	LEON QUARTERMAINE
Malvolio	. HENRY AINLEY
Fabian	H. O. NICHOLSON
Feste	. C. HAYDEN COFFIN
Priest	. EDGAR PLAYFORD
1st Officer	. FRANCIS ROBERTS
2nd Officer . . .	HERBERT ALEXANDER
Servant	. NEVILLE GARTSIDE
Olivia	. EVELYN MILLARD
Maria	LEAH BATEMAN HUNTER
Viola	. LILLAH McCARTHY

IT is a pleasure to record that Mr. Granville Barker's production—as the phrase now runs—of *Twelfth Night* at the Savoy yesterday evening was received with the greatest enthusiasm. There has, indeed,

[1] The most memorable and praiseworthy feature of the Granville Barker season at the Savoy was the rapid pace at which Shakespeare's words were spoken. It is one of the notorious faults of the English stage that its actors are lazy speakers (see *ante*, pp. 203–7). The three productions (*A Winter's Tale, Twelfth Night,* and *A Midsummer Night's Dream*) during this Savoy season were taken about one-third faster than was usual. I regard this *Twelfth Night* as the best Shakespeare production I have seen.—ED.

been no such first night this season. The word
'production' may perhaps in this case be justified.
In the main Mr. Barker follows the lines of his *A
Winter's Tale*. The decoration and the costumes are
again designed by Mr. Norman Wilkinson, who shows,
however, a more chastened mood. A curious pink
temple is rather trying, but the rest, whether it be
set-scene or painted-cloth, serves its artistic purpose
admirably, and some of the pictures are as delightful
as they are original. The costumes, too, are less
grotesque and eccentric. Mr. Barker again gives
practically the whole of the play as written, with,
however, two intervals instead of one. Even more
noteworthy is the fact that he has, quite rightly,
jettisoned the whole of the traditional 'business'.
In its place we have new 'business', which is not,
like so much new business, every bit as silly as the
traditional 'business', but is natural to the situation
and to the character. The result is as alive and alert
a performance of a play by Shakespeare as any that
one has known. It should be seen by everybody,
and the revival will doubtless enjoy a much longer
career than did its precursor, the play being so much
pleasanter and the mode of presentation so much less
curiously and distractingly perverse.

Mr. Barker points out in an interesting preface to
the sixpenny edition of the play to be had in the
theatre, and with much of which one can but agree,
that hitherto the practice has been to accentuate the
femininity of Cesario by dress and general appearance.
She has been represented less as a real boy than as a
'principal boy'. The Cesario of Miss Lillah McCarthy
might well deceive and awake love in a lady much
cleverer and much less susceptible than the Olivia
of Miss Evelyn Millard. Miss McCarthy's Viola is

the most rational one has ever encountered, and although the actress does not appear to have a very sensitive sense of rhythm there is no lack of either beauty or passion. At times, especially times of silence, her Cesario is strangely wistful and pathetic. Miss McCarthy is to be congratulated on by far the finest performance in poetic drama that she has yet given us. Miss Millard's Olivia is a beautiful, gracious, and elegant lady, but she strikes one as somewhat shallow in her feelings, in her grief as well as in her love. Maria is played with great zest and humour by Miss Leah Bateman Hunter, a grand-daughter of the Miss Bateman who shared in Irving's early triumphs at the Lyceum.

Another very fine and sensible performance is the Malvolio of Mr. Henry Ainley. It has become almost the fashion to represent Malvolio as flippant from the beginning. One famous Malvolio, for instance, took upon himself, in his first scene, to adjust his mistress's tresses, a proceeding which the Malvolio of Shakespeare would have assuredly regarded as an unpardonable liberty, if not as carnal. Malvolio may have his affectations, but they are all affectations of gravity and sobriety; his cumbrous pleasantries are those of one who regards himself as a sage rather than a wag. Against him are arrayed three or four, Sir Toby, Sir Andrew, Maria, and Feste, whose affectations are those of gaiety and joviality. They are 'shallow things' and not of his element, and they determine to infect him with their own frivolity and want of seriousness. This Mr. Ainley brings out splendidly. There is little that is fantastic about his Malvolio, whose dress and demeanour are sombre, whose movements are few and simple, whose discourse is studied, but spoken very quietly. He is a rather pallid, middle-aged man, a little owl-like in appearance, maybe, and on excellent, if not quite easy, terms with himself. The change wrought in Malvolio by the conspirators is more than a change of dress: it is a change of principles, almost a change of character. Of all three Malvolios, the righteous and self-satisfied steward, the egregiously deceived suitor, the pitiful and frenzied captive, Mr. Ainley gives a most notable account. The character is off his usual beat, but his impersonation ranks with the best Shakespearean impersonation of to-day.

There is not a part that is not capitally played, for though Mr. Hayden Coffin is not yet altogether sure of all his words he as Feste sings with great charm and acts with a spirit and vivacity one does not remember to have noticed before. Altogether admirable is the Sir Toby of Mr. Arthur Whitby, and no performance was more heartily received. Mr. Leon Quartermaine gives a very clever study of fatuousness as Sir Andrew, and in other parts Mr. Arthur Wontner, Mr. Denis Neilson-Terry, and Mr. H. O. Nicholson do their full share to making Mr. Barker's *Twelfth Night* as notable and as encouraging a Shakespearean production as any of our time.

THE MORNING POST, 16 November 1912

'THE PRETENDERS'

Haymarket Theatre, 13 February 1913

A WORLD of shrines and sanctuaries, a world where women must bear the ordeal of glowing iron on naked flesh, a world which will always be challenging its God to speak out what He knows, to make clear whom He has chosen, to accomplish His blessings on the pure in heart. Such simple faith is not what you think of as the inspiration of the children of Ibsen. But it is the creative spirit, the essential inherent energy of *The Pretenders*. With every art he had at his command, pageantry, fascination of story, mystery and magic of phrase, symbolism and character upon the titanic plan, he set himself to conjure up the greatest of the ages of faith, the mediaeval world.

It would be manufacture of misty paradoxes to argue that Ibsen, like some of the greatest men of the last century, was born to love the middle ages and republish their gospel to a generation of economists and calculators. All that he cared for in that or any other moment of the past was its capacity to produce the heroic character, the 'great man with a great thing to pursue'. But he was in every phase of his thought a dramatist. When he wanted to write the tragedy of a man, splendidly equipped in mind and heart, but cursed with lack of faith in himself and his mission, it was almost inevitable that he should put his hero against a world where the substance of things hoped for and the evidence of things not seen were to everyone real as life. We know that Skule, the soul-sick hero, and Hakon,

his prosperous antagonist, are in some sort presentments of Ibsen himself and Björnson. On such
identifications, interesting and important as these
are, it is always easy to lay too much stress. Very
often a great dramatist's creations must be suggested
by his own vicissitudes. But we mistake and mis-
understand the methods of art if we confound the
persons and do not divide the substance. In shaking
the doubts, distractions, and fears of Skule, Ibsen, as
Mr. Archer has well reminded us, delivered his own
soul. The calm self-confidence, the clear purpose of
Hakon may be something of a portrait of Björnson.
But Hakon and Skule have each individual life
which is independent of the modern reality. You can
imagine it argued, indeed, that they are modern men
with modern fashions of thought and feeling, for
all their mediaeval setting. That, again, is only
superficial truth. They are modern as Prometheus is
modern, as Macbeth is. They are not of an age, but
for all time. You see them *sub specie aeternitatis*. They
only have their full vigour, their plenitude of spirit
in that mediaeval world to which they belong. If
that is true of them, yet more potently it is true of the
third great creation of the play, Bishop Nicholas, a
very spirit of evil indeed, and as such in his nature
timeless, but a fiend fashioning himself to the conditions of the ages of faith.

In this memorable performance at the Haymarket one of the most impressive qualities is the
vivid realisation of the old unhappy far-off world of
mediaeval Norway. The pictorial element is, of
course, powerful. Scene after scene lingers in the
memory. The rude church and the fir trees, and the
glimpse of fjord and rock which we saw first gave in a
moment place and time and atmosphere, the stormy

northern kingdom, with its mountains of ambition and its childlike faith. The shadowy rough-hewn palace halls were the right homes for the banquets of these Wolf-skins and Birch-legs, men half-beast, half-divine. There was grave beauty in the room where the Queen sang to her King-child. The picture of the fir wood on the wintry hills had something of the bitterness and the dignity of the death of those

> Whom God has stripped so bare of everything
> Save the one longing to wear through their day
> In fearless wise.

The last scene of all, the courtyard of the convent from which Skule goes out to meet his doom, has a rarer and nobler grace. The gallery of arches aglow, and in the midst shadows, and all around an austere simplicity through which faint touches of clear colour came, made a deep harmony with the grandeur of the action. We do not recall decoration which interpreted and illustrated more perfectly the spirit of a play than this of Mr. Sime's and Mr. Harker's. With his costumes Mr. Sime was equally successful. Whether or no these breastplates and belted tunics, these splendid cloaks—blue like Odin's in the saga, or russet or saffron—these quaint mitres and helmets, be what thirteenth-century Norway wore, need concern no living soul. They are true to the spirit of the play. Just such barbaric magnificence must have been theirs, those chieftains and retainers who fought their lives out for a dream of greed and a fantastic faith. Set against the background of shadowy mystery, which suggests so well their pathless turmoil, their blind hopes and fears, they realise for you marvellously the age in which Barbarossa tried to be omnipotent and St. Louis died on his crusade.

With so much of the pictorial element in the performance we may have done. It would be blind to ignore its importance. It would be clumsy to say more. We must recognise that this wonderful realisation of the mediaeval spirit owes far more to the actors than to the consummate setting. The three who make the play, Mr. Laurence Irving's Skule, Mr. Basil Gill's Hakon, and Mr. William Haviland's Bishop Nicholas, are of their period without and within. One quality is common to them all—grandeur. They are not diminished by conventions, saving clauses of manner and spirit. They are what they are vehemently and upon the titanic scale. They are all, even at their subtlest, simple, in the sense that they know no reason why they should not be desperately in earnest. They are not careful about many things, but only about the things on which they have set their hearts or which have commanded their hearts in their own despite. This is the very spirit of the play, and the spirit of its time. It inspires in varying harmonious degrees the other actors, as well as the three chief combatants. Everybody is boldly drawn, urgent, swift. This effect is obtained—let us thank the producer, Mr. Lyall Swete—without injury to the text. There are all the five acts as you may read them in Mr. Archer's excellent translation, and we noted only one excision of importance. That was from the Bishop's ghost-walking, which, though we do not think so badly of it as some, is none the worse for diminution.

There can be no need now to do more than indicate the story. In one regard, though we have no emendation to offer, *The Pretenders* is an unfortunate title. It suggests ideas of Jacobites and Bonnie

Prince Charlie not at all to the purpose. The two Pretenders who concern us are Hakon and Skule. Skule had always coveted the crown, always seen it evade his grasp. He was a man with the power in him to be a great king, but unsure of himself. He would not play false, and was not quite sure that he would wrongly win. He had been regent, and when Hakon was made king by right of ordeal and election, he had still much honour and much power. But he coveted all still. He often believed himself the better man. Old Bishop Nicholas tempted him, old Bishop Nicholas who, born with a lust for power, found himself too weak to win or hold it, therefore hated all the world, and set himself to ruin Skule and Hakon both. Hakon was a man made for success, confident of himself, hard, egoistical, but with a clear vision of what his time needed. The Bishop pitted the two against each other, sowed in Hakon hate of Skule, and in Skule doubt of Hakon's divine right, and therewith, his work done as well as he could do it, he died. Skule made himself king, and for a while had the better of Hakon. But in the moment of peril he failed himself, and was overthrown. How on the verge of ruin his son came to him, how he nearly dragged the son down to hell with him, how at the last he redeemed his son, and his own soul, these things make the grand closing moments of the play.

Such a curt summary is, of course, utterly inadequate to express the masterly conduct of the plot or the poignant emotion of scene after scene. Different in almost every point of comparison from Ibsen's later work, *The Pretenders* shows all the technical dexterity, all the skill in the handling of intrigue, all the power of creating excited interest which have compelled those who like him little enough to hail him as a

consummate craftsman. To dwell upon that would
be to demonstrate the obvious. The higher qualities
of the play demand analysis.

In sheer force of effect upon the stage, as Mr.
Haviland showed us last night with accomplished art,
you must go to the greatest masters to find the equal
of Bishop Nicholas. The horror and terror, the
ghastly humour of his death leave your nerves
quivering. But Mr. Haviland did not fail to show us,
too, the majesty of evil in the character; its vast
intellectual stature. What is he, then, this bishop,
who boasts that he has 'hated much; hated every
head in this land that raised itself above the crowd'?
Not inhuman, to be sure. The malice, the mis-
anthropy of weaklings is a proverb. The Bishop is,
after all, but of the same temper as such a subaltern
rascal as Rashleigh Osbaldistone, hating all men
because they are not lame and halt as he. Of the
same temper—but of what different power! You
remember Odysseus in the *Philoctetes*, the cold,
efficient villain, with his 'Only—my will is to be
vanquished never'. So Bishop Nicholas might have
cried on his death-bed, exulting in the legacy of
disaster he was bequeathing, evil enduring through
the centuries at his command. But in the very
fury of his passion of malevolence there is something
superhuman. Almost verbally, altogether in spirit,
he challenges comparison with the lieutenant of
Milton's fiend. He will only be content if he can
'surpass common revenge'. He could heartily take to
himself the black creed of Mephistopheles:

> I am the spirit that denies;
> And rightly so, for all that from the Void
> Wins into life deserves to be destroyed.

Yet, to be sure, he believes and trembles. He must have masses said, and said again, and yet again, even while he jeers at the holy rite. Of this mingling of superhuman malignity and shuddering faith, Mr. Haviland made a wonderful reality, a piece of horror in which the tragic and the grotesque were united with arresting power. In the earlier scenes, when the Bishop, with his hold on life still secure, is but a grim, malicious diplomatist, with his veil still hiding the dark recesses of his soul, the actor was consummately skilful. The outward calm, the sly relish in each wriggle of his victims, were vivid, and the suggestion of passion concealed had power. The very aspect of the man, cadaverous already, with claw-like hands, dominated the fancy. But in his death there was a diabolical transfiguration. Everything that is evil and vile, envy, fear, cruelty, lust, if there be any vice and if there be any infamy, there was something of all in that passion of thwarted ambition. With fine imagination and masterly art the actor fired that scene.

The tyrant, says Plato, desires to be master of others when he is not master of himself. That is the tragedy of Skule. He is, as Mr. Irving was careful to make him, thoroughly at home with great affairs. He knows how to rule men and things. He is the stuff of which kings are made. That we are never allowed to doubt in Mr. Irving's acting. As clearly, as ably, he shows us the flaw in the man's soul—his lack of confidence in himself and his mission. This was very subtle work, and it triumphed in making us like the man as well as understand him. We had to feel, too—which is not quite inevitable in reading the play—that Skule's most disastrous fault, his blindness to anything beyond the power of the moment,

came naturally from his doubt of himself. He knows
how to be king, but not how to be king of anything
more than the turbulent Norway to which he was
born. He wants to be king, but only for the sake of
being king. Of a king's true duty, to bring peace to
a people rent and ravaged by civil war, he has no
conception till he hears of it from Hakon, and then
he can hardly believe in it. He is without the vision.
He never finds himself till the hour of his death.
The tragedy of that, the deeper tragedy which lies
in the man's half-consciousness of it, Mr. Irving
realised with appealing power. We have before noted
something of a mediaeval manner in his work. Here
it was splendidly in harmony. The profound simplicity, the ruggedness of his acting, its suggestion
of depths of feeling and aspiration had a rare force.
His bitter despair at failure in the hour of trial had
the quiver of agony in it. All the piteous, tragic
moments with his son, called up the tears of human
things. In the last scene of all, when Skule 'goes forth
into the great church to take the crown of life', the
noble emotion of action and words was played with an
austere passion, a dignity for which all praise is idle.

There are no mysteries, there is no tragedy in
King Hakon. He 'reads his title clear' to a crown on
earth and mansions in the skies, and never had much
doubt of it. But we need not write him off as a
shallow fellow because he was sure of himself and
what he had to do, and did it. He was selfish and
hard, to be sure, but as Carlyle would have said, he
'had fire in his belly'. As such Mr. Basil Gill played
him admirably, making a splendid kinglike figure to
the eye and a very credible master of men. You
never doubted that he was born for success, and that

he would make few mistakes in winning it. The man was there to the life. There are two other striking characters in the play, Vatgeir Skald, the minstrel who shows Skule something of the truth of himself and the world, and Peter, the son, who is Skule's one passionate follower to the last. Mr. Guy Rathbone played the first with pathos and force. Mr. Ion Swinley gave us a charming piece of work in the lad's desperate devotion, beautiful in its faith and tragedy. The ladies have but little part, but Miss Helen Haye, Miss Tita Brand, Miss Netta Westcott, and Miss Madge McIntosh all did admirably. It was a performance long to be remembered by its force and its fascination. Yet, as you think of it, for all the nobility of the play, for all its deep sincerity of thought and emotion, you may find it lacks something of the greatest art. Is it grace that you seek or mansuetude? Perhaps a richer humanity, a larger goodwill towards men.

THE DAILY TELEGRAPH, 14 February 1913

'THE BEGGAR'S OPERA': 20TH CENTURY[1]

Lyric Theatre, Hammersmith, 5 June 1920

Peachum	.	.	.	.	FREDERIC AUSTIN
Lockit	.	.	.	.	. ARTHUR WYNN
Macheath	.	.	.	.	FREDERICK RANALOW
Filch	.	.	.	.	ALFRED HEATHER
The Beggar	.	.	.	.	ARNOLD PILBEAM
Mrs. Peachum	.	.	.	.	. ELSIE FRENCH
Polly Peachum	.	.	.	.	SYLVIA NELIS
Lucy Lockit	.	.	.	.	. VIOLET MARQUESITA
Diana Trapes	.	.	.	.	BERYL FREEMAN
Jenny Diver	.	.	.	.	. NONNY LOCK

THE beggars have come back to Town, and have taken
up their abode at the Lyric Theatre, Hammersmith,
where, to judge from the enthusiasm of their welcome
on Saturday night, they should be able to disport
themselves for as long as they will. *The Beggar's
Opera* was revived in the only way possible to revive
it, with complete acceptance of its roguery and the
irresponsible delight in a world filled with knaves
but emptied of fools. Unless indeed Captain Macheath is a bit of a fool. Surely the hero of the highway
falls a prey to the plots of Peachum and Lockit and
the lures of his numerous ladies a little too easily
for a man of his experience. But, as he says himself,
it is the women who have unbent his mind and
'money is not so strong a cordial for the time'.
So Macheath comes to the gallows, or would do so
but for the actor's protest that an opera must end
happily and the Beggar's concession of a reprieve at

[1] See also *ante,* pp. 69-83 and 93-5.

the last moment. Villainy triumphs all the way and laughter follows its progress without a check.

Musically, too, the revival has taken the only possible course. The airs have been reset with dainty accompaniments which appeal at once to the modern ear, though the 18th century feeling is preserved by the use of appropriate instruments, strings, flute, oboe, and harpsichord, all of which were played by an accomplished orchestra of ladies under Mr. Eugene Goossens' direction. Mr. Frederic Austin, as well as taking the part of Peachum, first of the triumphant villains, has been the Dr. Pepusch of today and has made the arrangement of the music. Only once or twice did we feel that his skilful treatment brought a touch of descriptive colouring into the music which was foreign to the original spirit of the thing, and such touches were not unwelcome. For the music of *The Beggar's Opera* bears traces of every period from the undatable modal folksong to the street song of the 18th century, and why should it not gain something from the 20th? We should like, however, to have had Pepusch's overture complete with the slow movement which precedes the merry jig.

The artistic virtues of the actors and singers were as impossible to catalogue as their moral vices. The comedy of Miss Elsie French as Mrs. Peachum stood out above all others, and Miss Sylvia Nelis's treatment of the part of Polly (a sly puss, and no fool for all her circumspect air) was in perfect contrast to the bevy of brazen hussies surrounding her. She and Mr. Ranalow gave us the most delightful musical moments of the evening, particularly in their duet of 'Over the hills and far away.' But if we should begin to pick out songs there would be no stopping, for the opera is a string of gems and every one made the most of their opportunities.

Mr. Nigel Playfair is the 'John Rich' of this production, and is to be congratulated not only on having got together so admirable a company (for his success in that respect he made full acknowledgments to Sir Thomas Beecham in his speech at the close of the performance) but on the effective arrangement of simple scenery and dresses designed by Mr. C. Lovat Fraser. It was said of *The Beggar's Opera* originally that 'it made Gay rich and Rich gay'. If there is any justice in this world (and *The Beggar's Opera* declares that there is none) riches will continue to go hand in hand with gaiety in this new production.[1]

THE TIMES, 7 June 1920

[1] It ran for 1463 performances. The original run in 1728 was 62 nights, equally remarkable at that period.—ED.

THE TRAGIC ACTRESS

MISS GENEVIEVE WARD, who, if not the oldest living actress, is at any rate the oldest acting actress on the stage, has been speaking winged words on the decadence of our times. Interviewed on the occasion of her eighty-third birthday, she expressed strong views on the manners and customs of the young woman of the period, and went on to deplore the dearth of tragic actresses on our stage. 'The present-day actresses', she said, 'have not the physique for tragedy. The work in the old days was so much more strenuous for actresses than it is today, and in the past the women did not jump from tragedy to comedy and farce and back again as they do now. They stuck to their métier, and their art was all the better for it.'

There is certainly nobody who has a better right to speak on this subject than Miss Ward, who can look back upon her own long and triumphant career, first in grand opera and then in tragic parts, and with all confidence challenge the stage of this generation to produce anybody likely to rival her record. It is also true that we are not today rich in tragic actresses. But it is at least doubtful whether the reasons assigned by Miss Ward for the change are the real reasons. It is not even certain that the modern girl is lacking in physique; at any rate from her has been evolved that modern marvel of endurance, the cinema heroine. And it is at least an arguable view that the reason why the modern stage has few tragediennes is not lack of capacity so much as lack of demand.

Public taste in drama is subject to changes of fashion, and the fashion in drama has altered greatly, mainly because of the change in its public. Time was when the theatres appealed only to a certain limited class—the aristocracy—and all plays were written on that understanding. Playwrights were courtiers and dealt only with themes and characters such as might be acceptable to the Court. Tragedy then was all the rage; poor poets, their manuscripts sticking out of their pockets as inevitably as their elbows stuck out of their ragged sleeves, jostled one another in the endeavour to find some rich Mæcenas who would stand sponsor to their sad stories of the deaths of kings. Behind them they had the Greek tradition that the only fit theme for tragedy is the struggle of a human being of great position, cast in the heroic mould, and yet neither too good nor too bad to win our sympathy, against an adverse fate, which, in the end, proves itself too strong for even the mightiest mortal to contend with. Tragedy did not concern itself with little lives, nor with mean streets. Its hero might only excite our pity as a beggar if he had once been a king.

Such was the tradition as the Court dramatists accepted it, and it was preserved intact until long after their time. But with the use of a wider interest in the stage a change began to set in; the theatre became more and more a popular institution, and realised that it must deal with the themes that intrigued its public. Those themes gradually ceased to be the great problems of princes and became the little problems of ordinary men. Since, according to the ancient formula, tragedy cannot concern itself with such subjects, tragedy according to the ancient formula has ceased to be written

Realism has taken its place—a true attempt at the imitation of life as the plain man knows it. Since in life the tragic and comic elements are so knit together that they cannot be separated, so in the modern play the two are closely interwoven. Unlike its predecessors, modern drama cannot be divided off into two sharply contrasted heaps, labelled respectively 'Comedy' and 'Tragedy'.

There is another reason why the democratization of the theatre has driven tragedy out of favour. It has to some extent lowered the average intellectual standard of the man in the audience. A theatre which caters for the taste of a wide public must not be too sophisticated for its audience; and an audience must attain to a very considerable degree of sophistication before it can rise above an artless desire for happy endings. Appreciation or enjoyment of tragedy is an art which requires intellectual training and practice. It is true that there are many simple souls who 'go to the play for a good cry'; but their good cry comes usually from the contemplation of sentimentalisms—beautiful death-bed scenes to slow music, and so on—rather than the stark passions of tragedy. They go home with the easy tears on their cheeks, but with their souls unharrowed.

The plays and the public of today create a demand rather for all-round emotional actresses of quick human sympathy than for tragediennes; but here and there, even today, an actress of exceptional depth and power finds herself compelled to resuscitate the old fine tragic parts and pit herself against the great women who played those parts to bygone generations. At the present moment such a revival is being carried out by Miss Sybil Thorndike with such striking success that the modern stage may look to her to make possible in the near future a complete denial of Miss Ward's strictures.

Miss Thorndike has been known for some years as one of the most promising of the younger school of actresses, and as a prominent member of Miss Horniman's famous repertory company in Manchester she showed what she could do in modern realistic and introspective drama. It was recognized that in her we had an emotional actress of high merit, but it was not until she began to play her present series of parts that she gave a real indication of the true quality that is in her. In *Candida* and *Tom Trouble* she is, of course, seen in the kind of part with which she has been identified for a long time, and both are extremely clever, sincere, and thoughtful pieces of work. As Candida, indeed, she displays a tenderness and a sense of humour which are both admirable. But it is her work in her other two parts, and particularly as Hecuba, which lifts her into a new category altogether.

Euripides' two plays, the *Medea* and *The Trojan Women*, are specimens of the old type of tragedy at its purest. Both display, from beginning to end, the agonies of great souls in torment; neither Medea nor Hecuba is allowed a moment's respite. Either part subjects the tragic powers of an actress to the most searching test it is possible to imagine. Miss Thorndike passes this test with high honours. In the *Medea* she gives an exhibition of sheer power which is in itself enough to refute the criticism that the actress of today has not the physique for a tragic part. She begins the part at so high a pitch of emotion that it seems plainly impossible that she will be able to maintain it till the close without allowing the tension to drop; and, indeed, she does not quite succeed.

Nevertheless, none but an actress with a great tragic gift could come so near to complete success. Her failure to carry us with her quite to the end is due chiefly to her reading of the part. Her Medea is too inhuman to command sympathy. She is the barbarian sorceress, aching and thirsting for revenge, rather than the wronged wife seeking just retribution. 'Nobody', wrote Dr. Gilbert Murray once in a criticism of this play, 'can help siding with Medea.' To this extent, but only to this extent, does she fail of complete success. But her Hecuba is a really great achievement. It is quieter than the Medea; deeper and stronger, more intense and more moving. The tortures she has to bear are more varied and terrible, her method of bearing them more noble. It is, apart from its force, a notable piece of character acting; for in Medea the actress can appear in her own youth and strength and beauty, only adding a touch of the inhuman; but in Hecuba she is an old woman, her strength broken, her beauty faded—only her spirit still retains its old-time strength and dignity. But it is in the quietness of it that the power lies. Hecuba's most poignant moments are not when she is bewailing her own and her children's fate, nor yet when she is expressing her hatred of Helen and lust for vengeance upon her; they come when she is silent, listening to the pitiful outburst of Andromache. It is a real triumph of acting to achieve such a result by sheer unaided intensity of feeling, and the actress here raises her Hecuba to the position of a great part, greatly played.

Miss Thorndike has in these parts scored a great *succès d'estime*, which gives us reason to hope that it is only the earnest of still bigger things to come. Every natural advantage is hers; she is, like the parts she plays, cast in the heroic mould. It seems certain that she has only to be given a real chance to make a big popular success, which will draw even the present-day public to see her and will give her undisputed title to be called our foremost—Miss Genevieve Ward would probably say our only—tragic actress.

W. A. DARLINGTON: *Daily Telegraph*, 8 April 1920

'A BILL OF DIVORCEMENT'

14 March 1921

WHEN Miss Clemence Dane, already known as an accomplished novelist, stepped on to the stage of St. Martin's Theatre on Monday night and informed the audience, exceedingly enthusiastic about her play, that she could not make a speech (a statement which she very charmingly falsified) someone in the gallery gallantly and truly retorted, 'But you can write a play!' And, indeed, Miss Dane can write a play! The time she spent on the stage as an actress was clearly not wasted, and she has brought to the making of *A Bill of Divorcement* much knowledge of the theatre on its technical side. Her skill is so great that even when she commits grave errors, such as would involve another dramatist in disaster, she is able to retrieve her losses and skip easily into safety. Twice in the last act she nearly pushed her play over on to its side, and once in the second act she let it stagger dangerously; but she contrived to elude trouble, and the curtain finally descended amidst such applause as has rarely been heard in a London theatre, and has certainly not been heard there for some time.

A Bill of Divorcement is a piece of the theatre which looks uncommonly like a piece of life. It is a remarkable first play, although it is not so good as Miss Dane's first novel, *Regiment of Women*, in which she displayed very brilliantly that delight in dissection, that barbarous love of exposing a creature's writhings, which is characteristic of the ablest women novelists. The play has, I imagine, been written strictly to formula, just as Mr. William Archer has written his Indian melodrama, *The Green Goddess* (now enormously successful in New York) strictly in accordance with the principles laid down by him in *Play-Making*. A great deal of abuse has been bestowed upon machine-made plays, and perhaps deservedly, but for my part I discover much that is fascinating in them, even some of what Rupert Brooke called

the keen
Unpassioned beauty of a great machine.

It is very enjoyable to see Sardou making his wheels go round, and few people, if they are truthful, can deny that Sir Arthur Pinero, a more cunning craftsman than Sardou, excites them by that masterly scene of swift and changing sensations in *His House in Order* when Nina violently explodes in the presence of the Ridgeley family. Let anyone who is interested in dramatic craftsmanship study *His House in Order* or *The Gay Lord Quex*, and I do not doubt that he or she will discover there are few dramatists in England or out of it who know just how to get a theatrical effect with the skill that distinguishes Sir Arthur Pinero. Observe how he does it. First, there is a quiet spell, followed by a spell with a nervous jump in it. Then comes another quiet spell, but one in which the nervous jump is remembered. And then, biff! bang!! the whole thing goes up in wrath, as in *His House in Order*, or in terrific nervous excitement, as in *The Gay Lord Quex*, and the curtain is brought down with a rush before the audience can collect its senses. Sardou did this sort of thing fairly well, but he was a bungler compared with Sir Arthur Pinero, for Sardou not only made you aware of the wheels going round, but actually exhibited the entire works to you, whereas Sir Arthur almost persuades you that there aren't any wheels at all.

Miss Dane's play starts off as a piece of propaganda: it saves itself alive by becoming a piece of the theatre. 'The audience', according to the programme, 'is asked to imagine that the recommendations of the Royal Commission on Divorce have become the law of the land, and that the action of the play passes on Christmas Day, 1933.' But why *Christmas Day*? You, innocent of theatrical skill, will say that the situation described in the play would not be any less poignant or effective on, say, the Twelfth of July. And that is precisely where you, good innocent, would be in error. Miss Dane has the good sense to realise that she is entitled to employ any trick that will make her doctrine palatable, just as Mr. Shaw uses all the devices of scenic effects, strange situations, and pretty or unusual costumes as the jam for the powder of the Life Force. If you ask yourself why he suddenly puts Dolly and Philip Clandon into the costumes of columbine and harlequin, you are obliged to conclude that he does so for no other reason than to obtain a pictorial effect, to relieve the monotony of the argument with a piece of prettiness, or to break up a scene which is tending to drag, all of which is perfectly legitimate. Miss Dane opens her play on Christmas Day because she wishes to use all the associations of that day, already innately known to the audience, to help her in her work. She can get scenic effects with snow; she can get comic effects out of presents and religious orthodoxy and cold rooms; she can get sentimental effects with church bells; and so on. And she is quite right to do so.

The theme of the play in this: Margaret Fairfield,

who married Hilary Fairfield soon after the outbreak
of war in 1914, is living in a small country house
with her daughter, Sydney, aged seventeen, and her
sister-in-law, Hester, a narrow, doctrinaire, priest-
ridden spinster of a type that will, I trust, be totally
extinct in 1933. Hilary, member of a nervous
family with a tendency to 'queerness', sustained
shell-shock during the war and has, for sixteen years,
been confined in a lunatic asylum. His condition
is that of many victims of shell-shock, one of violent
revulsion from persons formerly loved, and, because
of the dangerous rage into which the mere sight of
her throws him, Margaret has not seen him for many
years. Sydney, the daughter, has never seen him at
all. The law of divorce has been amended so that
lunacy becomes a ground for dissolution of marriage.
When the play begins, Margaret has obtained a
divorce from Hilary, of which, owing to his condition,
he is ignorant, and she is within a week of being
married to Gray Meredith, who has wooed her for a
considerable time. The psychology of Margaret is a
little difficult to follow here. She is in love with
Meredith, and declares that she has never loved
Hilary. Why should she have delayed so long in
obtaining her divorce can only be explained by the
supposition that she is a woman of weak and cowardly
character, for there is no suggestion that she shares
the religious scruples of her sister-in-law. I think Miss
Dane detracts from the propaganda value of her play
by the introduction of this factor into the situation.
If Margaret had no love for Hilary and much love for
Gray, then the question of insanity has nothing whatever to do with the relationship of the three parties.

The daughter is a very advanced, downright young
woman with considerable strength of character. It

is she who appears to have urged her mother to the divorce and the engagement. Sydney is herself more or less engaged to Kit Pumphrey, a young man who is interested in eugenics, and is, unhappily for himself, the son of a High Church parson. News comes to Sydney, while her mother and Gray are at church, that Hilary has escaped from the asylum. It subsequently appears that he has recovered his sanity, although still in a highly nervous state, and that he would in all likelihood have been released within a short time. His return to the asylum, if he is captured, will only be for the purpose of formalities. Hilary comes to his home, and his mind is practically where it was on the day when he lost his senses. He loves Margaret still, and appears always to have loved her. This fact, and also the fact that there is no apparent ground for Margaret's lack of feeling for him—she must have had some sort of love for him when she married him—makes her position still more difficult to understand, and plays some havoc with the propaganda. The rest of the play deals with the reactions of the characters to this new situation. Margaret weakly wavers between Hilary and Gray, but finally decides to go to Gray, less on his persuasion than on that of Sydney, who has 'jilted' Kit, not because she no longer loves him, but because she will not pass on the taint of insanity to her children. She gives up her lover so that she may devote herself to the care of her father. Hester, invincibly obtuse, almost incredibly obtuse, makes some cruel comment on the selfishness of the younger generation which so lightly discards affection, and the play ends.

The propaganda is that lunacy is a just ground for divorce, and Miss Dane has very courageously tackled her problem by dealing with a hard case. Indeed, she very nearly ruins her argument by enlisting the sympathy of the audience almost entirely on the side of Hilary. The case against Hilary is that Life demands that he shall be sacrificed as a scapegoat, innocent as all scapegoats are. Margaret is a normal, healthy woman and the potential mother of normal, healthy children. Life demands that this woman shall not be bound to a man who may give her abnormal, unhealthy children or keep her infertile. Therefore, says Miss Dane, Margaret must divorce Hilary and marry Gray. That is the propaganda part of this play. The complications are the lack of love for Hilary by Margaret, and the question of heredity. Kit tells Sydney, before he is aware of the application of his argument to her, that a sane person ought not to take the risk of marrying one in whose family there is any mental derangement. She accepts him at his word and 'jilts' him. I do not know to what extent the alienists will support Sydney's sacrifice, and since I have very little acquaintance with theories on heredity, and particularly on insanity, I cannot argue about the subject here; but, writing as an entirely ignorant person, I am afraid I am left unconvinced by the necessity for Sydney's sacrifice. Nervousness, even 'queerness', is not necessarily productive of madness. It required a war to drive Hilary off his head, and even he recovered in time. Sydney was a strong-willed young woman, not any more 'queer' than a young woman of character is entitled to be, and Kit was a healthy phlegmatic sort of youth. In other words, the combination seemed to me admirable. The blend of quick character with somewhat beefy temperament should surely have produced very desirable babies.

The play had three bad moments. The first was in the second act, when Dr. Alliot was brought in to explain the views of the medical profession. Just what went wrong here, I do not know, but I fancy that Mr. Stanley Lathbury misconceived the part. On the other hand, Miss Dane did not do much to help him. The other bad moments were in the last act, the first of the two being when Sydney 'jilts' Kit. This scene was too long and not very skilfully handled by Miss Dane, but it suffered from a more serious defect in that Miss Dane compelled Sydney, a quite candid and truthful girl, to play a trick of insincerity on Kit. I am not convinced that Sydney ought to have jilted Kit, but assuming that her behaviour in doing so was right, she ought to have told him the true reason for her refusal to marry him. This was a singular lapse for Miss Dane to make, but it is easily put right. The second of these two bad moments was in the scene in which Gray is told that Margaret has decided to stay with Hilary. The speeches put into Gray's mouth were so obscure in meaning and made him seem so cruel and thick-skulled that the play very nearly made a sensational collapse at this point. This flaw can also be very easily removed, and probably by this time has been. Mr. Aubrey Smith's acting at that point was, from the technical point of view, the best acting in the play, for he had to do what was almost impossible, retain sympathy for a sympathetic character at a moment when that character is behaving in an incomprehensible and unsympathetic fashion.

The play is superbly acted. Apart from Mr. Aubrey Smith's really remarkable performance in the scene to which I have just referred, there were three supremely good pieces of acting. Miss Lilian Braithwaite, who played the part of Margaret, revealed an aspect of her acting with which we are not familiar, the power to express intense emotion. The weak, wavering character of Margaret, swung from one mood to another, constantly in need of support and counsel, was perfectly portrayed. Miss Braithwaite has put lovers of good acting deeply in her debt. In addition to her fine performance, there were those of Miss Meggie Albanesi as Sydney and of Mr. Malcolm Keen as Hilary. Miss Albanesi's acting in the final scene of the play was easily the best performance that has been given by any young actress in England in the whole of my experience as a playgoer; and there are not many older actresses who could excel her in that scene. The reticence with which she expressed her deep emotions was abandoned just for a moment or two, exactly at the right moment and for the right length of time; and we were allowed to see a young girl's suffering, not to the point of being embarrassed or humiliated by it, but of being left in clear understanding of it. This was a very distinguished piece of work. Mr. Malcolm Keen is a young actor narrowly known. He stepped at one bound from a place of obscurity to a place of high degree on Monday night. His Hilary was beautifully—there is no other word for it— beautifully done. Both Miss Albanesi and he made one feel proud of young English actors and actresses. These two do not waste their time on golf courses! The remainder of the company were excellent, although I am dubious of Mr. Lathbury's interpretation of the doctor.

ST. JOHN ERVINE: *The Observer*, 20 March 1921

THE SEARCH FOR THE MASTERPIECE

IF the business of criticism be the discovery of masterpieces, how comes it about that our dramatic critics express no concern at the failure of masterpieces to appear, and, when one of these rarities occurs, do not notice its advent? I need give no examples—the crucial ones of Ibsen and the early Shaw will suffice—but it might be interesting to suggest why the attitude of expectation that some day the best kind of dramatic writing will appear, and that the whole world of the theatre will be rejoicing in it, is so rare. I insist on the great importance of such a disposition. To my mind the critic of the drama should be continually reverting to the mood of the Jewish people about the Messiah. 'Art thou he that should come, or do we look for another?' said the pious Jew. 'Is this the mantle of Shakespeare, or even the hem of his garment?' should be the keynote of that minute and painstaking research to which the true lover of letters is committed. For when the standard of the best is set up, the criticism of the second-best, or of the positively bad, becomes (if the literary equipment be adequate) a fairly simple matter. And how fruitful must this method be upon the sensitive material of the artist's mind! How it must encourage and stimulate him! How seriously must he take his profession! And what a vastly heightened affair must the immortal quest of the crown of wild olive henceforth become!

Now I decline to put down this incuriousness about dramatic masterpieces to want of ability in our critics. There are many powerful and keenly analytical minds at work on the drama in London and elsewhere. But I do suspect one specially predisposing cause (there are others) in the mechanism of their profession. That is their occupation with this kind of writing to the exclusion of other literary interests. Just as I, who write much on politics, often find my mind ceasing to work with freedom upon that subject, so do our specialists of the stage neglect the fertilization of their minds with soil drawn from other fields of thought. Is that a paradox? I do not think so. The Drama is not Art. It is a form of art. It is not Life. It is an expression of life. And if it is treated as the thing in itself, the study of it tends to become an expert examination of its rules and conventions, instead of a continual reference to its place in the general scheme of art, to poetry, music, painting, and sculpture, and no less to religion, to history, and to politics. In a word, I believe that in the narrow *expertise* of our times, the dwindling power shrinks and is finally lost.

I venture to apply these remarks to the criticisms of Sir James Barrie's *Shall We Join the Ladies?* at the St. Martin's Theatre. For the most part this work is dismissed as a 'practical joke' (in indifferent taste), 'a Barrie', indeed, but a wrong, because an unexpected, an uncontracted-for, 'Barrie'. The joke is that the author, meaning to write a three-act play, produces a single-act farce, and thus palms an unfinished work on the public. Now it happens that *Shall We Join the Ladies?* is finished to the last hair, and that its dramatic scheme and critical intention end with the fall of the curtain. But my point is that the error of the critics arises from a misconception, not of the method of the play, but of its meaning. It is assumed that *Shall We Join the Ladies?* is an unconcluded crime-story. It is, in fact, a parable. There is no single murderer to be discovered. The guests at Sam Smith's Round Table are all murderers. Or rather they, like their Inquisitor, are spiritual, or, like the dream-people in Poe's stories, apparitional figures. They are all the world, or all society. They are the sheep of the weekly admonition in the Common Prayer Book. They are the individual conscience —the guilty soul of our old friend Everyman.

For this sudden dive of Barrie's into morals, philosophy, religion, all in the guise of a wicked-looking and witty farce, his critics were, I suggest, unprepared, because they were thinking, not of the mind of the artist and its incurable habit of becoming a law unto itself, but of its familiar and customary mould. Which is as much as to say that because Shakespeare had written *Romeo and Juliet*, where love is everything, he had no business to write *Hamlet*, where love is nothing. On the contrary, if our critics had sought for the stamp of genius instead of merely examining the hall-mark of use and wont, they must, I think, have divined that this strange, and even cruel, fantasy obeyed all the higher laws of the dramatic art. Note, for example,

1. Its use of the element of surprise.

2. The attitude of terrified expectation, aroused in the actors, and transferred to the audience.

3. The employment of simple physical means— the courtesies of the dinner-table, and the passage of the meal itself—the higher the moral and symbolic effect of the drama. (Compare the porter's speech and the knocking in *Macbeth*.)

4. The resort to familiar comic effects (*e.g.* the superstition of the thirteen diners) to prepare the mind for the tragic ones.

5. The hint of the supernatural (*e.g.* the 'dark passage', and the forced assemblage in the 'butler's room') so as to emphasize the visible and material terrors of the scene.

6. The rapid and continuous evolution of the characters of the actors (*e.g.* the increasing desire of one criminal to betray another, the husband to give away the wife, the 'brother' the 'sister').

7. The economy of the dialogue joined to its appositeness.

I have six other points, but I reserve them. Let me merely add that the gaiety of the audience showed them to be of the critics' opinion, not of mine. They treated *Shall We Join the Ladies?* as a good, if puzzling, 'Barrie'.

H. W. MASSINGHAM: *The Nation and The Athenæum,*
18 March 1922

'PEER GYNT' AT THE OLD VIC

ONE of the advantages of being an advocate of the
Old Vic is that your client gives you such superb
backing. A few weeks ago we urged that this people's
theatre in the Waterloo Road should, on the strength
of its Shakespeare performances, receive a national
or municipal status. Since we wrote, it has trebled
the weight of our plea by carrying through, without a
touch of self-advertisement, an enterprise from which
the commercial theatre would recoil in horror, and
giving an astonishingly beautiful performance of a
great part of *Peer Gynt*. The difficulties of this task
probably only those concerned in it can appreciate.
(We believe that the mere procuring of a proper
score of the full Grieg music was a baffling quest,
and after that the whole problem of orchestration
had to be faced.) There was no tradition, be it remembered, to help the producer in visualizing this
vast panoramic fantasy, which unrolls its endless
episodes in Norway, Morocco, Egypt, on the sea, in
mountains of the imagination, in the haunts of
trolls, elves, and wraiths, and in places such as the
void where Peer wrestles with the Boyg, to which
perhaps not even the author was able to assign a
shape or character. Yet it has been done, and with
what results? That select gatherings of Ibsenites
have sprinkled the benches and murmured their
applause? Not a bit of it. The doors have been
besieged with crowds which any manager of a
popular *revue* would be glad to see thronging his own
vestibule, the large auditorium has been packed
with attentive and delighted listeners, and a dramatic

critic who had missed the first night had to sue for a
corner in the management's private box.

In the face of these really amazing facts we cannot
do less than once again urge the necessity of rescuing
this theatre from its financial difficulties, and that
by the only satisfactory way of public recognition.
Since our last article on the subject, the reception
given to the Geddes Report has shown that the nation
is decisively opposed to the policy of buying immediate economic relief by mortgaging its educational
and cultural future.   After that there need be less
hesitation in urging that an opportunity should be
taken by adopting the Old Vic, which if neglected
may be long sought for a second time in vain.
The union of artistic purpose and popular appreciation which it has brought about is a thing that the
most lavishly endowed national theatre in the unde-
fined future might spend years without accomplishing,
would, indeed, perhaps for ever fail to attain. This
most difficult spade work has already been done; it
is now for the community to use or to waste it.

We have mentioned economy. What an economist
Mr. Robert Atkins, the producer of *Peer Gynt*, may
claim to be! With what trifling resources he has built
up a spectacle of memorable art! There is a simple
'cut scene', as the old toy theatres used to call it,
affording a glimpse into the depths of a steep Norwegian valley which has more atmosphere about it
than some elaborate 'sets' in the West End that have
probably cost ten times as much; the mountain cleft
(consisting, it may be, of a couple of curtains)
where the Dövre King holds his obscene rout, is a
grandiose nightmare like some of the chapters in
Mr. Wells's moon-romance; out of a parasol, a yellow
rug, and a blue skyground, the whole Moroccan

desert is deftly conjured. Even more impressive is the scene of Ase's death in the mountain hut, with the coursing shadow on the wall giving ghostly life to Peer's fancied drive up to Heaven-gates. Here all conspires—the genius of the poem, the majestic pulse of the dirge in the orchestra, the tact of the producer, and the acting (at its finest in this episode) of Miss Florence Buckton as Ase and Mr. Russell Thorndike as Peer. Mr. Thorndike's attack upon his colossal task is a wonderful evidence of his vitality and incisive strength as an actor; his Peer seemed to us, however, rather too sharp and sinister a rogue. Peer Gynt, after all, is just ordinary human nature.

It would be a long list that would pick out all the performances of minor parts deserving notice. Miss Gladys Dale was splendidly passionate in the brief tragedy of Ingrid, the bride seduced by Peer, and Miss Frances Petersen altogether eerie and disquieting in her clever conception of the Green-Clad One, the snout-faced troll Princess. The Dövre King was richly played by Mr. Andrew Leigh, and Mr. Reyner Barton's Herr von Eberkopf was a delightful thumb-nail sketch of Prussian professorialism. But perhaps the best of all was Mr. Rupert Harvey's fine performance of the Button Moulder. No fire-breathing messenger from Hell was ever so alarming as he is in his gentle implacability. The character is, of course, a creation of genius, a wonderful personification of the apparent disinterestedness of Fate. A mistake on Mr. Harvey's part might have ruined the truth of it, but his perceptions are delicate and he did not make that mistake.

D. L. MURRAY: *The Nation and The Athenæum,*
25 March 1922

MARIE LLOYD

WHEN, in the Tottenham Court Road, I saw, tucked under the newsboy's arm, the sheet which announced that Marie Lloyd was dead,[1] everything around me became still. The street lost its hubbub, and for a space I was alone with a personal sorrow. In moments of emotion one is apt to notice the little things, and at once I remarked that, on the poster, the artist's name was prefaced with the word 'Miss'. Death, it seemed, laying his hand upon her who was known over the whole English-speaking world as 'Marie', must use more ceremony. 'Marie'—pronounced with the broad vowel beloved of the Cockney—was in everybody's mouth that day, in club and barrack-room, in bar-parlour and in modest home. On the high seas 'Marie's dead' would be droned from ship to ship. Returning from Kempton a party of bookmakers fell to speaking of the dead artist. One said, with tears in his eyes, 'She had a heart, had Marie!' 'The size of Waterloo Station,' another rejoined. Her abounding generosity was a commonplace of the profession. She would go down to Hoxton, where she was born, and make lavish distribution to the street-urchins of boots and shoes which she fitted with her own hands. She had numberless pensioners dependent upon her charity. She earned some two hundred thousand pounds, and gave it all away. 'God rest her,' said the bookmaker who had first spoken, and bared his head. That night, at Blackfriars Ring, a bruiser with the marks of many fights declared: 'We shan't none of us see

[1] On 7 October 1922, aged 52.

the likes o' Marie again. She was a great artist.'
Those who know that soundness must underlie a
boxer's brilliance before he receives the title of
'artist', will recognize the force of this tribute. If
the music-hall singer, embodying a social stratum to
those who know it like their hand, had deviated
from truth by so much as a finger's breadth, she
would not have received this highest meed of praise.
To those whose verdict is based upon the most
positive of evidence such fancy things as implications
are without meaning. Facts are facts, alike in the
New Cut or in Leicester Square. Marie Lloyd's
characters knew no parishes but these; they were born
in one and rose to the other. 'Sank', the moralist will
exclaim, true to his eternal preoccupation, and for
ever beside the point. Morality is a philosophy of
life; this realist presented types of human character
and drew no moral.

It was not, however, from a world of bullies or
the lower deck that Marie Lloyd drew her chief
support. She was enormously popular with the
class which lives in villas and makes a fetish of
respectability. To placate these, would-be apologists
have pleaded that 'whilst many of the songs were in
themselves offensive, the manner of their delivery
took away the offence'. This is the purest nonsense.
The genius of this *diseuse* consisted in the skill and
emphasis with which she drove home the 'offensive'
point. She employed a whole armoury of shrugs
and leers, and to reveal every cranny of the mind
utilized each articulation of the body. Frank in
gesture as Fielding was in phrase, her page of life
was as outspoken and as sure. Hottentot and
Eskimo knowing no English, the respectable burgess
priding himself on his ignorance of the way of the

saloon-lounge, would yet recognize from the artist's
pantomime the burden of her song. She gave you
the frankly raffish wink which the courtesan tips to
her *gigolo*, together with the hard stare of the streets;
and thus made you free of an old profession. 'No
one was ever the worse for her performance.' Everything depends, surely, upon what these squeamish
critics mean by 'offensive' and 'worse'. It will not be
claimed, I think, that *A Little of What you Fancy Does you
Good* turned the young men out of the heated music-
hall into the Strand determined to look neither to the
right nor to the left. Marie Lloyd sang, as Rabelais
wrote, for good Pantagruelists and no others, and
chastity had to look elsewhere for a minister.

> Inside the Horsel here the air is hot,
> Right little peace one hath for it, God wot,

was the last reflection conveyed from that Hill of
Venus which was the stage of the Tivoli Music Hall.
Hoxton's daughter was as much the embodiment
of her period as some more pretentious folk. She
reduced to the comprehension of butcher's-boy and
clerk, those limbs moving 'as melodies yet' to quite
unpardonable music, all that meaningless tosh about
'curing the soul by means of the senses'. Little
patience, we may be sure, had the comédienne with
the original form of these nostrums for sick minds.
She translated them into tonics for the healthy body;
she preached the world and the flesh, and gloried in
their being the very devil. None ever left the theatre
feeling 'better' for her songs. From that blight, at
least, they were free. That which she sang was an old
hymn which, on the music-hall stage, will not be
repeated. *Explicit Laus Veneris.*

From any cold-blooded, reasoned immorality her
songs were entirely free. Flaubert, you remember,

makes one of his characters conjure up the red lamp
of a brothel with the reflection that of all life's
experiences this youthful one was the most truly
happy. Marie Lloyd's honest spirit would have
utterly disdained so pitiful a philosophy. The sailor
of whom she sang might, as the result of an encounter
in Piccadilly, miss his ship, but a mere incident would
not turn him, like Flaubert's sentimental fellow,
eternally adrift. There was no decadent Latin taint
about Marie; she was almost saltily British. Villadom
accepted her in the way it accepts the gay dog who
makes no secret of his gaiety. Villadom will have
nothing to do with the sad fellow whose pleasure is
furtive, and it recognized that there was nothing sad
or secret about its idol. Marie knew that the great
English public will open its arms to vice, provided
it is presented as a frolic. She knew, though she
could not have put her knowledge into words, that
her art was one with the tradition of English letters,
which has always envisaged the seamy side of life
with gusto rather than with deprecation. Yvette
Guilbert harrowed the soul with the pathos of her
street walkers; Marie Lloyd had intense delight in
her draggle-tails. She showed them in their splendour,
not in their misery; the mopishness and squalor of
their end were not for her. And that is why, when
she came to the portrayal of elderly baggages, she
refrained from showing them as pendants to her
courtesans. A French artist would have insisted upon
the inevitable descent to the procuress, whereas the
English artist rejected even Mother Peachum. Instead she gave happy life to battered harridans
ludicrous in the sight of man, if not of God; diving
into their very entrails for the unstilled riot which
made old Jenny steal from her husband's bed to

dance at the ball. Again she proved herself an infinitely greater realist than others more highly esteemed. She depicted the delight of humble life, the infinite joy of mean streets. When some jovial crone, emerging from the wings, flung at an unseen, routed foe a Parthian 'And it wouldn't take me long, neither!' you settled in your stall to listen to a reading from the Book of Low Life. There was unction here, and a smack of the lips over a Vulgate the accuracy of which, divined by the boxes, was eagerly checked by the gallery. Was Marie Lloyd vulgar? Undoubtedly. That jovial quality was her darling glory. She relished and expounded those things which she knew to be dear to the common heart.

Marie had the *petite frimousse éveillée*, the wideawake little 'mug' which Sarcey noted in Réjane. Her 'dial', as the Cockney would put it, was the most expressive on the halls. She had beautiful hands and feet. She knew every board on the stage and every inch of every board, and in the perfection of her technical accomplishment rivalled her great contemporary of another world, Mrs. Kendal. Briefly, she knew her business. But it is not my purpose to talk now of technical excellence. Rather would I dwell on the fact that she was adored by the lowest classes, by the middle people, and by the swells. 'I hope,' she said in a little speech before the curtain at her last appearance at the Alhambra, 'I hope I may, *without bigotry*, allude to my past triumphs.' Poor soul, it is we who should ask to be delivered from that vice. Marie broadened life and shared it, not as a mean affair of refusal and restraint, but as a boon to be lustily enjoyed. She redeemed us from virtue too strait-laced, and her great heart cracked too soon.

JAMES AGATE: *At Half-Past Eight*, 1923

'THE WAY OF THE WORLD'

CHARLES LAMB did a world of mischief when he put before his most famous essay the title *On the Artificial Comedy of the Last Century*. Sitting at this performance of the greatest prose comedy in the English language, I could not, for the life of me, see anything artificial in the personages beyond their inessentials—dress, speech, and polite notions. Manners change, but not the man who wears them. If Lady Wishfort is artificial, then so, too, is Falstaff. I see equally little reason why Congreve's hot-handed widow should be so superfluous to demand the time of day, except for the causes assigned to that other gormandiser. Wishfort is all appetite, and as real as any canvas of old Hogarth or modern page of Zola. One of her kind attends dinner parties to this day, less her candour and wit.

Millamant, too, could go into any novel of Meredith, *mutatis mutandis*, and having regard to the topics which a more generous age has conceded to the sex. Wit of Millamant's order is imperishable, for the simple reason that her creator gave her a mind. Lamb's celebrated excuse for compunctionless laughter is that these creatures never were. The truth is that they are, and always will be. 'The effect of Congreve's plays,' says Hazlitt, 'is prodigious *on the well-informed spectator*.' It is easy to pronounce as artificial a world of which you are ignorant; in the Hebrides *Our Betters* would doubtless be dubbed fantastic. There are more Wishforts and Millamants about town to-day than there are Hedda Gablers.

Mirabell is a poseur, but he does not date one-tenth as much as Wilde's Lord Henry Wotton. And as for Sir Wilfull Witwould, one of his kidney sold me a horse no later than Wednesday last. Congreve, in a word, was the natural well from which Sheridan, Wilde, and our own Somerset Maugham have drawn their 'natural table-waters'. Without, alas, quite so much naturalness.

How is the piece played at Hammersmith? For all it is worth, is the answer; and perhaps just a teeny-weeny bit popularised. We could do without that business with the chandelier and the bewigged orchestra. The play is keyed up to the highest pitch known to classic comedy. It may be that Mr. Playfair was afraid to trust us with the pure distillation of the Comic Spirit; it is much more probable that he recognised that in Miss Margaret Yarde he had a Wishfort who must prove a moral and physical eruption in—to use Prince Hal's phrase—flame-coloured taffeta. It was a first-class performance, striking alike to eye and ear. The simpering of this hag-ridden beldam would have brought down the comminations of a Lear. There was cut-and-come-again, you felt, in the way of grotesque, unbridled fancy. Sobriety could not hold the stage against this monstrously comic obsession. And therefore was sobriety not attempted.

But what of Millamant? Almost everything, is our answer this time. Never can actress have spoken the epilogue with less belief in its aptness.

> There are some critics so with spleen diseased
> They scarcely come inclining to be pleased

was not true of those who on Thursday came to see, not only the old piece, but the speaker of the epilogue

fulfil prophecy. Let me not mince matters. Miss
Edith Evans is the most accomplished of living and
practising English actresses. Leaving tragedy to
Miss Thorndike, she has a wider range than any
other artist before the public, and is unrivalled alike
in sentimental and adamantine comedy. A year or
two ago there were seen at intervals upon the London
stage elderly spinsters with white hair purring the
fire out in vacuity. These tabbies were all Miss
Evans. Her *dévote* in *Les Trois Filles de M. Dupont* and
her housemaid in *I Serve* showed a quality of pathos
which, one thought, had left the scene with Mrs.
Kendal. This actress's Cleopatra in *All for Love*
might, though tragedy is not her *forte*, have hung
without discrepancy among the Lelys at Hampton
Court. Her performances in *Heartbreak House* and
Back to Methuselah are too glitteringly new to need
recalling. Her Mistress Page was the quintessence
of gaiety.

I am tired of recounting all this, but the thing has
got to be persisted in. Miss Evans has simply to be
dinned into the most insensitive of auricular appen-
dages—the ear of the West End manager. They
say that, by the tape-measure, this actress has not
the fashionable type of feature, for all the world as
though her business was to grin before a camera.
Bluntly and frankly, I will agree that if I wanted to
hire a chit to carry a banner in a pantomime I should
not engage this artist. But if she does not possess rare
beauty in the highest sense, then I know not that
quality. This countenance is replete, as was said
of Congreve's style, 'with sense and satire, conveyed
in the most pointed and polished terms'. This
acting is 'a shower of brilliant conceits, a new triumph
of wit, *a new conquest over dullness*'. You could hang

any one of this player's portraits on the sky, and challenge the Zodiac.

And why?

Her Millamant is impertinent without being pert, graceless without being ill-graced. She has only two scenes, but what scenes they are of unending subtlety and finesse! Never can that astonishing 'Ah! idle creature, get up when you will' have taken on greater delicacy, nor 'I may by degrees *dwindle* into a wife' a more delicious mockery. '*Adieu*, my morning thoughts, agreeable wakings, indolent slumbers, all ye *douceurs*, ye *sommeils du matin, adieu*'—all this is breathed out as though it were early Ronsard or du Bellay. And 'I nauseate walking,' and 'Natural, easy Suckling!' bespeak the very genius of humour. There is a pout of the lips, a jutting forward of the chin to greet the conceit, and a smile of happy deliverance when it is uttered, which defy the chronicler. This face, at such moments, is like a city in illumination, and when it is withdrawn leaves a glow behind.

One fault I find, and one only. Millamant's first entry bears out Mirabell's announcement: 'Here she comes, i' faith, full sail, with her fan spread and her streamers out.' The actress makes her appearance something lapwing fashion, a trifle too close to the ground. It is possible, too, that Mrs. Abington gave the whole character a bigger sweep. Miss Evans conceives her as a rogue in porcelain, and keeps her within that conception. Walpole, one feels sure, would have had civil things to say of this performance of which the perfect enunciation is one of the minor marvels.

The Mirabell of Mr. Robert Loraine was a trifle on the sober side, but showed distinction if a trifle too much heart. The part was beautifully spoken, and the actor used only the suavest and most gentle notes in his voice. He listened exquisitely. Miss Dorothy Green made great music of her lines, and Messrs. Playfair and Norman enjoyed themselves hugely.

10 February 1924

JAMES AGATE: *The Contemporary Theatre 1924*

'HAMLET' IN MODERN DRESS

Claudius, King of Denmark	. FRANK VOSPER
Hamlet	COLIN KEITH-JOHNSTON
Polonius, Lord Chamber-lain	A. BROMLEY-DAVENPORT
Horatio, Friend to Hamlet	. ALAN HOWLAND
Laertes, son to Polonius .	. ROBERT HOLMES
Osric	. GUY VIVIAN
Ghost of Hamlet's father .	. GROSVENOR NORTH
First Player . . .	. TERENCE O'BRIEN
First Gravedigger . .	. CEDRIC HARDWICKE
Fortinbras, Prince of Norway	. DONALD FINLAY
Gertrude, Queen of Den-mark . . .	DOROTHY MASSINGHAM
Ophelia, daughter to Polonius . . .	. MURIEL HEWITT

Kingsway Theatre

Do you know what it is when some scheme, thought of its nature to be beyond attainment, is suddenly, to use a phrase eternally current in political circles, 'brought within the bounds of practical politics'? It is, I assure you, a highly exhilarating feeling. There must always have been among those who feel any curiosity about *Hamlet* at all, a curiosity to be able to judge *Hamlet* as though, by some inconceivable flight of burning genius, a modern playwright, say Tchekhov, had written it. All the idea needed, as it happens, was a few dress suits and a few Court uniforms. But no one before Sir Barry Jackson happened to think of it, and now Sir Barry Jackson and his company have done it.

This production so pleased me and excited me, so amused me and thrilled me, that I find it difficult to collect my thoughts about it or to become articulate on the subject. Early in the proceedings I ceased to be an intelligent spectator with an account to render afterwards. I merely enjoyed, and lost myself in enjoyment. There was quite enough of the new and the unexpected to absorb, and to take all one's faculties of absorption. I can only give a scattered note to explain why the present *Hamlet* at the Kingsway is the richest and deepest *Hamlet* I have ever seen. It is rarely that one is profoundly moved in a theatre, and, when one is, the pleasure is so great that an unreadable notice at the week-end seems a small price to pay for it.

To begin with, there is a difference between '*Hamlet* in Modern Dress' (as the production calls itself), and '*Hamlet* as a modern play', as it actually is played. The one suggests Daisy Ashford and Mr. Salteena—which is far from the truth. We are quite simply at a little modern Catholic court—say of Ruritania, say of any small Baltic Kingdom. The King and his ladies and gentlemen, his secretaries and officials, wear evening dress or morning dress. (Hamlet, as befits his status of antagonist and intellectual, never gets beyond a dinner jacket and a soft shirt.) The younger men from the 'Varsity, Laertes, Rosencrantz, Hamlet himself, show a predilection for tweeds. There is a sprinkling of uniforms at the Court. And that is really all that need be said in the matter of costumes. They are easy, natural, appropriate. None of them gets a laugh, and none of them is meant to. They merely transport us to the modern world. But, as Wordsworth said,

> Oh, the difference to me!

The difference in the main is not to Hamlet himself,

who at once becomes easier to play because his surroundings become ten times as interesting, but in the others, who surprise one by suddenly leaping to life. (Mr. Colin Keith-Johnston, a really impressive and inspiring young Hamlet, must have tribute returned him. But I may say at once that I felt he was on to such a chance and opportunity as no actor had never had before him.)

The King is the main beneficiary. Ordinarily, I am never so bored as when the King in *Hamlet* is speaking. He seems indistinguishable from the Player King except for his longer part. I now doubt if I was ever so interested in any modern gentleman as I was in Mr. Frank Vosper (clean-shaven, well dressed, easy in manner, a polished and dignified usurper) speaking the same lines at the Kingsway. Polonius, by the same treatment—the venerable dotard, choked with beard, becomes the dapper little middle-aged Secretary of State—loses nothing, and gains much (and Mr. Bromley-Davenport, much worked up by the general atmosphere of high comedy and excitement that the piece created), has never given a more inspiriting performance). Laertes also. Laertes ordinarily emerges a lay figure readymade from the property room. Who has ever before violently cared what Laertes does or thinks? And yet, once make him an ordinary decent undergraduate, warped by a rancorous hatred in his heart for the young man who he thinks has seduced his sister—let him once be seen as a young man of to-day, and not as a walking costume—and I know that the Laertes of the trunk-hose, or, alternatively, of the winged-helmet Viking tradition, is a creature I never want to endure again in a modern theatre.

What exactly Sir Barry Jackson and his company

have done is to show that *Hamlet* in all its parts is a great deal better play than any company of actors have ever dared to think it before. The breathless, deathless beauty of the language, the language of fire and dew, of boldness, of subtlety, of soaring loveliness, is not lost by being set among a master-piece of modern drama. It merely puts the dialogue of most modern drama to blush by its magnificence. It is the old supreme virtue to which all the other virtues have now been added.

By doing *Hamlet* in modern clothes, the Birmingham company have shown how the ideas of later centuries were ransacked for its making. Imagine the play to be by Tchekhov. This is not mere flippancy. I beg you to go to this *Hamlet* and imagine that Tchekhov wrote it. Imagine that he composed that talkative, idiosyncratic, extraordinarily vivid and mercilessly observed crowd of struggling figures. The canvas is larger than he would have attempted. The boldness of its lights and shades is a world different from his quiet monotone. But in the strange harmony by which all art that is great is seen to have an underlying unity with all other art that is great, it is possible to see that Tchekhov, by a heightening of his genius, might have composed such a *Hamlet*. The difference is in degree, not in kind.

It has always been possible to see that *Hamlet* contained in it the germs or fragments of ideas of nearly all other plays that have ever been written, much as *David Copperfield* can be found to contain the germ of many other great novels besides itself, and all musical combinations can be found to occur in Bach. But never till now has it been possible to see that *Hamlet*—played as it should always now be played, as a play of contemporary life—could make one huge bonfire of the lot and soar aloft in the combined radiance of them all.

HUBERT GRIFFITH: *The Observer*, 30 August 1925

A CREATOR

I suppose that every ordinary regular theatre-goer
has his complaints about the dramatic critic, and
most certainly, every dramatic critic has his complaint about the ordinary theatre-goer.

Myself, I love the dramatic critic, especially when
he tells me how desperately full his daily letter-bag is.
All I want is to see him happy, and for one's letter-
bag to be full is apparently, for a dramatic critic,
the height of happiness! But at times I would like
a point to be made that isn't made. The critics say
so many things about the theatre, are, on the whole,
so lively and amusing and interested, that it seems
churlish to complain, but I do feel that there is only
one of them who ever distinguishes between uncreative
acting and creative acting.

By creative acting I mean, I suppose, the ability
of the actor to make something out of the material
given to him that is a created work *additional* to his
material. Irving, whom alas! I never saw, was, I
believe, a master creator, and one leading actor of
our day is exactly the opposite of this: that is, he
shows you to perfection the material that he has been
given, neither more nor less.

He is so perfectly accomplished that you don't
ask him to do more than he does, but the old pantomime men—Dan Leno, Herbert Campbell and the
rest—were masterly creators in the sense that they
created a great deal out of nothing at all; indeed, as
I get on with my subject I am beginning to wonder
whether the actor as creator is not always at his best
when he has almost nothing to work on.

There I'm held up by the thought that some of the finest creative work done by actors during the last three or four years has been witnessed at the Old Vic—is to be witnessed at this moment, where John Gielgud is making some magnificent creation out of *Hamlet,* imposing his *new* art on the old one. Strange, by the way, that this extraordinary performance at the Old Vic of *Hamlet* in its entirety, witnessed from 6.30 to 11.30 by a packed and excited house, receives almost no notice in the Press, while a scratch matinée at the Haymarket of the same play receives columns!

However, to return to my subject, I am sure that *creative* acting is rarer in England than in America, France or Germany, and, to show more plainly what I mean, I will give some examples. Réjane and the elder Guitry were supreme creative actors; Alfred Lunt, Ethel Barrymore, George Arliss are American examples. Friedrich Schorr and Lottie Lehmann are examples in opera. The supreme instance in England at this moment is Charles Laughton. I am not saying that in my opinion Laughton is our finest actor—far from it. Cedric Hardwicke, Nicholas Hannen, Godfrey Tearle, Tom Walls—there are many more who are, I think, in the general round at present finer actors. But he is our supreme creator.

Laughton works on his part as a novelist does on a novel or a painter on a picture, and he is at his best, as I believe Henry Irving was, when he has almost nothing to work on. I don't mean that he is at his best on conventional machine-made 'Theatre'; he would, for instance, make little or nothing of *The First Mrs. Fraser,* but the two parts in which to my mind he has conspicuously failed are the football hero of *The Silver Tassie* and *Pickwick.* I know that many people thought him very fine in the first of these, and that nearly everyone was agreed that he did not succeed in the second, but I am sure that in both cases too much creative work of the first order had already been done before he got to it.

No; where you can see him setting to with the eagerness and excitement of an artist who needs only a nod to foresee a masterpiece is in plays like my own *Man with Red Hair*, in Bennett's comedy,[1] in a cheap murder play, in Edgar Wallace's excellent *On the Spot*. In all these plays creative work had already occurred, but it was *unfinished* creative work. In the case of my own little play I had the opportunity of catching him in the act. My hero (or villain as you prefer) had been intended originally as a puppet twopence-coloured. I never dreamed that anyone could take him seriously. Laughton took him very seriously indeed, not for my sake or the play's sake or for art's sake, but simply because he had the clay in his hands, and must add a pinch here, make a false eyebrow there, lengthen the nose, twist the mouth, knowing that, as he did so, a created figure, waiting and long imprisoned, would be liberated and escape to the chimney pots like a ghost in Stravinsky's Ballet. Had the rehearsals continued another month heaven knows what my Crispin would have grown to.

He works, of course, in the dark, and it is with the shadows of darkness yet clinging to them that his figures emerge. In the murder-play of a season or two ago (*Alibi* was, I think, its name) he played the part of a French detective. The character was in itself nothing. Dennis Eadie (in his own manner often a splendid actor) played almost at the same time, I remember, a French detective in a drama by

[1] *Mr. Prohack*, by Arnold Bennett.—ED.

A. E. W. Mason, and made nothing but the conventional stage-detective out of it.

Alibi had a dreadfully bad first act, as clumsy and maladroit an affair as I can remember, but Laughton was terrific from his first entrance, not only in make-up—of which he is sometimes a master and sometimes not—but also in all the hints he gave you as to the soul of his strange off adventures. The plot that the detective had to unravel was less than nothing; he was never more thrilling than in the last act when, his problem solved, with no beauty, no voice, no kind of charm, he made love to a pretty girl. The scene should have been revolting. You should have pitied the girl and agonized for her escape, but in truth you felt that she was fortunate to have the opportunity of living with so adventurous a spirit. She would find, you felt, everything bad and everything good in this man. She would have her shocks, she would have also her enchanting hours.

Laughton is always sinister when he is happily engaged. In this present play of Edgar Wallace's he is loathsome and lost. But he is much more than that. He is a poet and a creator of beauty. Every squirm, every husky whisper is a key to an important truth—and a truth we feel he is showing us for the first time.

Thus it is to be a real creator.

HUGH WALPOLE: *The Week-end Review*, 10 May 1930

BIBLICAL
'TOBIAS AND THE ANGEL'

The Bible only fails the modern author when he tries to be biblical. Let him attempt a pastiche of the trope and the rhythm of the Authorised Version and defeat is certain. That was the sad fate of a play about Samson and Delilah which Miss Edith Evans produced not long ago. The modern mummer who wanders about in a formidable beard crying 'O Rose of the Valley of Sharon' is bound to fail. He becomes a talkie version of the oleographic illustrations in the popular Bibles printed about 1880. Another method, once favourite, now certain to provoke derision, was the Livestock Parade. As a boy I used to attend all the productions of Mr. Beerbohm Tree. But compulsory Bible at school made me carefully omit to visit *Joseph and his Brethren*. What I do remember is the spectacle of camels waiting under English skies at the stage-door of His Majesty's Theatre. They displayed a discreditable patience. No doubt the wretched animals did carry the play on their backs. But they would scarcely manage it to-day. The theatre audience does grow up. To make the Muse collide with a menagerie is no longer a certain way to fill the house.

We know now that if the legends are to be used they must be used without pedantic or pretentious archaism. That was the earliest way. The authors of the Mystery Cycles had no English Bible on which to work; but they had the stories and they transferred them quite simply into the chatter of English working men. The Wakefield Nativity Play, for instance, is full of complaints about agricultural wages, and Mac, the sheep-stealer, is just the eternal poacher of the English countryside who finds it better to wring a questionable living from a dark night than to live laborious days as the honest hind of another and a richer man. It was the business of the Elizabethans to make the drama secular and professional; naturally they chose non-biblical themes, but had they turned to scripture they would surely have created the characters in the image of themselves. Shakespeare was no lover of archaism; his Lear, Caesar, Hamlet, and English monarchs all speak the same idiom and probably they borrowed from the same wardrobe. when we reach our own time we find that that is the only way; the dramatist may use the scriptural names and chronicles, but he must speak his own mind in his own way.

That is what Mr. Shaw did when he turned back to the legends. In *Back to Methuselah* he created Eve in his own image, with the curious result that she is far more life-like than any of the real people in the later reaches of the play, Burge, Lubin, and the rest. Eve is just a good intelligent member of the I.L.P. and the Women's International League. She is disgusted alike with the natural serf who is Adam and the vain-glorious man-eater who is Cain—that is, with the too patient proletarian and the ramping militarist. In something of the same way Mr. Marc Connelly in *The Green Pastures* presented the nigger-heaven as Louisiana sees it, complete with banquet-ings of fish-fry and a God who talks coon-stuff to his darkie-angels. Accordingly, the play is as reverent in its own way as the Nativities are in theirs. The one irreverent way of dramatising scripture is to be heavily scriptural and to have a fling at reinstating Solomon in all his verbal glory.

The Apocrypha, with its magic and its wonderments and its fearful tales of lust and blood, must exercise a natural lure over the theatre. But here also it is useless to attempt to recapture the original atmosphere and to call in the antiquarian expert, who will tell you the exact components of Judith's wardrobe and kitchen cupboard. I have seen two *Judith* plays and both failed. They were wrapped in semibiblical language, while semi-biblical fine linen flapped expensively over the laboriously-painted limbs of very English actors. The result was totally detached from all worlds, ancient, modern, terrestrial, and celestial. Mr. James Bridie knows better. He has attempted, as he says, 'a speech belonging to no particular period—a speech that might equally well have been used by a pupil of Swift and an apostle of Arnold Bennett'. Consequently, his rendering of the book of Tobit comes alive from the start and stays alive. He is concerned only to tell the story and not to make it a plinth for a doctrinal superstructure. Mr. Shaw would have used the modest house in Nineveh as an excuse for a lecture on Imperialism, Subject Races, and the Housing Question in the Middle East; old Tobit's passion for burying stray corpses would have become a text for disquisition on social hygiene; the Archangel would have offered a grand opportunity for further observations on the superman. Mr. Bridie does, indeed, come to the foothills of such metabiological mountains when his Archangel talks to Sara about the nature of 'daemons'.

A daemon is a creature by whose agency you write immortal verse, go great journeys, leap into bottomless chasms, fight dragons, starve in a garret. . . . It is, perhaps, fortunate that daemons are too much occupied to visit, or to concern themselves with, the bulk of mankind. . . . When it is necessary to Jahveh's purpose they make contact, often with extremely disturbing results; for daemons are not all equally expert and conscientious, and their material is not invariably well chosen. I could talk for a thousand years on the methods and the shortcomings of daemons.

An Archangel of Mr. Shaw's would, of course, so continue, if not for the whole æon suggested. But Mr. Bridie denies his Raphael the pleasures of garrulity.

In a way, we are disappointed. For Mr. Bridie, who is that most interesting of human species, a doctor with a general education, seeing beyond the flesh and the pharmacy to the wider reaches of the soul and of society, could doubtless compose a disquisitive drama of great pith and moment. But he has elected to retell quite simply this lovely story of little Tobias, and there is wisdom in that. For Tobias is naturally a good theatre man. Who can resist the humble fellow who deems himself, and to us appears, to be a timid wretch and then turns out to be a lion-hearted hero who will suffer all for love, even the indescribable death by the strangling hand of the devil, Asmoday? Tobias is the kind of cleric one might have met in the earlier stories of H. G. Wells, a Mr. Hoopdriver of Nineveh, who sets out for Ecbatana much as Hoopdriver rode on that summer day and on the unaccustomed bicycle along the Portsmouth Road with Guildford as the scarcely achievable goal of labour on the wheels of chance. Mr. Frederick Piper plays the lad very nicely in just that temper; one can imagine him emerging from some den of ledgers at noon on Saturday, blinking a little at the strangeness of the sun, but rapturous and wondering whether any girl will smile for him.

Tobit, too, can hardly go wrong. The benign senior under curse of blindness is another trump card, and Mr. Morland Graham plays the part delightfully. Sara is the only questionable figure. She proclaims herself (and in the Apocrypha she appears to be) a person of distinction. 'I loved beauty, grand, absolute beauty.' How reconcile that with the 'smooth, weak, meaningless face' and the air of a sulky, spoilt baggage which is also in the part? Miss Hermione Baddeley emphasises the latter aspect. But it does not come right. What does come superbly right is Mr. Ainley's Archangel Raphael, in outline a superb commander of any celestial legion, in speech a wit, in demeanour as fine a gentleman as ever fardels bore for the necessary service of divine command.

IVOR BROWN: *The Week-end Review,* 19 March 1922

'TWELFTH NIGHT' AT THE OLD VIC

1933

SHAKESPEAREANS are divided, it is well known, into three classes; those who prefer to read Shakespeare in the book; those who prefer to see him acted on the stage; and those who run perpetually from book to stage gathering plunder. Certainly there is a good deal to be said for reading *Twelfth Night* in the book if the book can be read in a garden, with no sound but the thud of an apple falling to the earth, or of the wind ruffling the branches of the trees. For one thing there is time—time not only to hear 'the sweet sound that breathes upon a bank of violets' but to unfold the implications of that very subtle speech as the Duke winds into the nature of love. There is time, too, to make a note in the margin; time to wonder at queer jingles like 'that live in her; when liver, brain, and heart' . . . 'and of a foolish knight that you brought in one night' and to ask oneself whether it was from them that was born the lovely, 'And what should I do in Illyria? My brother he is in Elysium.' For Shakespeare is writing, it seems, not with the whole of his mind mobilized and under control, but with feelers left flying that sport and play with words so that the trail of a chance word is caught and followed recklessly. From the echo of one word is born another word, for which reason, perhaps, the play seems as we read it to tremble perpetually on the brink of music. They are always calling for songs in *Twelfth Night*, 'O fellow come, the song we had last night.' Yet Shakespeare was not so deeply in love with words but that he could turn and

laugh at them. 'They that do dally with words do
quickly make them wanton.' There is a roar of
laughter and out burst Sir Toby, Sir Andrew, Maria.
Words on their lips are things that have a meaning;
that rush and leap out with a whole character packed
in a little phrase. When Sir Andrew says 'I was
adored once', we feel that we hold him in the hollow
of our hands: a novelist would have taken three
volumes to bring us to that pitch of intimacy. And
Viola, Malvolio, Olivia, the Duke—the mind so
brims and spills over with all that we know and guess
about them as they move in and out among the lights
and shadows of the mind's stage that we ask why we
should imprison them within the bodies of real men
and women? Why exchange this garden for the
theatre? The answer is that Shakespeare wrote for
the stage and presumably with reason. Since they
are acting *Twelfth Night* at the Old Vic, let us compare the two versions.

Many apples might fall without being heard in
the Waterloo Road, and as for the shadows the
electric light has consumed them all. The first
impression upon entering the Old Vic is over-
whelmingly positive and definite. We seem to have
issued out from the shadows of the garden upon the
bridge of the Parthenon. The metaphor is mixed,
but then so is the scenery. The columns of the bridge
somehow suggest an Atlantic liner and the austere
splendours of a classical temple in combination. But
the body is almost as upsetting as the scenery. The
actual persons of Malvolio, Sir Toby, Olivia and
the rest expand our visionary characters out of all
recognition. At first we are inclined to resent it.
You are not Malvolio; or Sir Toby either, we want
to tell them; but merely impostors. We sit gaping

at the ruins of the play, at the travesty of the play. And then by degrees this same body or rather all these bodies together, take our play and remodel it between them. The play gains immensely in robustness, in solidity. The printed word is changed out of all recognition when it is heard by other people. We watch it strike upon this man or woman; we see them laugh or shrug their shoulders, or turn aside to hide their faces. The word is given a body as well as a soul. Then again as the actors pause, or topple over a barrel, or stretch their hands out, the flatness of the print is broken up as by crevasses or precipices; all the proportions are changed. Perhaps the most impressive effect in the play is achieved by the long pause which Sebastian and Viola make as they stand looking at each other in a silent esctasy of recognition. The reader's eye may have slipped over that moment entirely. Here we are made to pause and think about it; and are reminded that Shakespeare wrote for the body and for the mind simultaneously.

But now that the actors have done their proper work of solidifying and intensifying our impressions, we begin to criticize them more minutely and to compare their version with our own, We make Mr. Quartermaine's Malvolio stand beside our Malvolio. And to tell the truth, wherever the fault may lie, they have very little in common. Mr. Quartermaine's Malvolio is a splendid gentleman, courteous, considerate, well-bred; a man of parts and humour who has no quarrel with the world. He has never felt a twinge of vanity or a moment's envy in his life. If Sir Toby and Maria fool him he sees through it, we may be sure, and only suffers it as a fine gentleman puts up with the games of foolish children. Our Malvolio, on the other hand, was a fantastic complex creature, twitching with vanity, tortured by ambition. There was cruelty in his teasing, and a hint of tragedy in his defeat; his final threat had a momentary terror in it: But when Mr. Quartermaine says 'I'll be revenged on the whole pack of you', we feel merely that the powers of the law will be soon and effectively invoked. What, then, becomes of Olivia's 'He hath been most notoriously abused'? Then there is Olivia. Madame Lopokova has by nature that rare quality which is neither to be had for the asking nor to be subdued by the will—the genius of personality. She has only to float on to the stage and everything round her suffers, not a sea change, but a change into light, into gaiety; the birds sing, the sheep are garlanded, the air rings with melody and human beings dance towards each other on the tips of their toes possessed of an exquisite friendliness, sympathy and delight. But our Olivia was a stately lady; of sombre complexion, slow moving, and of few sympathies. She could not love the Duke nor change her feeling. Madame Lopokova loves everybody. She is always changing. Her hands, her face, her feet, the whole of her body, are always quivering in sympathy with the moment. She could make the moment, as she proved when she walked down the stairs with Sebastian, one of intense and moving beauty; but she was not our Olivia. Compared with her the comic group, Sir Toby, Sir Andrew, Maria, the fool were more than ordinarily English. Coarse, humorous, robust, they trolled out their words, they rolled over their barrels; they acted magnificently. No reader, one may make bold to say, could outpace Miss Seyler's Maria, with its quickness, its inventiveness, its merriment; nor add anything to the humours of Mr. Livesey's Sir Toby. And Miss Jeans, as

Viola, was satisfactory; and Mr. Hare, as Antonio, was admirable; and Mr. Morland's clown was a good clown. What, then, was lacking in the play as a whole? Perhaps that it was not a whole. The fault may be partly with Shakespeare. It is easier to act his comedy than his poetry, one may suppose, for when he wrote as a poet he was apt to write too quick for the human tongue. The prodigality of his metaphors can be flashed over by the eye, but the speaking voice falters in the middle. Hence the comedy was out of proportion to the rest. Then, perhaps, the actors were too highly charged with individuality or too incongruously cast. They broke the play up into separate pieces—now we were in the groves of Arcady, now in some inn at Blackfriars. The mind in reading spins a web from scene to scene, compounds a background from apples falling, and the toll of a church bell, and an owl's fantastic flight which keeps the play together. Here that continuity was sacrificed. We left the theatre possessed of many brilliant fragments but without the sense of all things conspiring and combining together which may be the satisfying culmination of a less brilliant performance. Nevertheless, the play has served its purpose. It has made us compare our Malvolio with Mr. Quartermaine's; our Olivia with Madame Lopokova's; our reading of the whole play with Mr. Guthrie's; and since they all differ, back we must go to Shakespeare. We must read *Twelfth Night* again. Mr. Guthrie has made that necessary and whetted our appetite for the *Cherry Orchard*, *Measure for Measure*, and *Henry the Eighth* that are still to come.

VIRGINIA WOOLF: *The Death of the Moth*, 1943

'MURDER IN THE CATHEDRAL'

THE Festival of Music and Drama, organized by
the Friends of Canterbury Cathedral, began on
Saturday, and will continue throughout the present
week. A new play, *Murder in the Cathedral*, by Mr.
T. S. Eliot, was performed during the evening in a
setting designed by Mr. Laurence Irving to accord
with the existing decoration of the Chapter House.
The action, which is accompanied throughout by
the tragic comments of a chorus of Canterbury
women, describes Becket's return to England, his
resistance to the persuasions of four Tempters, who
represent the innermost working of his own mind,
his death, and his murderers' attempt to justify their
action. The play is an exposition, in Becket, of the
nature of saintliness, and contains an urgent suggestion that the problems by which he was beset are
present to-day. In form it is something between a
Morality and a chronicle play, the use of introspective
symbols being subtly interwoven with a simplified
historical narrative.

Recognizing the necessities of the dramatic
medium, Mr. Eliot has put away from him, except
on rare occasions, the use of private symbols and
has written in a way that may be generally understood. There are certain passages of which, though
the meaning is plain, the aesthetic purpose remains
obscure—namely, those in which Mr. Eliot employs
a limping jingle that reminds the hearer of nothing
so much as the 'book' of a pantomime. In some
instances the intention appears to be satirical, the
speaker (for example, one of the Tempters) being

made to use language which, though its argument is serious, argues against itself by its sound:—

> And later is worse, when men will not hate you
> Enough to defame or to execrate you,
> But pondering the qualities that you lacked
> Will only try to find the historical fact:
> When men shall declare that there is no mystery
> About this man who played a certain part in history.

But sometimes the same jingle is used when there can be no satirical intention—perhaps simply to avoid stateliness of phrase in connexion with commonplace subjects. The Archbishop, encountering the murderers, says to his priests:—

> On my table you will find
> The papers in order, and the documents signed.

Why, here, the rhyme? And, when a Tempter says:—

> Hungry hated
> Will not strive against intelligent self-interest

—on what system of prosody is the statement divided into two lines?

These are surviving mannerisms. For the greater part of the play Mr. Eliot has succeeded in combining lucidity and precision with an uncommon vigour that fully justifies his departure from the customary forms of dramatic verse. The Chorus is never a group of women dully chanting. Taught by Miss Fogerty how to use Mr. Eliot's rhythms, it has at once dramatic and intellectual impact. Becket himself has a corresponding freedom from stately monotony. As represented by Mr. Speaight he is extraordinarily rich in spiritual vitality, and one has an impression, particularly when he preaches his sermon on the nature of martyrdom, of being admitted to his mind and of seeing the world with his eyes. Over modern religious drama there is often spread a kind of pious mist, timid, and thickly traditional. This has been cast off. Mr. Eliot's writing and Mr. Martin Browne's production are continuously keen and clear, but it is, perhaps, worth remarking that the peril to Mr. Eliot's dramatic method is in his rhymes, and that its merits most movingly appear in the prose sermon and in those passages of verse that are direct in their attack and are not twisted to irony or humour.

THE TIMES, 17 June 1935

'AS YOU LIKE IT' AT THE OLD VIC

November 1936

THE Old Vic's latest production of *As You Like It* is
sombre in tone and pace. There is no indication in
the text that it was October in Arden, or that they
fleeted the time carelessly in a world of dusk and
yellowing leaves. Yet here is no sunshine, and hardly
a scene of normal daylight. There is a great deal of
moonshine, and some total darkness relieved by the
lanterns of the exiled courtiers. It is all too slow.

The costumes are more in keeping with the play,
and it is not at all unhappy to begin on a note of
Watteau with the ladies embarking for Arden as if
it were Cythera, and Touchstone in very likeness of
the famous Gilles in the Louvre. Many of the
performances accord too surely with the direction
which has wrongly ordered this comedy to march
to its end rather than dance. Exceptions are Miss
Eileen Peel's clear-cut Celia, the determinedly
nimble Touchstone of Mr. Milton Rosmer, and the
wondrous blank that Mr. Alec Guinness makes of
the rustic William.

But the major exceptions have to be, and they
blissfully are, the Rosalind and the Orlando. In the
latter Mr. Michael Redgrave cuts a charming figure
and solves the problem of the later scenes by appearing to think the ladies' make-believe rather silly.
This Orlando would rather pine for Rosalind than
woo her by proxy, and he quite surprisingly persuades
us to realise that this was his author's intention.
Shakespeare's intentions are seldom envisaged by
actors.

Miss Edith Evans played Rosalind at the Vic a little over ten years ago. She begins this revival by suggesting that time has been unkinder than it need have been by combing her hair straight back from her forehead and piling some foolish blossoms on her crown. But no sooner is the masquerade entered upon than we are wooed and eventually won even more willingly than her lover in the play. Miss Evans draws and paints a Meredithean lady rich in mind. No other actress has such raillery, and in the sham love-making her lapses into tenderness when the handsome boy turns from the sport are wholly exquisite. This is the virtue of her Rosalind, that she is constantly able to deck her passion in those humorous similes wherein this part abounds. It is a romantic and a witty performance that in its great moments must long be remembered; and in the end the audience is made one Orlando.

ALAN DENT: *Preludes and Studies,* 1942

EDITOR'S NOTE

Principal works consulted in the preparation of the Descriptive Index to this volume:

JOHN DOWNES. *Roscius Anglicanus.* 1708

DAVID ERSKINE BAKER. Biographia Dramatica. 1782

The Thespian Dictionary. 1802

JOHN GENEST. *Account of the English Stage from 1660 to 1830.* 1832

CHARLES EYRE PASCOE. *The Dramatic List.* 1879

WILLIAM DAVENPORT ADAMS. *Dictionary of the Drama.* Vol. I, 1904 (no others published)

DESMOND MacCARTHY. *The Court Theatre: 1904-7.* 1907

JOHN PARKER. *The Green Room Book.* 1907

SIR PAUL HARVEY. *The Oxford Companion to English Literature.* 2nd edn. 1937

JOHN PARKER. *Who's Who in the Theatre.* 9th edn. 1939, and earlier editions

The Dictionary of National Biography

Chambers's Biographical Dictionary

Who Was Who. 1897-1915. 1916-28. 1929-40

Who's Who. 1944 and earlier annual issues

DESCRIPTIVE INDEX

ABBREVIATIONS: app., appearance(s), appeared; incl., including; perf., performed, performing; Sh., Shakespeare, Shakespearean. CG, Covent Garden Theatre; DL, Drury Lane Theatre; Hay., Haymarket Theatre; LI, Lincoln's Inn Fields Theatre. AEFH, Miss A. E. F. Horniman's Company at the Gaiety Theatre, Manchester; FRB, F. R. Benson's Shakespeare Company; OUDS, Oxford University Dramatic Society; OV, Old Vic Company; RADA, Royal Academy of Dramatic Art; VB, Vedrenne-Barker season at the Court Theatre 1904-7. B.Op., *The Beggar's Opera* (Gay); LL, *Love for Love* (Congreve); SC, *She Stoops to Conquer* (Goldsmith); SS, *The School for Scandal* (Sheridan); VP, *Venice Preserved* (Otway); WW, *The Way of the World* (Congreve).

Place and date of a performer's first known appearance on the professional stage shown thus: Margate 1874. Principal companies with which a performer appeared, thus: FRB, Tree, Forbes Robertson, VB, OV. Principal playwrights in whose works a performer appeared, thus: Sh., Sheridan, Shaw, Galsworthy, Barrie.

Individual characters in plays are indexed only when their identity is not evident in the context.

A